ANDRÉ GIDE

If It Die . . .

André Gide was born in Paris in 1869 and died there in 1951. He was awarded the Nobel Prize for Literature in 1947. His works include *The Immoralist, The Counterfeiters, Lafcadio's Adventures, Strait Is the Gate, The Cellars of the Vatican,* and his three volumes of *Journals.* He also wrote plays, essays, short stories, and books of travel.

INTERNATIONAL

ANDRÉ GIDE

If It Die . . .

AN AUTOBIOGRAPHY

Except a corn of wheat fall into
the ground and die, it abideth
alone: but if it die, it bringeth
forth much fruit.
JOHN XII, 24.

Translated by Dorothy Bussy

Vintage International
VINTAGE BOOKS
A DIVISION OF RANDOM HOUSE, INC.
NEW YORK

FIRST VINTAGE INTERNATIONAL EDITION, MAY 2001

The Library of Congress has cataloged the Modern Library edition as follows:
Gide, André, 1869–1951.
If it die . . . an autobiography ; translated by Dorothy Bussy.
3-331 p. 24 cm.
1. Gide, André, 1869–1951. 2. Authors, French—20th century—Biography.
PQ2613.I2 Z52 1935

Vintage ISBN: 978-0-375-72606-4

www.vintagebooks.com

146028962

I

I WAS BORN ON NOVEMBER 22ND, 1869. MY parents at that time lived in the Rue de Médicis in an apartment on the fourth floor which they left a few years later and of which I have kept no recollection. Stay though, I do remember the balcony, or rather what could be seen from the balcony—the bird's-eye view of the Place with its ornamental piece of water and fountain; or rather, to be still more exact, I remember the paper dragons which my father used to cut out for me and which we launched into the air from the balcony; I remember their floating away in the wind over the fountain in the Place below and being carried away as far as the Luxembourg Gardens, where they used sometimes to catch in the top branches of the horse-chestnut trees.

I remember too a biggish table—the dining-room table, no doubt—with its table-cloth that reached nearly to the ground; I used to crawl underneath it with the *concierge's* little boy, who sometimes came to play with me.

"What are you up to under there?" my nurse would call out.

"Nothing; we're playing." And then we would make a great noise with our playthings, which we had taken with us for the sake of appearances. In reality, we amused ourselves otherwise, beside each other but not with each other; we had what I afterwards learnt are called "bad habits."

Which of us two taught them first to the other? I have no idea. Surely a child may sometimes invent them for himself. Personally, I cannot say whether anyone instructed me in the knowledge of pleasure or in what manner I discovered it—I only know that as far back as my recollection goes, I cannot remember a time without it.

I perfectly realise, for that matter, that I am doing myself harm by relating this and other things that follow; I foresee what use will be made of them against me. But the whole object of my story is to be truthful. Put the case that I am writing it for a penance.

One would like to believe that in that age of innocence the soul is all sweetness, light and purity, but I can remember nothing in mine that was not ugly, dark and deceitful.

I used to be taken for my outings to the Luxembourg; but I would not play with the other children; I kept sulkily apart with my nurse and watched their games. I remember once they were making mud-pies with their pails . . . All of a sudden, when my nurse was looking another way, I dashed up and trampled all the pies underfoot.

The only explanation I can think of for this behaviour is that I must have gone up to one of the children and asked to be allowed to play with them. It was their refusal that enraged me so and made me want to destroy their game.

The other incident I must relate is still odder, for which reason, no doubt, I am less ashamed of it. I often heard my mother tell the story later on, so that it kept fresh in my memory.

It happened at Uzès, where we used to go once a year to visit my father's mother and other relations—amongst them my de Flaux cousins, who owned an old house and garden in the heart of the town. It was in the de Flaux' house that it happened. My cousin was a very beautiful person and she

4

knew it. Her black hair, which she wore parted in the middle and smoothed down on either side of her face, set off the perfection of her cameo-like profile (I have seen a photograph of her since then) and the dazzling whiteness of her skin. I remember the dazzling whiteness of her skin very well—and I remember it especially well because the day I was taken to see her she was wearing a low-necked dress.

"Go and give your cousin a kiss," said my mother, as I came into the drawing-room. (I couldn't have been much more than four years old—five, perhaps.) I went obediently up and she drew me towards her; but at the sight of her bare shoulder and its dazzling whiteness, some sort of craziness possessed me; instead of putting my lips to the cheek she offered me, fascinated by her dazzling shoulder, I gave it a great bite with my teeth. My cousin screamed with pain and I with horror. She began to bleed and I to spit with disgust. I was speedily carried off and I really believe they were all so astounded that they forgot to punish me.

I have found a photograph of myself taken at that time; it represents me half hidden in my mother's skirts, frightfully dressed in a ridiculous little check frock, with a sickly, ill-tempered face and a crooked look in my eyes.

I was six years old when we left the Rue de Médicis. Our new apartment, the second floor of No. 2 Rue de Tournon, was at the corner of the Rue Saint-Sulpice, on to which the windows of my father's library looked; my own room gave on to a large courtyard. I particularly remember the ante-room of this flat, because that was where I spent most of my time when I was not at school or in my bedroom; when mamma was tired of me she would tell me to go and play with "my little friend Pierre," which meant in other words—by myself. There was a gaudy coloured carpet in this ante-room, covered

5

with large geometrical patterns, and it was great fun playing at marbles on it with "my little friend Pierre."

I had a special little string bag for my best and finest marbles. They had been given me one by one and I kept them apart from the ordinary ones. Some were so lovely I could never touch them without being enraptured afresh by their beauty—in particular, a little one of black agate with a white equator and two tropics; and I had another of translucent cornelian, the colour of light tortoise-shell, which I used as a taw. Then there was the common herd of grey marbles which I kept in a coarse linen bag and which were sometimes won and sometimes lost and served as stakes when later on I had real playmates.

Another plaything I adored was that worker of marvels called a kaleidoscope—a kind of toy telescope, looking through which one sees at the other end a constantly changing rose pattern, made of loose bits of coloured glass imprisoned between two transparent plaques. The inside of the telescope is lined with looking-glass, so that the phantasmagoria of the coloured pieces, altering with every little movement of the hand, is multiplied into a symmetrical design. The shifting of the rose patterns filled me with unspeakable delight. I can still recollect accurately the colour and shape of the bits of glass: the largest was a light ruby, triangular in shape; owing to its weight, it was always the first to move, jostling and tumbling over the rest of them. There was a very dark garnet, almost round; an emerald, shaped like a scythe; a topaz, whose colour is the only thing I can remember about it; a sapphire and three little gold-brown fragments. They were never all on the stage together; some of them kept completely out of sight; others were partially hidden in the wings on the other side of the looking-glasses; the ruby alone was so large that it never disappeared entirely.

My girl cousins shared my liking for this toy, but they were less patient than I; they used to give it a shake each time so as to get a complete change. My method was different; without taking my eyes off the pattern for a moment, I turned the kaleidoscope very, very gently and watched the rose as it slowly altered. Sometimes the hardly perceptible displacing of one piece brought about the most startling consequences. I was quite as curious as I was wonder-struck and soon resolved to make my toy give up its secret by force. I took out the bottom, counted up the bits of coloured glass and removed the three looking-glasses from their cardboard sheath; then I put them back, but only three or four bits of coloured glass with them. The colour scheme was poor; the changes had ceased to be surprising; but how easy now to follow the action of the different parts! how clearly one understood the reason of one's pleasure!

Then it occurred to me to replace the little bits of glass by all sorts of different objects—a nib, the wing of a fly, a match-end, a blade of grass. The effect was dull, no longer the least transparent or fairy-like, but the reflections in the looking-glasses gave it a kind of geometrical interest . . . In short, I passed hours and days over this amusement. I think it is unknown to the children of the present day, which is why I have said so much about it.

The other amusements of my early childhood—games of patience, transfers, bricks, were all solitary. I had no playfellows . . . Yes, though; I can recall one small friend, but alas, he was not a playfellow. When Marie took me to the Luxembourg Gardens, I used to meet a child there of about my own age, a delicate, gentle, quiet creature, whose pallid face was half hidden by a pair of big spectacles, the glasses of which were so dark that one could see nothing behind them. I cannot remember his name, perhaps I never knew it. We used to call him Mouton because of his little white woolly coat.

"Mouton, why do you wear spectacles?"

"I have bad eyes."

"Let me see them."

Then he had lifted the frightful glasses and the sight of his poor blinking, weak eyes had made my heart ache.

Not that we played together; I cannot remember that we did anything but walk about hand in hand without saying a word.

This first friendship of mine lasted only a short time. Mouton soon stopped coming. Oh, how lonely the Luxembourg seemed then! . . . But my real despair began when I realised that Mouton was going blind. Marie had met the little boy's nurse in the street and she told my mother what she had learnt; she spoke in a whisper so that I should not hear; but I caught these words: "He can't find the way to his mouth!" An absurd remark, assuredly, for of course there is no need to see in order to find the way to one's mouth, as I immediately reflected, but nevertheless it filled me with dismay. I ran away to cry in my room and for several days I practised keeping my eyes shut and going about without opening them, so as to try and realise what Mouton must be feeling.

My father was taken up preparing his lectures at the Faculty of Law and gave very little of his time to me. He spent most of the day shut up in a vast and rather dark study, into which I was only allowed when he expressly invited me. I have a photograph which keeps me in mind of my father with his square-cut beard and rather long curly black hair; without this picture I should only have had the recollection of his extreme gentleness. My mother told me later that his colleagues had surnamed him *Vir probus;* and I learnt from one of them that they often had recourse to his advice.

I had a veneration for my father which was slightly mixed with fear and which was enhanced by the solemnity of this abode. I went into it as into a temple; the bookcase rose out of the gloom like a tabernacle; a thick carpet of a dark rich colour stifled the sound of my footsteps. There was a reading-desk near one of the two windows; in the middle of the room stood an enormous table covered with books and papers. My father would go and fetch some big volume, a *Coûtume* of Burgundy or Normandy, and open the heavy folio on the arm of an easychair, so that we might follow from page to page the persevering labours of a gnawing bookworm. While he was consulting some ancient text, the learned jurist had admired these little clandestine galleries and had said to himself, "Ah! this will amuse my small boy." And it did amuse me very much, and the amusement he seemed to take in it as well, increased my own.

But my recollection of the study is especially bound up with his reading aloud. My father had very special ideas as to what should be read to me—ideas that were not shared by my mother; and I used often to hear them discuss what was the proper nourishment for a child's mind. Similar discussions sometimes arose on the subject of obedience, my mother holding that a child should obey without trying to understand, my father always inclining to explain me everything. I remember very well that then my mother would compare the child I was to the people of Israel and declare that before living in grace it was good to have lived under the law. I think to-day that my mother was right; nevertheless my attitude to her at that time was constantly marked by discussions and frequently by insubordination, while a single word from my father would have obtained anything he pleased from me. I think it was inclination rather than principle that kept him from holding up for my admiration or amusement anything he did not himself like and admire. French literature for children at that date was almost wholly inept, and I think he would have been pained to see some of the books that were put into my hands later on—Madame de Ségur's for instance, though I must confess that, like nearly all the children of my generation, I took a good deal of pleasure in them—foolish pleasure but fortunately not greater than the pleasure I had before taken in hearing my father read aloud to me certain scenes from Molière, certain passages of the *Odyssey*, *Pathelin's Farce*, the adventures of Sindbad or Ali Baba and some of the harlequinades of the Italian Comedy that are to be found in Maurice Sand's *Masques*; in this book there were pictures for me to admire too of Harlequin, Columbine, Punchinello and Pierrot, after I had listened to them discoursing in my father's voice.

The success of these readings was such and my father's confidence in me so great, that one day he ventured on the first part of the Book of Job. This was an experiment at which my mother wished to be present; and so it took place not in the library, like the other readings, but in a small drawing-room which was more particularly in my mother's domain. I would not swear of course that I at once understood the full beauty of the sacred text! But the reading certainly made the deepest impression on me, not only because of the solemnity of the story, but because of the gravity of my father's voice and my mother's expression, as she sat with her eyes closed, in order alternately to signify or to shield her pious absorption, and opened them only to cast a questioning glance on me, full of love and hope.

Sometimes on fine summer evenings, when we had not supped too late, and when my father was not too busy, he used to say:

"Would my little friend like to come for a walk?"

He never called me anything but his "little friend."

"You'll be sensible, won't you?" said my mother. "Don't come in too late."

I liked going out with my father; and as he rarely gave me any of his time, the few things we did together had an unfamiliar, solemn and rather mysterious air about them which delighted me.

Playing as we went at some game of rhymes or riddles, we would walk up the Rue de Tournon and then either cross the Luxembourg Gardens or follow the part of the Boulevard St. Germain that skirts them, until we reached the second garden near the Observatory. In those days the land that faces the School of Pharmacy had not yet been built over; the School itself in fact did not exist. Instead of the six-storied houses that stand there now, there were nothing but temporary wooden booths, stalls for the selling of old clothes, and sellers or hirers of second-hand velocipedes. The asphalt—or perhaps macadam—space which borders the second Luxembourg was used as a track by the devotees of this sport; they sat perched up aloft on those weird, paradoxical machines which were the ancestors of the bicycle, circled swiftly past us and disappeared into the darkness. We admired their boldness and their elegance. The frame-work and the minute back wheel on which the equilibrium of this aerial apparatus depended were scarcely visible. The slender front wheel swayed to and fro; the rider seemed some fantastic creature of a dream world.

As the night fell, it intensified the lights of a *café-concert* a little further on, whose music attracted us. We could not see the gas globes themselves, only the strangely illuminated horse-chestnut trees above the palisade. We drew near. The planks were not so well joined as to prevent one from getting a peep here and there between two of them, if one put one's eye close enough: I could just make out over the dark swarming mass of the audience, the wonderment of the stage, on which some music-hall star was warbling her absurdities.

Sometimes we still had time to walk back through the big Luxembourg Gardens. But a rub-a-dub of drums soon gave notice it was closing time. The last visitors reluctantly turned towards the exits, with the park-keepers close at their heels, and behind them the broad garden walks, now left deserted, filled slowly up with mystery. On those evenings I went to bed intoxicated with darkness, sleep and strangeness.

When I was five years old, my parents sent me to some children's classes held by Mademoiselle Fleur and Madame Lackerbauer.

Mademoiselle Fleur lived in the Rue de Seine. While the little ones, of whom I was one, were poring over their alphabets or copy-books, the elders—or rather the elder girls (for Mademoiselle Fleur's classes were attended by a good many girls but only by little boys) were in great excitement over some theatricals to which the children's parents were to be invited. An act of *Les Plaideurs* was being rehearsed; I saw the girls trying on their false beards and envied them for being allowed to dress up; nothing, I thought, could be more delightful.

I can remember nothing at Madame Lackerbauer's but an old electric apparatus (a Ramsden machine) which made me desperately curious, with its glass disk, on to which were stuck little metal plaques, and a handle to make the disk go round; it was expressly forbidden to touch it "on pain of death," as the notices on high-power transmission posts say. One day the mistress tried to make the machine work; we children stood round in a big circle very far off, because it was highly alarming; we expected to see the mistress struck dead;

and she certainly trembled a little as she put the knuckle of her forefinger to the brass knob at the end of the apparatus. But not the smallest spark flashed from it . . . Oh! how relieved we were!

I was seven years old when my mother thought it necessary to supplement Mademoiselle Fleur's and Madame Lackerbauer's classes by Mademoiselle de Goecklin's piano lessons. One could not help suspecting this innocent lady to be less devoted to the arts than in extreme need of earning her living. She was a slight, pale little creature and always looked on the point of fainting. I think she can never have had enough to eat.

When I was well-behaved, Mademoiselle de Goecklin used to present me with a picture which she drew out of a small muff. The picture in itself might have seemed ordinary enough and I might almost have turned up my nose at it; but it was scented—extraordinarily scented—in remembrance, no doubt, of the muff; I used hardly to give it a glance; I just sniffed it; then I stuck it into an album with other pictures, which the big shops used to give their customers' children— but which were not scented. A little while ago, I opened the album to amuse a small nephew: Mademoiselle de Goecklin's pictures are still perfumed; they have perfumed the whole album.

After I had done my scales, my arpeggios and a little solfège and drummed over again and again some piece out of *The Young Pianist*, I gave up my place to my mother, who sat herself down beside Mademoiselle de Goecklin. I think it was from modesty that Mamma never played alone; but in duets she was magnificent! As a rule it was a part of some Haydn symphony they played, preferably the finale which, so she thought, needed less expression because the time was so quick —and she hurried it more and more the nearer she came to

13

the end. She counted aloud from one end of the piece to the other.

When I was a little older, Mademoiselle de Goecklin stopped coming to us; I used to go to her for my lessons. She lived in a tiny apartment with an elder sister, who was either an invalid or a little feeble-minded and had to be looked after. In the first room, which probably served as the dining-room, there was a cage full of bengalis; in the second room stood the piano; some of the notes in the upper register were horribly out of tune, which considerably damped any preference I might have had for taking the treble in our duets. Mademoiselle de Goecklin had no difficulty in understanding my repugnance and she would say in a plaintive voice and a kind of abstracted manner, as if she were giving a discreet order to a spirit: "We must really send for the piano-tuner." But the spirit never did the errand.

My parents had taken to passing the summer holidays in Calvados at La Roque Baignard, a country place which had come into my mother's possession at my grandmother Rondeaux' death. The Christmas holidays we spent at Rouen with my mother's relations, and the Easter ones at Uzès with my paternal grandmother.

Nothing could be more different than these two families, nothing more different than the two provinces of France which combine their contradictory influences in me. I have often thought that I was driven into the field of art by my consciousness that only in this way should I find it possible to reconcile these discordant elements which would otherwise have led to a state of perpetual warfare or at any rate antagonism. No doubt the only natures capable of asserting themselves powerfully are those having behind them one undeviating urge of heredity. On the other hand, arbiters and artists are, I imagine, produced when cross-breeding encourages the simultaneous growth and consequent neutralisation of opposing elements. I am very much mistaken if examples could not be found to bear me out.

But the law which I here adumbrate has hitherto, it would seem, occupied historians so little that not a single one of the biographies I have consulted at Cuverville, where I am writing this, not a single dictionary, not even the enormous *Biographie Universelle* in fifty-two volumes, not one of them, I say, look where I may, so much as mentions the maternal origins of a single great man or single hero. Some day I shall return to this subject.

My great-grandfather, Rondeaux de Montbray, counsellor, like his father before him, at the Cour des Comptes, (his fine town house still stood in the Place Notre-Dame opposite the cathedral) was Mayor of Rouen in 1789. In '93 he was thrown into prison at Saint-Yon with M. d'Herbouville, and M. de Fontenay, who was considered more *advanced*, succeeded him in his post. On leaving prison, he retired to Louviers. It was there, I think, that he married for the second time.[1] He had had two children by a previous marriage; and up till that time the Rondeaux family had been wholly Catholic; but Rondeaux de Montbray's second wife was a Protestant, Mademoiselle Dufour, who bore him three more children, of whom Edouard, my grandfather, was one. These children were baptised and brought up in the Catholic faith. But my grandfather also married a Protestant—Julie Pouchet, and this time the five children, of whom my mother was the youngest, were brought up as Protestants.

At the time of my story, nevertheless, that is to say at the extreme limit of my memories, my grandparents' house had reverted to Catholicism and had become indeed more Catholic

[1] For this information and that which follows I am indebted to my aunt, Madame Rondeaux, from whose dictation I took it down during her last stay at Cuverville.

and *bien pensant* than it had ever been before. My uncle Henri Rondeaux who, after my grandmother's death, lived in it with his wife and two children, had been converted when he was still very young and long before he had thought of marrying the very Catholic Mademoiselle Lucile K.

The house was at the corner of the Rue de Crosne and the Rue de Fontenelle. Its carriage entrance gave on to the latter street and most of its windows on to the former. I thought it enormous—and so indeed it was. Downstairs, as well as the porter's lodge, the kitchen, the stables and the coach-house, there was a warehouse for the *rouenneries* or printed linens which my uncle manufactured in his factory at Le Houlme, a few kilometres outside Rouen. Next to the warehouse there was also a little office into which we children were forbidden to go, and which, for that matter, was forbidding enough of itself, with its smell of stale tobacco and gloomy, cheerless aspect. But on the other hand, how delightful the house was! Even as one stepped over the threshold, the deep soft-toned bell seemed to be giving one a welcome. To the left, under the arched entrance way and three steps up, was the porter's lodge, from which the porter's wife smiled down at one through her glass door. Opposite lay the courtyard, where all sorts of decorative green plants, ranged in pots against the further wall, were enjoying the air for a little before going back to the greenhouse at Le Houlme, out of which they had been taken and to which they would shortly be sent back for their health's sake—meanwhile taking it in turns to have a little rest here, after their service indoors. And indoors! Oh, how warm, how soothing, how discreet it all felt! A little severe perhaps, but so comfortable, so dignified and pleasant! The well of the staircase was lighted below by the arched entrance way, and at the top of the house by a glass roof. On every landing there were long benches, covered with green velvet,

16

where it was delightful to lie on one's stomach and read. But one was still more comfortable between the second and last floors, sitting on the steps themselves, which were laid with a black and white speckled carpet, bordered with wide strips of red. The light that fell from the glass roof was soft and peaceful. I sat on one step and leant my elbow on the one above, which also served as a reading desk, as it slowly dug into my ribs.

I mean to write down my recollections just as they come, without trying to arrange them in any order. The most I can do is to group them round places and persons; my memory seldom goes wrong about places but often confuses dates. I am lost if I attempt to take count of chronology. When I think over the past, I am like a person whose eyes cannot properly measure distances and is liable to think things extremely remote which on examination prove to be quite near. This is how for a long time I was convinced I remembered the entry of the Prussians into Rouen.

It was night time. A military brass band was playing; one could see it from the Rue de Crosne balcony as it marched past; and the walls of the houses were whipped into astonished life by the flickering lights of resinous torches.

My mother to whom I spoke of this in later years convinced me that, first of all, I was much too young to have any recollection whatever of that time, and secondly, that no inhabitant of Rouen, or at any rate no member of my family would ever have gone on to the balcony to look out, even if Bismarck or the King of Prussia himself had ridden by, so that if the Germans had got up a procession, it would have passed through streets of closed shutters. What I remembered must certainly have been the military torchlight processions which used to go up and down the Rue de Crosne every Saturday evening, long after the Germans had left the town.

"That was what we used to show you. And, do you remember, we used to sing:

> "*Hey diddle day! Hey diddle day*
> *See the fine soldiers marching away!*"

And suddenly the song came back to me as well. Everything returned to its proper place and proportions. But I felt as if I had been a little defrauded; it seemed to me I had been nearer the truth in the first instance and that what my youthful senses had invested with such importance deserved to be a historical event. Hence the unconscious necessity I had felt of making it unduly remote, so that it might be magnified by distance.

It was the same with the ball at the Rue de Crosne, which my memory obstinately placed in my grandmother's lifetime; but as she died in 1873, when I was not yet four years old, I must have been thinking of the party which my uncle and aunt Henri gave three years later, on the occasion of their daughter's coming of age.

I had gone to bed, but was prevented from sleeping by strange rumours—a thrill of agitation that ran through the house from top to bottom, accompanied by waves of harmonious sound. No doubt I had noticed some preparations during the day. No doubt I had been told there was to be a ball that evening. But could I have any idea what a ball was? I had not given the matter a thought and had gone to bed as usual. But now came these strange rumours . . . I listened, trying to catch some sound that would be more distinct, trying to understand what was happening. I strained my ears with all my might and main. Finally, unable to resist any longer, I got up and groped my way out of the room along the dark passage, till I reached the lighted staircase. My room was on the

18

third floor. The waves of sound rose from the first; I felt I must go and see; and as I got nearer, creeping downstairs step by step, I began to distinguish the sounds of voices, the rustling of dresses, whispering and laughter. Nothing wore its usual look; I felt as if I was going to be suddenly initiated into another life—a mysterious, differently real, more brilliant, more exciting life, which began only after little boys had gone to bed. The passages on the second floor were deserted; the party was downstairs. Should I go on? I should be caught if I did. I should certainly be punished for not going to sleep, for having ventured to look. I slipped my head between the iron bars of the bannisters to take a peep. At that very moment some of the guests were arriving—an officer in uniform, a lady all in ribbons and silk; she was holding a fan in her hand; the man-servant—my friend Victor—whom I did not recognise at first because of his knee-breeches and white stockings, was standing by the open door of the drawing-room and announcing the guests. All of a sudden someone pounced down on me—it was my nurse Marie, who was trying to peep like me and had ensconced herself a little lower down, at the first turn of the stairs. She seized me in her arms and I thought at first she was going to carry me back to my room and shut me up; but no, on the contrary, she took me down to the place where she had been watching and from which it was just possible to catch a tiny whiff of the festivities below. I heard the music perfectly now. I saw the gentlemen whirling round to the sound of invisible instruments, with beautifully dressed ladies, who were all far more lovely than in the daytime. Then the music ceased; the dancers stopped; and there was a noise of voices instead of the sound of instruments. My nurse was on the point of taking me back to bed, when just at that moment one of the lovely ladies who was standing leaning by the door and fanning herself caught sight of me. She came up

19

to where I was and kissed me, laughing because I did not recognise her. She was evidently the friend I had seen that morning calling on my mother; but all the same I was not really and truly sure of it. When I got back to my bed, my brain was in a turmoil, and before sinking into sleep, I thought in a confused way—there is reality and there are dreams; and there is *another* reality as well.

The vague, ill-defined belief that something else exists alongside the acknowledged, above-board reality of every-day life, inhabited me for many years; and I am not sure that even to-day I have not still some remnants of it left. It had nothing in common with tales of fairies, ghouls or witches, nor even with Hoffmann's or Hans Andersen's stories. No, I think it was more a kind of unskilful desire to give life more thickness—a desire that later on religion was better able to satisfy; and also a sort of propensity to imagine a clandestine side to things. After my father's death, for instance, big boy as I was, I took it into my head, that he was not really dead, or at any rate—how can I put this kind of apprehension?— that he was only dead to our visible, diurnal life, but that at night he used to come secretly while I was asleep and visit my mother. In the daytime, my suspicions wavered, but at night, just before going to sleep, I felt them grow more vivid and more certain. I did not try to unravel the mystery; I felt I should put an abrupt stop to anything I might try to discover; no doubt, I was still too young, thought I, and then my mother was too much in the habit of saying about too many things, "You will understand it when you are older"—but on certain nights, as I dropped off to sleep, I really had the feeling that I was making way—giving up my place.

I must return to the Rue de Crosne. I can see the schoolroom on the second floor at the end of a passage into which the bedrooms open; it is more comfortable, cosier than the big drawing-rooms downstairs, so that my mother prefers sitting here and keeping me with her. A big cupboard, which serves as a bookcase, takes up the end wall. The two windows look on to the courtyard; one of them is double and in between the two frames are pots and saucers in which there are flowering bulbs—crocuses, hyacinths, "Duke of Tholl" tulips. On either side of the fireplace are two large tapestry armchairs, worked by my mother and aunts. My mother is seated in one of them. Miss Shackleton, on a mahogany chair covered with crimson rep, is sitting at the table, busied with her filet embroidery. The little square of filet she is adorning—a spider's web over which her needle runs industriously to and fro—is stretched on a metal frame; Miss Shackleton sometimes consults a pattern, on which the design is traced in white on a blue ground. My mother looks at the window and says:

"The crocuses are out; we shall soon be having fine weather."

Miss Shackleton corrects her gently:

"Oh, Juliette, how like you! It is because the weather is fine already that the crocuses have come out. Surely you know they don't start it."

Anna Shackleton! I recall your calm face and pure brow, the slight severity of your mouth, your smiling eyes that showered such loving-kindness on my childhood. I wish I could invent fresh words in which to speak of you—more moving, more respectful, tenderer words. Shall I some day tell the story of your modest life? I should like your humility to shine as resplendently in my story as it will shine before God on the day the mighty are cast down and the lowly magnified. It is not the great and glorious of this world that I have ever felt inclined to portray—no, but those whose truer glory is hidden from sight.

I cannot say what reverses of fortune had brought the Shackleton children out of the depths of Scotland and cast them on the continent. Pastor Roberty, who himself married a Scotchwoman, was, I believe, acquainted with the family and it was no doubt he who recommended the eldest daughter to my grandmother. Needless to say, I only learnt all that follows much later, either from my mother herself or from my elder cousins.

It was really as my mother's governess that Miss Shackleton entered our family. My mother was then nearly old enough to be married and many a one thought that the presence of Anna Shackleton—young herself and moreover extremely pretty—might not be very advantageous for her pupil. Young Juliette Rondeaux, it must be confessed, was not a very easy person to manage. Not only did she constantly retire into the background and efface herself when she ought to have been cutting a figure, but she never lost an opportunity of pushing forward Anna, to whom she had almost immediately become devotedly attached. Juliette could not endure to be better dressed than her friend; she considered everything that drew attention to her position or her fortune shocking, and a continual battle waged between her on one side, and her mother and elder sister Claire, on the other, about questions of precedence.

My grandmother was assuredly not a hard-hearted woman; but though not exactly over-proud of her position, she had a very lively sense of social hierarchies. Her daughter Claire had this same sense (she had indeed very little other) but not her mother's kindness of heart. She was irritated to find her sister was without it, and to be met instead by a temper which, if not actually rebellious, was at any rate far from submissive—a temper which was probably not natural to Juliette, but which had apparently been fostered by her friendship for

Anna. Claire found it difficult to forgive Anna her sister's friendship; she considered that friendship comports degrees and shades and that it was not proper Miss Shackleton should forget she was a governess.

"What!" thought my mother, "am I handsomer? or more intelligent, or better? Is my fortune or my name any reason I should be preferred?"

"Juliette," Anna would say, "you must give me a tea-coloured silk gown for your wedding-day, and I shall be completely happy."

.   .   .   .

For a long time Juliette Rondeaux had disdained the most brilliant matches in Rouen, when one day people were surprised to hear she had accepted a penniless young professor of law, from the depths of Provence, who would never have dared to ask her hand if good Pastor Roberty, by whom he had been introduced into my mother's family, and who knew her views, had not encouraged him to do so. When six years later, I made my appearance, Anna Shackleton adopted me as she had adopted, one after the other, my big cousins. As neither beauty, nor grace, nor kindness, nor cleverness, nor virtue can compensate for lack of money, it was never Anna's lot to know anything of earthly love but a pale reflection, nor to have any other family but the one my relations provided her with.

My memory of her recalls a face with features already a little hardened by age and a slightly severe mouth; her eyes alone had kept their smile—a smile that at any trifle was ready to break out into laughter, so fresh and pure, that it seemed as though neither sorrows nor disappointments had been able to lessen the extreme amusement it is natural for a human being to take in life. My father too had the same laugh and sometimes Miss Shackleton and he went off into fits of childish merriment, in which I cannot remember my mother's ever joining.

Anna (with the exception of my father, who always said Mademoiselle Anna, we all called her by her Christian name, and I used even to say "Nana"—a childish habit I only gave up when a book by Zola came out with this name for title)— Anna Shackleton wore a kind of indoors cap, made of black lace, with two lappets that fell on each side of her face and framed it rather oddly. I do not know when she took to this headdress, but I cannot remember her without it, and she is wearing it in one or two photographs I have of her. Though the expression of her face, her bearing and whole way of life were so tranquil and harmonious, Anna was never idle; she kept her interminable embroidery for the time she spent in company and devoted her long hours of solitude to translation; for she read English and German as well as French, and knew Italian very tolerably.

I have kept some of these translations, which were never printed; they are written in her fine regular handwriting and fill several stout copybooks to the last line. All the works she translated in this way have since appeared in other translations—better perhaps; and yet I cannot bring myself to throw away these copybooks which tell such a tale of patience, love and probity. The one among them I am especially fond of it Goethe's *Reineke Fuchs*, of which Anna used often to read me passages. After she had finished this work, my cousin Maurice Démarest, gave her a present of a set of little plaster heads of all the animals mentioned in the old *fabliau*; Anna had hung them all round the frame of the glass over the mantelpiece in her room, and they were a constant delight to me.

Anna drew too and painted. She made some sketches of La Roque, conscientious, harmonious, modest sketches, which still hang in my wife's room at Cuverville; and another of La Mivoie, a place which belonged to my grandmother on the right bank of the Seine above Rouen. (It was sold shortly after her death and I should scarcely remember it except for the fact that every time I go to Normandy, I can see it from the train near Saint-Adrien's hill, and above the church of Bon-Secours, a few moments before one crosses the bridge.) In Anna's water-colour, it still has the graceful balustrade and the *Louis XVI* façade, which its new owners promptly ruined by adding to it a massive pediment.

But Anna's principal occupation, her dearest study was botany. In Paris she assiduously attended M. Bureau's lectures at the Natural History Museum, and in the spring, she used to join the botanising excursions organised by M. Poisson, his assistant. I make a point of not forgetting these names which Anna referred to with such veneration, and which wore the halo of a great prestige in my eyes. My mother thought this would be an opportunity of getting me to take a little exercise, and allowed me to join these Sunday excursions, which gave me the romantic feeling of a scientific voyage of discovery. The band of botanists was composed almost entirely of old maids and harmless monomaniacs. We used to meet at some station and take the train together; we all wore, slung over our shoulders, a tin box painted green, in which to put the plants we proposed to study or dry. Some of us had pruning scissors as well, and some, butterfly nets. I was among the latter, for I was not interested in flowers at that time so much as in insects and especially in beetles of which I was beginning a collection; and my pockets were stuffed with boxes and glass bottles in which I poisoned my victims by means of benzine fumes or cyanide of potassium. At the same time I hunted for plants as well; more nimble than the elderly explorers, I ran on ahead, left the beaten track to ransack the copses and fields, and trumpeted my discoveries, bursting with pride when I was the first to catch sight of a rare species; the other members of our little troop came up to admire it afterwards—rather vexed, some of them, when the specimen was unique, while I took my prize off in triumph to Anna.

In imitation of Anna and with her help, I made a herbarium; but I more especially helped her to complete hers, which was very large and remarkably well arranged. Not only had she succeeded by dint of patience in getting the finest examples of each variety, but they were marvellously set up: thin strips of gummed paper were used to keep the most delicate little stalks in place; the build and carriage of the plant were carefully respected; the bud, the full-blown flower and the seed were all shown together, and the names underneath were written in copper-plate. Sometimes the designation of a doubtful variety necessitated the most careful and minute investigations. Anna bent over her microscope, armed herself with pincers and tiny scalpels, opened the flower delicately, spread its organs under the objective glass and showed me some peculiarity of the stamens or what not, which her *Flora* had not mentioned and which M. Bureau had pointed out.

It was especially at La Roque, where Anna came with us every summer, that her botanising activities reached their height and the herbarium grew fat. She and I never went out without our green boxes (for I had mine too) and a kind of special trowel which enabled us to dig up the plant without injuring its root. Sometimes we watched one particular plant day after day; we waited for the flower to come to perfection and were in real despair when on the last day we found perhaps that it had been half eaten by caterpillars, or maybe a sudden storm kept us in.

At La Roque the herbarium reigned supreme; everything connected with it was performed with the zeal and gravity pertaining to a rite. On fine days, the leaves of grey paper, between which the plants were to be dried, were spread out on all the window-sills and on the sunny parts of tables and floors. Some of them—those that were slender or fibrous—required only a few leaves of paper; but there were others—fleshy ones, juicy with sap—which had to be pressed between thick mattresses of very dry, spongy paper that had to be changed every day. All this took a considerable amount of time and needed much more room than Anna was able to find in Paris.

She lived in the Rue de Vaugirard, between the Rue Madame and the Rue d'Assas, in a little flat of four poky rooms that were so low you could almost touch the ceiling with your hand. The apartment, however, was not badly situated, opposite the garden or courtyard of some scientific institution, which gave us an opportunity of witnessing the first trials of those strange affairs—solar boilers. They were like enormous flowers, with a corolla made of mirrors; the pistil, at the point where the rays of light converged, contained the water which had to be brought to the boil. No doubt the attempt was successful, for one fine day, one of the boilers burst, terrifying the whole neighbourhood, and breaking the window-panes in Anna's drawing-room and bedroom, which both looked on to the street. The dining-room and a study where Anna usually sat, looked on to a courtyard; it was here that she preferred to receive the few intimate friends who came to see her; and I should no doubt have forgotten the drawing-room, if it had not been there that a little folding bed had been put up for me when once, to my great joy, my mother had entrusted me for a few days to her friend's care, for some reason or other which I cannot remember.

When I began going to the Ecole Alsacienne, my parents having, I suppose, come to the conclusion that the education I was getting with Mademoiselle Fleur and Madame Lackerbauer was no longer adequate, it was settled I should have lunch with Anna once a week. It was on Thursdays, I remember, after the gymnastic lesson. The Ecole Alsacienne was not then as flourishing as it afterwards became and had no special room for physical drill, so that its pupils used to be sent to Pascaud's Gymnasium, a few doors from Anna's, in the Rue de Vaugirard. I used to arrive at her rooms still dripping with perspiration, and all in disorder, my clothes full of sawdust and my hands sticky with rosin. What was there so charming about those luncheons? Chiefly, I think, Anna's untiring attention to all my most foolish chatter, the feeling that I was important in her eyes, that I was awaited, considered, made much of. It was for my sake the room filled with welcome and smiles and the lunch was especially good. How I wish that in return I could remember one gracious act, one look or word of childish affection . . . But no; the only thing I can recall is an absurd sentence, worthy of the dense boy I then was; I blush to repeat it—but this is no romance I am writing and I have determined not to flatter myself in these memoirs, either by adding anything agreeable or hiding anything painful.

As I was eating that morning with an excellent appetite and it was clear Anna, with her small means, had done her best:

"Oh, Nana!" I cried, "I shall eat you out of house and home!" (the words are still ringing in my ears) . . . At any rate, I had no sooner pronounced them, than I felt that no one of any delicacy of heart could have said such a thing, that Anna was hurt by them, that I had a little wounded her. This was, I think, one of the first flashes of my conscience—a fugitive gleam, too fitful and too feeble as yet to pierce the thick darkness that still wrapped my tardy childhood.

II

I can imagine my mother's bewilderment when for the first time she left her comfortable surroundings in the Rue de Crosne to accompany my father to Uzès. The progress of the age seemed to have passed by this little Provençal town, situated off the beaten track and unaware of the surrounding world. The railway only went as far as Nîmes, or at most to Remoulins; and from there one had to finish the journey in a crazy shandrydan. It was considerably longer to go by Nîmes but the road was much more beautiful. It crossed the Gardon by Saint Nicholas' bridge and then one entered Palestine and Judaea. The rough glen or *garrigue* smelt sweet of lavender and was bright with tufts of white and purple cistus. A dry, exhilarating air blew overhead, which cleared the road but covered everything round with dust. Our carriage often started numbers of enormous grasshoppers, which spread their blue, red or grey membranes and shot up into the air, gay butterflies for a single moment, but falling down the next with their brightness dulled, and indistinguishable from the stones and scrub amongst which they lay.

Asphodels grew on the banks of the Gardon; and in the river-bed itself, which was almost everywhere dry, the flora was quasi-tropical . . . Here, I leave the shandrydan for a moment; there are memories I must snatch in passing or I shall not know where else to place them. As I have already said, I fit them less easily into time than into space; for instance, I cannot say what year it was that Anna came to visit us at Uzès, which my mother no doubt was anxious to show her; but what I do remember very clearly is the excursion we made with her one day from Saint Nicholas' bridge to some village not far from the Gardon, where the carriage was to pick us up.

In the narrow parts of the valley, at the foot of the cliffs burning with the reverberated heat of the sun, the vegetation was so luxuriant it was difficult to make one's way through it. Anna was in ecstasies at the many plants that were unknown to her, and kept recognising one or another she had never before seen growing wild—I was going to say "at liberty"— as, for instance, those triumphant daturas, sometimes called "trumpets of Jericho," which, with the oleanders, have remained so deeply engraved on my memory for their splendour and strangeness. We advanced cautiously on account of snakes, and saw several, though mostly harmless ones, which glided out of our way. My father, who found something to amuse him at every turn, was inclined to loiter and linger. My mother, aware of the lateness of the hour, tried in vain to hurry us on. The evening was already closing in when we came out from between the high banks of the river. The village was still a long way off and the angelic sound of its bells reached us only faintly; the road that led to it was nothing but an ill-defined path, wavering uncertainly through the brushwood . . . The reader will suspect perhaps that I am adding all this after the event; but no; the sound of the angelus is still in my ears; I can still see the delightful path, the rosy sunset and the darkness marching up behind us from the bed of the Gardon. At first I was amused by the long shadows we cast; then everything vanished in the grey of twilight and I felt my mother's anxiety growing upon me too. But my father and Anna, intent on the beauty of the hour, still dawdled, regardless of time. I remember they were repeating poetry; my mother thought "it was not the moment" and cried:

"Paul, you can say that when we get in."

In my grandmother's apartment all the rooms communicated, so that in order to get to their bedroom, my parents had to go through the dining-room, the drawing-room and another smaller drawing-room, where a bed for me was put up. If you finished the round, you came to a little dressing-room and then to my grandmother's room, which could be reached from the other end as well, by passing through my uncle's room. This latter opened again on to the landing, as also did the kitchen and the dining-room. The windows of the two drawing-rooms and my parents' room looked on to the esplanade; the others opened on to a narrow courtyard, round which the apartment was built; my uncle's room alone overlooked a dark alley, at the further end of which could be seen a corner of the marketplace. My uncle cultivated strange objects on his window-sill; he had a collection of mysterious glass jars and in these were stuck a number of rigid stems round which crystallised what he explained were salts of zinc, copper and other metals: he told me that according to the name of the metal, these implacable growths were called trees of Saturn, Jupiter, etc. My uncle had not then begun to take an interest in political economy; I heard later that his real hobby at that time was astronomy, to which study he was drawn by his taste for figures, a habit of taciturn contemplation and that denial of individuality and psychology of any kind, which eventually turned him into a being with less knowledge of himself and other people than anyone I have ever known. He was then a tall young man, with long strands of black hair plastered back behind his ears, rather short-sighted, rather queer, chary of words and incredibly alarming. He was greatly irritated by my mother's constant attempts to thaw him; though full of good intentions, she was not very adroit, and my uncle, unable or unwilling to take the will for the deed, was even then beginning to be impervious to the blandishments of anyone who was not a humbug. It seemed as if my father had absorbed all the family stock of amiability and that none was left to moderate the crabbed humours of its other members.

My grandfather died some time before I was born; my mother had, however, known him, for I was not born till six years after her marriage. She described him to me as a typical Huguenot, single-minded and austere, very tall, very strong and angular, inflexible, scrupulous to excess, and with a confidence in God which he pushed to sublime extremes. He had formerly been a president of the Uzès tribunal, and at the time she knew him was almost entirely taken up by good works and by the moral and religious instruction of his Sunday-school pupils.

Besides my father, Paul, and my uncle, Charles, Tancrède Gide had had several children who had died in infancy, one from a fall on the head, another from sun-stroke, yet another from a neglected cold—neglected apparently for the same reason that he neglected his own health. When he fell ill, which seldom happened, he refused to have recourse to anything but prayer; he considered the intervention of the doctor officious, not to say impious, and died without allowing one to be sent for.

Some people may wonder that these impracticable and almost antediluvian forms of humanity should have survived so long; but the whole small town of Uzès was in itself a survival, and my grandfather's extravagances were certainly not conspicuous in a place where everything was of a piece, where everything accounted for them, explained them, encouraged them and even made them appear natural; and what is more, I think that almost identical conditions would have been found over the whole Cévennes district, which even as late as this had barely recovered from the cruel religious dissensions by which it had been so long and so severely tormented in the past. A strange adventure of my own, which I must relate here, though it belonged to my eighteenth year, or there-abouts, makes me think I am right.

I had started from Uzès one morning in answer to an in-vitation from my cousin, Guillaume Granier, a pastor in the neighbourhood of Anduze. I spent the day with him. Before letting me go, he had preached to me, prayed with me and for me, and blessed me or at least prayed God to bless me . . . But this has nothing to do with my story. The train was to take me back to Uzès for dinner; but I was reading *Le Cousin Pons*. Of all Balzac's many masterpieces, it is perhaps my favourite; at any rate it is the one I have read oftenest. Now it was on that very day that I discovered it. I was in a seventh heaven of de-light, beside myself, oblivious of the world . . .

The approach of night at last interrupted my reading. After abusing my carriage for not being lighted, I noticed it was stationary; the railway people, thinking it was empty, had shunted it on to a siding.

"Didn't you know you had to change?" they asked. "You must be deaf! Or perhaps you were asleep. You had better take another nap, for there is no train from here now till to-morrow morning."

The prospect of passing the night in a dark railway car-riage had no charms for me; and besides, I had not dined. The station was a long way from the village and I felt less at-tracted by the inn than by the chance of an adventure; be-sides, I had no more than a few pence in my pockets. I started walking along the road, trusting to luck, and decided to knock at a fairly large *mas* or farm-house which looked clean and inviting. A woman opened the door and I told her I had lost my way, that the fact of having no money did not prevent me from having an appetite, and that perhaps they would be hospitable enough to give me something to eat and drink; and then I would go back to my railway carriage and wait patiently till morning.

The table was already laid, but the woman who had opened the door at once set another place. Her husband was away; her old father, who was sitting by the fire, for the room where they sat was the kitchen as well, remained bending over the hearth without speaking, in what seemed a disapproving silence which made me feel uncomfortable. All of a sudden I noticed a big Bible on a kind of shelf, and realising I was in a Protestant household, I mentioned the name of the person I had been visiting. The old man sat up at once; he knew my cousin, the pastor; he even remembered my grandfather very well. I realised from the way he spoke of him how much unselfishness and kindliness may lie under the roughest exterior, and this applied to my grandfather as much as to the old peasant. My grandfather must have resembled him, I thought, in his look of extreme robustness, his voice which, though not melodious, was clear and ringing, and his straightforward, uncompromising glance.

In the meantime the children came in from work—a grown-up girl and three boys; more delicately built than their grandfather; good-looking young people, but with grave faces for their age, and even perhaps a touch of sternness on their brows. Their mother placed the steaming soup on the table and stopped me in the middle of a sentence with a quiet motion of her hand, while the old man said the *benedicite*.[1]

It was during supper that he spoke of my grandfather; his language, though precise, was full of imagery; I am sorry not to have noted down some of his phrases. "Can this be really

[1] It has been pointed out to me that this word is never used except by Catholics. I must wait until Protestants provide me with another to designate the short prayer that precedes a meal. *(Author's note)*

English Protestants have provided the word *grace!* But I keep the original *benedicite* for the sake of Monsieur Gide's curious note. *(Translator's note)*

nothing but a family of peasants?" I kept saying to myself. "What distinction they have, what vivacity, what dignity compared to our loutish, stolid Normandy labourers!" At the end of supper, I got up to go; but my hosts would not hear of it. The mother was already setting about her preparations; the eldest son would sleep with one of his brothers; I should have his room and his bed, which she spread with clean coarse sheets, smelling deliciously of lavender. With them, they said, it was early to bed and early to rise, but as for me, I might sit up and read, if I felt inclined to.

"But," said the old man, "you will allow us to follow our usual custom—which will not astonish you, as you are Monsieur Tancrède's grandson."

Then he fetched down the big Bible I had noticed and put it on the table which had been cleared. His daughter and grandchildren sat down again on either side of him at the table in an attitude of devotion that came naturally to them. The grandfather opened the Holy Book and read aloud a chapter of the Gospels in a solemn voice, and then a psalm; after which, they all, with the exception of himself, knelt down in front of their chairs. I saw that he remained standing, with his eyes shut and his hands laid on the closed book. He uttered a short prayer of thanksgiving, very dignified and very simple, with no requests in it, and I remember he thanked God for leading me to his door, and in such a tone that my whole heart responded to his words. To end up with, he said the Lord's Prayer; then there was a moment's silence before each of the children rose. It was all so noble and so calm, the kiss of peace he put on the forehead of each so beautiful, that I too went up with the others and in my turn offered him my forehead.

There was still alive among my grandfather's generation the memory of the persecutions that had dealt so unsparingly with their ancestors, or at any rate a certain tradition of resistance. A great stubbornness of spirit had resulted from the attempt to bend them. Each one of them clearly heard Christ's words addressed to him and to all the little martyred flock: "Ye are the salt of the earth: but if the salt have lost his savour wherewith shall it be salted?" . . .

And it must be acknowledged that the Protestant service in the little chapel of Uzès still kept a particularly racy flavour in the days of my childhood. Yes, it fell to my lot to see the last representatives of that generation of men who addressed God as "thou", attending divine service with their great felt hats on their heads, raising them each time the pastor pronounced the name of God, and only taking them off during the Lord's Prayer . . . A stranger would have been shocked at what looked like irreverence, if he had not known that these old Huguenots kept their heads covered in memory of the open-air services, held under a burning sky, in the secret recesses of the mountains, at a time when their ritual carried with it the danger of a capital penalty.

Then, one after the other, these megatheria disappeared. Their widows survived them for some time. They had ceased going out, except to chapel on Sundays, which meant to meet each other as well. There was my grandmother, her friend Madame Abauzit, Madame Vincent, and two other old ladies whose names I have forgotten. A little before the service began, their servant-maids, as old nearly as their mistresses, brought in the ladies' foot-warmers and placed them in their pews. Then, punctually to the minute, the widows made their entrance and the service began. Half blind as they were, they did not recognise each other outside the door, nor till they were safely in their pews, when carried away by the pleasure of meeting their cronies, they set up a chorus of extraordinary greetings—a mixture of congratulations, enquiries and an swers; each of them as deaf as a post, hearing nothing her gossip said to her, so that for some moments the noise of their united voices completely drowned that of the unfortunate pastor. Some people, who might otherwise have been indignant, forgave the widows in memory of their husbands; others, less strict, were amused; some of the children burst out laughing; as for me, I felt so uncomfortable that I asked not to sit next my grandmother. This little performance was repeated every Sunday; it was at once more grotesque and more touching than can well be imagined.

I could never make you understand how very old my grandmother was. As far back as I can remember there was nothing left in her by which one could possibly guess or imagine what she had once looked like. She had an iron constitution and outlived not only her husband, but her eldest son, my father, as well; and for a long time after his death, my mother and I went back to Uzès year after year to find her the same as ever, barely a little deafer—for as to being more wrinkled, it was impossible.

The dear old lady certainly put herself out in every possible way to entertain us; which is precisely the reason I am not quite sure that we were very welcome. That, however, was not the point; what my mother desired was not so much to give pleasure as to accomplish a duty, a rite—as for instance, the solemn letter she obliged me to write to my grandmother every New Year and which completely spoilt the holidays for me. I began by trying to get out of it.

"But what difference can it make to grannie whether she gets a letter from me or not?"

"That is not the question," said my mother; "you have not got so many obligations as all that in your life; you must not shirk them."

Then I would burst into tears.

"Come, darling," she began again, "be sensible; think of your poor grannie and remember you are her only grandson."

"But what in the world am I to say to her?" I wailed through my sobs.

"Anything. Tell her about your cousins—about your little friends, the Jardiniers."

"But she doesn't know them."

"Tell her what you are doing."

"But you know quite well it won't interest her."

"It's not the slightest good talking, my dear. You won't leave this room (it was the Rue de Crosne school-room) till you have written the letter."

"But . . ."

"No, my dear, I am not going to argue."

After which my mother retired into a stony silence. I dawdled a little longer and then began to rack my brains over my sheet of white paper.

The fact is that nothing seemed capable of interesting my grandmother any more. And yet whenever we went to stay at Uzès, out of kindness, I think, to my mother, who would sit beside her with her needlework or her book, grandmother would put a great strain on her memory and every quarter of an hour or so would at last recollect the name of one of my Normandy cousins and come out with:

"And how are the Widmers?"

My mother answered her with infinite patience and then returned to her reading. Ten minutes later:

"And Maurice Démarest, he's not married yet?"

"Yes, mother; Albert is the one who isn't married. Maurice has three children—three daughters."

"Dear, dear, Juliette! Did you ever!"

This interjection did not imply any doubt. It was simply an

exclamation fitted for every occasion; my grandmother used it to express astonishment, approbation or admiration, so that it came as the immediate reflex to whatever one said; and for a little time after she had launched it, grandmother's head still kept wagging meditatively up and down; one saw her ruminating the piece of news in a sort of empty mastication, during which her poor old wrinkled chaps alternately sank in and puffed out. Finally, when it was all thoroughly absorbed and she had given up for the time any attempt to think of fresh questions, she took up her interrupted knitting again.

Grandmother knitted stockings; it was the only occupation I ever saw her engaged in. She knitted all day long in the manner of a diligent insect; but as she continually got up to go to the kitchen to see what Rose was doing, she often left her stocking straying on some piece of furniture or other and I really believe she was never known to finish one. There were beginnings of stockings in all the drawers, into which Rose used to tidy them away when she did the drawing-room in the morning. As for her knitting needles, grandmother always carried a sheaf of them stuck behind her ear, between her little beribboned cap and the meagre strand of her yellowish grey hair.

My aunt Anna, her new daughter-in-law, had not the same affectionate and respectful indulgence for grandmother that my mamma had; she held her mother-in-law responsible for everything about my uncle that she disapproved of or that irritated her. I think she only came to Uzès once while my mother and I were staying there; she had no sooner arrived than we caught her making a raid on the stockings.

"Eight! I've found eight of them!" she said to my mother, at once amused and exasperated by such thriftlessness. And in the evening, she could not resist asking my grandmother why she never finished any of them.

The poor old thing tried at first to smile; then she turned anxiously to my mother:

"Juliette, what does Anna mean?"

But my mother preferred to keep out of it and my aunt went on louder than ever:

"I was asking, mother, why you never finish one stocking before starting on so many fresh ones?"

Then the old lady, a little vexed, pursed up her lips and retorted snappily:

"Finish! Finish! . . . It's all very well for Anna! . . . But one must have time!"

My grandmother suffered from the constant fear that we should not have enough to eat (though she herself hardly ate anything), and my mother had the greatest difficulty in persuading her that four dishes to a meal were enough for us. More often than not she refused to listen to her protests and hurried off, as soon as my mother's back was turned, to have a mysterious colloquy with Rose. My mother in her turn would catch Rose before she started on her marketing, would revise the menu and suppress three-quarters of it.

"Well, Rose, what about those spring chickens?" cried my grandmother at lunch.

"But, mother, we've already had cutlets this morning. I told Rose to keep the spring chickens for to-morrow."

The poor old dear was in despair.

"Cutlets! Cutlets!" she would repeat, affecting to laugh. "Lamb cutlets! It takes six of them to make a mouthful . . ."

Then, by way of protest, she would get up and go to a little cupboard at the other end of the dining-room and, in order to make up for the wretched inadequacy of the menu, would fetch out a mysterious pot of some delicacy or other which had been prepared against our coming. As a rule it contained succulent morsels of pork, stuffed with truffles and preserved in lard, known as *fricandeaux*. My mother of course refused.

"Tut, tut! But the boy would like some at any rate."

"I assure you, mother, he has had plenty already."

"But you don't want him to die of hunger, do you?" . . .

(According to her, every child that was not bursting with fat was perishing. When later on she was asked how her grandsons, my cousins, were, she invariably pulled a long face and answered: "Sadly thin!")

One good way of escaping my mother's censorship was to order some dish from the Hotel Béchard—a tender fillet of beef *aux olives*, a *vol-au-vent* full of *quenelles*, or a flaky *brandade*, or the traditional *croûtillon au lard* from Fabregas', the pastrycook's.

My mother, in the name of hygiene, made war too against my grandmother's favourite dishes; and in particular against the habit she had when she was helping the *vol-au-vent* of keeping a bit of the bottom crust for herself.

"But, mother, you're taking the very richest bit!"

"Oh!" said my grandmother, who cared not a snap for hygiene, "the bottom crust . . ."

"Let *me* help you."

And the poor old thing had to submit to seeing her favourite morsel taken off her plate.

It was Fabregas too who supplied the sweets, which were very praiseworthy, but not very varied. To tell the truth they always resolved themselves into the *Sultana*, which none of us were particularly keen about. The *Sultana* took the shape of a pyramid, sometimes topped, for the sake of swagger, with a little angel made of some white inedible substance. The pyramid was composed of minute *choux à la crème*, with a tough coating of caramel on them, welding them together so firmly that they had to be broken through with the spoon instead of being elegantly divided. A cloud of caramel threads enveloped the whole and removed it from the regions of greed with a poetical, if sticky, veil.

Grandmother wished us to understand it was only for want of something better that she offered us a *Sultana*. She used to make a face and say:

"Oh! Fabregas! . . . Fabregas! He hasn't much choice!"

Or again:

"He's getting careless."

How long those meals lasted for a boy like me, who was always impatient to get out! I was passionately fond of the country round Uzès, of the valley of the Fontaine d'Eure and above all of the *garrigue*. In the first years, our maid Marie came with me on my walks. I used to drag her up Mont Sarbonnet, a little limestone hillock just outside the town, a delightful place for caterpillars. The hawk-moth caterpillar, which looks like an untwisted turban and has a kind of horn on its hinder part, was to be found on the great milky-juiced euphorbias; and there were other caterpillars of the swallow-tail variety, which lived on the fennel in the shadow of the pines, and which, if one teased them, reared up from the backs of their necks a kind of forked trunk with a strong smell and an astonishing colour. If you followed the road that goes round the Sarbonnet, you reached the green meadows watered by the Fontaine d'Eure. The wettest of these meadows were enamelled in springtime with the graceful white narcissus, known as "the poet's narcissus" and called by the people of those parts the *courbadonne*. The inhabitants of Uzès never dreamt of picking them and would not turn out of their way to look at them; so that there was always an extraordinary profusion of them in these solitary meadows; the air was perfumed with their scent for a long way round; some of them stooped their faces over the water, as in the legend I had been taught, and those I would not pick; others grew half-hidden in the thick grass; but as a rule each flower, erect on its stalk, shone like a star on the dark background of the turf. Marie, like the good Swiss girl she was, loved flowers; we used to carry them home in armfuls.

The Fontaine d'Eure is that constant river the Romans captured and brought as far as Nîmes by the famous aqueduct of the Pont du Gard. The valley, through which the stream flows, half-hidden by alders, closes in as it approaches Uzès. O little town of Uzès! if you were in Umbria, how the tourists would flock from Paris to visit you! Uzès lies on the edge of a rock, whose steep slopes are partly covered with the thick woods of the Duchy gardens; the big trees that grow at the bottom shelter the river crayfish in their tangled roots. From the terraces of the Promenade or public Gardens, one can look across the tall Duchy nettle-trees and see facing one, on the other side, a still steeper and more rugged rock, riddled with caves, arches, needles and escarpments, like those one sees in sea-shore cliffs; then, above them and beyond, lies the harsh, hoarse *garrigue*, laid waste by the sun.

Marie, who was constantly complaining of her corns, professed very little enthusiasm for the stony paths of the *garrigue;* but the time came when my mother let me go out by myself and I could climb the rocks to my heart's content.

After walking for some time along the edge of the rock, where it was worn smooth by footsteps, and climbing down the steps that had been cut in its face, you crossed the river at the *Fon di biau* (I do not know whether I have spelt this name, which in Mistral's language means *Oxen fount*, correctly). It was a fine sight to see the washerwomen slowly planting their bare feet on the steps, as they came home from work in the evening, walking with their upright and noble gait that came to them from carrying their load of white linen, antique fashion, on their heads. As *Fontaine d'Eure* is the name of the river itself, I cannot be quite sure that the words *fon di biau* actually mean a fountain: what I remember is a water-mill, which was also a farm, shaded by immense plane-trees; in between the stream and the mill-race lay a sort of little island in which the farmyard poultry disported themselves. I used to go and dream or read at the extreme point of this little island; perched on the trunk of an old willow and hidden in its branches, I watched the adventurous games of the ducks and was deafened deliciously by the purring of the mill, the clatter of the water in the wheel, the myriad whispers and chatter of the river, while from further away, where the washerwomen were washing, came the rhythmic slapping of their bats.

But much more often, I would cut the *Fon di biau* and make straight for the *garrigue* at a run, drawn to it already by that strange love of the inhuman and the arid which for so long made me prefer the desert to the oasis. The great dry, perfumed gusts of wind, the blinding reverberation of the sun on the bare rock, were as intoxicating as wine. And how much I enjoyed climbing the rocks; hunting for the praying mantis (the people there call it the *prega-Diou*), whose conglutinated eggs were such a puzzle to me when I found them hanging on some little twig or blade of grass; or lifting up the stones to discover the horrible scorpions, centipedes and millipedes that crawled underneath them!

On rainy days, when I had to stop indoors, I hunted mosquitos, or else pulled grandmother's clocks to pieces, as they had usually all gone wrong since our last stay; I found this finicky job most absorbing, and how proud I was after I had set them going, to hear grannie say, when she was able to tell the time again:

"Oh, Juliette! Did you ever! That boy . . ."

But what I liked best in rainy weather was the time I spent in the loft, of which Rose lent me the key. (That was where I first read *Stello*, when I was older.) From the loft window, one could look down on to the neighbouring roofs; there was a large wooden cage, covered with a sack, near the window; it was there grandmother fattened her chickens for the table. I was not much interested in the chickens, but if one kept quite still for a little, there peeped out from among the piles of trunks, of nameless, useless objects, of all sorts of dusty lumber, or from behind the store of logs and kindling wood, the funny little faces of Rose's kittens, still too young to prefer, as their mother did, the warm peaceful kitchen, Rose's petting, the heat and smell of the joint turning in front of the wood fire, to the chaotic medley of their native loft.

Without having seen my grandmother, you might have supposed there could be nothing older in the world than Rose; it was a miracle she was still able to do any work; but grandmother wanted so little, and when we were staying there, Marie helped her with the rooms. Finally, however, Rose retired, and a series of the weirdest specimens succeeded each other as maid-servants, before my grandmother could be persuaded to go and live at Montpellier with my uncle Charles. One cheated, another drank, the third was disreputable. I remember the last; she belonged to the Salvation Army and it really seemed as if she were going to give satisfaction, when my grandmother, one sleepless night took it into her head to go to the drawing-room to fetch the stocking she was eternally knitting. She was dressed in her under-petticoat and night-gown; and, I suppose, had wind of something queer; she cautiously opened the door of the drawing-room and found it ablaze with lights . . . The Salvation Army lassie was holding a reception—which she did twice a week; the meetings in my grandmother's rooms were both edifying and popular, for after hymns were over, tea and refreshments were handed round. One can imagine my grandmother's entry into the midst of this assembly in her night attire! . . . It was shortly after this that she left Uzès for good.

Before leaving Uzès with her, I must speak of the door of the cupboard in the dining-room. This door was very thick and had what is called a knot in it, or to be more accurate, a spot in the sap-wood which had been the starting place of a little branch. The end of the branch had disappeared so that a round hole was left; it was about the size of a little finger and ran obliquely up and down in the thickness of the door. At the bottom of the hole, could be seen something round and smooth and grey which greatly puzzled me.

"Do you want to know what that is?" said Rose, as she was laying table one day, for I was busily engaged in sticking my little finger into the hole so as to get into contact with this strange object. "It's a marble your papa slipped into the hole when he was a little boy your age, and it has stayed there ever since."

This explanation satisfied my curiosity but only by exciting me in a different way. I was always fidgeting round the marble; by pushing my little finger right down, I could just reach it; but every effort I made to get it out merely made it roll round on itself and my nail slid over the smooth surface with a little squeaking noise, which was exasperating . . .

Next year as soon as we arrived at Uzès, I tried again. In spite of mamma's and Marie's laughter, I had let my little fingernail grow to an inordinate length on purpose, and now I managed without difficulty to slip it under the marble—a quick jerk, and out it shot into my hand.

My first impulse was to run to the kitchen and proclaim my triumph; but the prospective pleasure of Rose's congratulations all at once struck me as so very slight, that I stopped short on the way. I stood a few moments opposite the door gazing at the grey marble in the hollow of my hand; but henceforth it was like all its fellow marbles—it had no further interest for me the moment it had been brought to light. I felt uncommonly silly and small over my would-be smartness . . . Blushing, I slipped the marble back into its hole again (where it probably is to this day) and went off to cut my nail without speaking of my exploit to anyone.

Some ten years ago, as I was passing through Switzerland, I went to see my poor old Marie in her little village of Lotzwyl, where she still manages to keep alive. She talked to me about Uzès and my grandmother and freshened up some of my faded memories.

"Every time you ate an egg," she told me, "whether it was boiled or fried, your grannie never missed saying, 'Oh, leave the white, dearie; its only the yolk that's any good!'" And Marie, like a good Swiss woman, added: "As if the good Lord hadn't made the white to be eaten too!"

This is not a literary composition; I am just writing down my recollections as they come to me, so now I pass from my grandmother to Marie.

I remember the day it suddenly occurred to me that Marie might be pretty; it was one summer's day at La Roque; (what a long time ago!) she and I had gone out together to pick flowers in the meadow that lies in front of the garden; I was walking on ahead and had just crossed the stream; I turned round; Marie was still standing on the little bridge made of a tree-trunk, and in the shadow of an ash which overhangs the stream just at that place; another step or two and suddenly she was in a blaze of sunlight; she was holding a bunch of ox-eye daisies in her hand; her face, shaded by a broad-brimmed hat, seemed all one smile.

"What are you laughing at?" I called out.

"At nothing," she answered. "It's a fine day."

And all of a sudden the valley brimmed over with love and happiness.

In my family the servants were always kept very strictly. My mother, who was disposed to think she had a moral responsibility for the people she was interested in, would never have tolerated an intrigue that was not to be eventually consecrated by the ties of Hymen. This was no doubt why I never knew Marie with any other passion than the one which I accidentally discovered she had for Delphine, our cook, and which my mother would certainly never have dared to suspect. Needless to say, I myself did not realise it at the time and it was not till long after that the explanation of the transports I overheard that night occurred to me; some obscure instinct, nevertheless, kept me from speaking about them to my mother.

My room in the Rue de Tournon, as I have said, gave on to the courtyard, and was a little apart from the others; it was a fairly large room and, like all the others in our apartment, had a very lofty ceiling; next door to me, at the end of the passage that connected my room with the rest of the flat, was a kind of large closet, used as a bathroom (I afterwards conducted my chemical experiments in it), and above that the height of the ceiling gave space enough for Marie's bedroom. This bedroom was reached by a staircase starting in reality from my room, but cut off from it by a partition at the back of my bed. The closet and Marie's room had also another exit on to the back-stairs. Nothing is more difficult or more tedious than a description of places, but I think it necessary here in order to explain what follows . . . I must also say that our cook, Delphine, had just become engaged to the coachman of neighbours of ours in the country. She was on the point of leaving us for good. Now, on the night before her departure, I was awakened in the middle of the night by the most extraordinary noises; I was just going to call Marie, when I became aware that the noises were proceeding from her room; for that matter, they were more peculiar and mysterious than alarming—like a kind of dirge for two voices, which I can compare now-a-days to the *keening* of the Arab women I have heard in Algeria, but which seemed to me then like nothing on earth : a melancholy chant, interrupted spasmodically by sobs and cluckings and cries; I listened for a long time, sitting up in the dark and feeling in some inexplicable fashion that this was the expression of something more powerful than decency or sleep or the darkness of night; but at that age there are so many inexplicable things that—well!—I shook it all aside and sank off to sleep again; next morning, I did my best to account for it as an extravagance due to the uncontrolled behaviour of servants in general—of which I had lately had an example at the time of my uncle Démarest's death.

Ernestine, the Démarests' maid, while the mourners of the family in the drawing-room were restraining their tears in the presence of my aunt, who sat there mute and motionless and reduced to a shadow—Ernestine, seated in an armchair in the next room and sobbing loudly, kept ejaculating at intervals :

"Oh, my kind master! Oh, my dear master! My revered master!"

And she shook and heaved and carried on in such a way that I felt at first as if Ernestine was bearing all the weight of my aunt's grief, and that my aunt had got rid of it on to Ernestine, much as one hands a travelling bag over to a porter.

I could not understand at that age (I was ten years old)

49

that Ernestine's lamentations were addressed to the gallery, while Marie only raised hers because she thought no one heard them. But at that time I was not in the least inclined to be sceptical and besides was utterly ignorant, and even incurious of the works of the flesh.

It is true that in the Musée du Luxembourg, where I used sometimes to go with Marie (I imagine my parents had taken me there for the first time themselves, with the desire of cultivating my taste for lines and colours), I cared much less for story pictures—notwithstanding the pains Marie took to explain them—for that very reason, perhaps—than for pictures of nudes—to Marie's great scandal, who proceeded to inform my mother of the fact; and I was still more attracted by statues. The sight of Idrac's *Mercury* (if I am not mistaken) threw me into a stupor of admiration, out of which Marie had the greatest difficulty in arousing me. But it was not images such as these that gave me sensual pleasure, any more than pleasure evoked such images. Between the one and the others there existed no connection. Sexual excitement was caused by quite different things: most often by a profusion of colours or of unusually shrill sweet sounds; sometimes also by the idea of some urgent and important act which I ought to perform, which was expected of me, which I did not perform, and instead of performing only imagined; and also by the very kindred idea of destruction, which took the shape of spoiling a favourite toy: for the rest, there was no real desire, no attempt at contact. Anyone who is surprised at this can know very little about the matter: without examples and without object, what would sensual enjoyment become? Daydreams are its servants; they feed it at random with senseless luxuries, absurd prodigalities—an extravagant expenditure of life . . . But to show how greatly a child's instinct may go astray, I will mention more particularly two of the themes

that gave me physical enjoyment: one was furnished me very
innocently by George Sand in her charming story of
Gribouille. Gribouille throws himself into the water one day
that it is raining very hard, not to avoid the rain, as his wicked
brothers say, but to avoid his brothers, who are laughing at
him. For some time, he struggles in the water and tries to
swim; then he lets himself go; and as soon as he lets himself
go, he floats; then he feels himself becoming tiny, light, odd,
vegetable; leaves sprout out of him all over his body; and
soon Gribouille turns into a slender, graceful sprig of oak,
which the water gently deposits on the bank of the stream.
Absurd! But that is my very reason for telling it; I say what
is true and not what I think may redound to my credit. No
doubt "the grandmother of Nohant" had not the slightest intention of writing anything demoralising; but I bear witness
that no schoolboy was ever troubled by any page of *Aphrodite*
so much as I—ignorant little boy that I was—by the metamorphosis of Gribouille.

There was also a stupid little play of Madame de Ségur's
called *Les Dîners de Mademoiselle Justine*. There is a passage in it where the servants take advantage of their masters'
absence to have a bout of gormandising; they ransack the cup-
boards; they gorge themselves with food; then suddenly, as
Justine is stooping to lift a pile of plates out of the cupboard,
the coachman steals up behind her and puts his arm round
her waist; Justine is ticklish and drops the pile. Crash! The
whole of the crockery is smashed to pieces. This disaster made
me swoon with delight.

About this time, a little workwoman, whom I used to see
at my aunt Démarest's too, was in the habit of coming to sew
in my mother's house. Her name was Constance. She was a
little hunchback, with a bright colour, a roguish eye, a limp-
ing gait, very clever with her hands, reserved in her speech

in my mother's presence, but extremely free and easy as soon as she had turned her back. For convenience sake, she was put to work in my room, where the light was better; she spent whole afternoons there and I spent hours in her company. How was it that my mother, who was usually so scrupulous, so attentive, whose anxious care I soon found actually irksome, how was it that my mother allowed her vigilance to flag upon this occasion? But if Constance's conversation was not all it should have been, I for one was far too dense to understand it, and when Marie sometimes exploded into her handkerchief, I had no notion why. But Constance talked much less than she sang; her voice was pleasant and singularly full for so small a body; she was all the more vain of it as it was the only thing about her she could be vain of. She sang all day long; she used to say she could not sew properly unless she sang; she never stopped singing. Heavens! what songs! Constance might have declared with truth that there was nothing immoral about them. No, what fouled my brain was their stupidity. If only I could have forgotten them! Alas! while the most exquisite gems of music have fled my memory, these wretched vulgar songs sound in my ears as distinctly as on the first day I heard them. What! Rousseau in later life could still remember with emotion the charming airs his aunt Gancera had sung him to sleep with in infancy, and must I till the end of my days hear Constance's common voice singing to a waltz tune such words as these?

> *"I say, Mammy, what a lark!*
> *Do we know this sweet young spark?*
> *Isn't he a lollipop?*
> *Isn't he a real cough-drop?"*

What a to-do about a harmless popular song!

Yes, I know. And it is not the song I object to, but the amusement I took in it, in which I seem to see the dawning of a shameful taste for indecency, stupidity and the worst vulgarity. I am not too severe on myself. I shall soon show that there were elements in my disposition which, unperceived as yet, would eventually incline me to virtue. In the meantime my mind was still desperately benighted. In vain I search the past for some glimmer of promise in the dull lad I then remember. Heart and head seemed equally plunged in darkness. I have already related my clumsy response to Anna's kindness. Another memory of the same period will give even a better idea of that stage of undevelopment in which my childhood still lingered like the veriest grub.

My parents had sent me, as I have said, to the Ecole Alsacienne. I was eight years old. I was not put into the tenth class in which the smallest children were taught their rudiments by Monsieur Grisier, but into the one above under Monsieur Vedel, a worthy roundabout little man from the South of France, upon whose brow rose an unexpectedly romantic crest of black hair, contrasting strangely with the rest of his colourless and placid person. A few weeks, or a few days, before the incident I am going to relate, my father had taken me to be introduced to the head-master. As the term had already begun and I was a late-comer, the boys whispered, as they stood aside to let us pass through the playground, "A new boy! A new boy!" while I clung nervously to my father's side. Then I took my place among the others, though, for reasons I shall soon be obliged to tell, only for a short time. On that particular day, Monsieur Vedel was teaching his class that there are sometimes several words in a language to denote the same object and that then they are called synonyms. And he gave as an example the word *cou-*

53

drier and the word *noisetier* which both mean *nut-tree*. Then, in order to vary the lesson a little, he passed from teaching to questioning and asked the new boy Gide to repeat what he had just said . . .

I did not answer. I could not answer. But Monsieur Vedel was kind; with all the patience of a good teacher, he repeated his definition and gave the same example; but when he asked me again to tell him the synonym for *coudrier* I again held my tongue. Then, for form's sake, he grew a little angry and ordered me to go outside into the playground and repeat twenty times running that *coudrier* was the synonym of *noisetier*.

My stupidity had sent the whole class into ecstasies. If I had wanted to cut a dash, it would have been very easy, when Monsieur Vedel called me back after my penance and asked me for the third time the synonym of *coudrier*, to have answered "cauliflower" or "pumpkin". But no; I did not want to cut a dash and I disliked being laughed at; I was simply stupid. Perhaps I had taken it into my head to be obstinate? No, not even that; I really think I did not understand what I was wanted or expected to do.

As impositions were not customary in this school, Monsieur Vedel had to content himself with giving me a "nought for conduct." The punishment however was none the less rigorous, for being purely moral. But it had not the smallest effect on me. Every week regularly I had my "nought for conduct" or for "order and cleanliness"; sometimes both. It was a dead certainty. Needless to add I was among the lowest in the class. I repeat, I was still asleep—unawakened—unborn.

A little later I was sent away from school for quite different reasons, which I must pluck up my courage to tell.

III

It was clearly understood that I was only to be sent away from school temporarily. Monsieur Brunig, the head of the lower school, gave me three months to get cured of "the bad habits" Monsieur Vedel had discovered—easily enough, for I was at no particular pains to hide them, not having grasped how reprehensible they were; for I was still living (if one can call it living) in the half-awakened state of imbecility I have described.

My parents had had a dinner-party the evening before; I had stuffed my pockets with the sweetmeats that had been left over from dessert, and that morning, while Monsieur Vedel was exerting himself at his desk, I sat on my bench, enjoying alternately my pleasure and my chocolates.

Suddenly I heard myself summoned.

"Gide! You look very red? Come here and speak to me a minute."

My cheeks became redder still, as I went up the four steps of the desk and my schoolfellows tittered.

I did not attempt to deny it. At the first question Monsieur Vedel put me in a whisper, as he bent down towards me, I nodded my acquiescence; then I went back to my desk more dead than alive. Nevertheless it did not occur to me to think that this interrogatory would be followed by any consequences; before putting his question, had not Monsieur Vedel promised to say nothing about it?

Notwithstanding which, that very evening my father got a letter from the head asking him not to send me back to school for three months.

The Ecole Alsacienne had a reputation for conduct and morals; it was their specialty. Monsieur Brunig's decision on this occasion therefore was not in the least surprising. My mother told me later, however, that my father had been indignant at his letter and at the abruptness and rigour of the punishment. He concealed his anger from me of course, though he showed me his distress. After serious consultations with my mother, it was decided to take me to the doctor's.

My parents' doctor at that time was no less a person than Dr. Brouardel, who shortly after became celebrated as an expert in medical jurisprudence. I think my mother did not expect much more from this consultation than a moral effect and perhaps a little good advice into the bargain. After she had had a few minutes' private conversation with Brouardel, she left the consulting-room and he called me into it.

"I know all about it, my boy," he said, putting on a gruff voice, "and there's no need to examine or question you. But if your mother finds it necessary to bring you here again, that is, if you don't learn to behave, look behind you!" (and his voice became truly terrible). "Those are the instruments we should have to use—the instruments with which little boys like you have to be operated on!" And he rolled his eyes at me ferociously as he pointed out a panoply of Touareg spearheads hanging on the wall behind his chair.

This threat was really too thin for me to take it seriously. But my mother's obvious anxiety, together with her admonishments, and my father's silent distress, at last penetrated my torpor, which had already been considerably shaken by my dismissal from school. My mother extracted promises from me; she and Anna exerted themselves too to invent distractions for me. The Great Universal Exhibition was on the point of opening and we used often to walk as far as the palisades and watch the preparations . . .

Three months later, I took my place again on the school benches; I was cured—at any rate as much as one ever is. But not long after, an attack of measles left me in weak health, and my parents decided to take me away from school again until the following year; I should then be able to start from the beginning once more, in the same class of which I had missed so much the year before. They carried me off to La Roque without waiting for the holidays to begin.

When in 1900 I determined to sell La Roque, I swallowed down my regret out of bravado, confidence in the future, and the vain and rather theoretical hatred of the past which bolstered it up (futurism, it would be called nowadays). In reality, my regret was much less lively at the time than it afterwards became. Not that the place owes any of its beauty to memory; when, something more of a traveller, I saw it again in after years, I was better able to appreciate the intimate charm of the little valley, which, in those days of swelling hopes and desires impressed me chiefly with a sense of its narrowness.

"And skies too little over trees too big"

as Jammes says in one of the Elegies he wrote when he was staying with us.

It is this valley and our house that I have described in the *Immoraliste;* the outer aspect of the country furnished me with the scenery of the book, but throughout its pages I have endeavoured to trace a deeper resemblance.

The place was bought by my grandparents. A black marble slab over the postern bore the following inscription:

CONDIDIT A 1577 NOB. DOM. FRANCISCUS

LABBEY DO ROQUÆ.

MAGNAM PARTEM DESTRUXIT A 1792

SCELESTE TUMULTUANTIUM TURBA

REFECIT A 1803 CONDITORIS AT NEPOS

NOBILIS DOMINUS PETRUS ELIAS MARIA

LABBEY DO ROQUÆ, MILES

57

I have copied it word for word and take no responsibility for the Latin.

At any rate, it was only too obvious that the principal block of the buildings was much later in date, its only charm consisting in its drapery of wistaria. The kitchen buildings, on the other hand, and the postern were of small but exquisite proportions, and built, according to the charming style of the earlier period, in alternate courses of brick and stone. The whole building was surrounded by a widish moat of some little depth, supplied with running water from the river; a rivulet, flowery with forget-me-nots, brought it in and poured it into the moat in a waterfall. As her room was near by, Anna called it "*my* waterfall"; to enjoy a thing is to make it your own.

The chatter of the river was mingled with the song of the waterfall and the ceaseless murmur of a little spring which gushed up outside the island, opposite the postern; it was there we got our drinking-water, which was icy cold, and in summer covered the water-bottles with mist.

Flocks of swallows whirled incessantly round the house; their clay nests were built for the sake of shelter under the eaves of the house and in the embrasures of the windows, so that one could watch the young broods. When I think of La Roque, I first of all hear the swallows' cries; they seemed to split the azure as they flew past. I have often seen swallows elsewhere; but never anywhere else have I heard them give exactly that cry; I think they uttered these cries as they flew circling round, each time they passed their nests. Sometimes they flew so high that one's eyes dazzled following them; that was on the finest days; when the weather changed, their flight fell barometrically. Anna explained to me that the tiny insects they pursue so swiftly fly higher or lower according to the pressure of the air. I have sometimes seen a swallow swoop

58

low enough to cut the surface of the water with a daring stroke of its wing.

"There's going to be a storm," my mother and Anna would say then.

And suddenly the sound of rain was added to the other liquid sounds of stream, spring and waterfall; it fell with a silvery patter on to the water of the moat. Leaning with my elbows on the sill of one of the windows that opened on to it, I was never tired of watching the myriads of little circles which kept forming, spreading, intersecting each other and disappearing, with sometimes a great bubble that burst in the middle of them.

When my grandparents came into possession of the property, the only access to it was through fields, woods and farmyards. My grandmother and Monsieur Ch . . .,[1] his neighbour, laid out a road, which branched off from the high road between Caen and Lisieux at La Boissière, and served first Blancmesnil, where Monsieur Ch . . . lived, and then La Roque. When La Roque had been connected with the rest of the world by road, my grandfather built a brick bridge in place of the little drawbridge, which was expensive to keep in order and never raised.

What words can describe the delight for a child of living on an island—a tiny island—from which moreover he can escape whenever he pleases? A brick wall, serving as a parapet, circled it and connected the different portions of the building; this wall was thickly overgrown with ivy on its inner side and was wide enough to walk along quite safely; but if you wanted to fish, you were too much in view and the better plan was simply to lean over it; the outer surface dipped straight into the water and was ornamented here and there with wall-plants, valerians, strawberries, saxifrage, some-

[1] The celebrated statesman and historian Guizot.   *(Translator's note)*

59

times even with a little bush, which mamma looked at dis-
approvingly because it loosened the brickwork, but which
Anna would coax her to spare, because a tit had nested in it.

A courtyard in front of the house, between the postern and
the kitchen buildings, left the eye free to roam over the
moat-parapet and across the garden into the depths without
end of the valley beyond—a valley which would have seemed
narrow, had the hills that enclosed it been higher. On the
right, a road that wound along the hillside led to Cambremer
and Léaupartie and then on to the sea; one of the thick-set
hedges, which in those parts mark the meadow boundaries,
hid this road from sight almost the whole way; and, vice
versa, La Roque was only visible from the road in sudden
snatches, when, for instance, the hedge was interrupted by a
gate leading into the fields that sloped gently down to the
river. A few fine clumps of trees, the peaceful cattle resting
under their shade, or here and there an isolated tree on road
or riverside, gave the whole valley the smiling, placid appearance of a park.

The open space inside the island, which for want of a better
name I call the courtyard, was spread with gravel; this was
kept at due distance from the house by a few flower-beds,
laid out in front of the drawing-room and dining-room windows, and planted with geraniums, fuchsias and dwarf rose-
trees. Further back was a little triangular lawn, where grew
an immense *acacia sophora*, which was far taller than the
house. It was under this tree—the only one in the island—
that we generally sat during the fine days of summer.

It was only downstream that the view opened out, that is
to say, only in front of the house; in this direction the valley
widened at the juncture of two streams; one came from
Blancmesnil, flowing through woods, the other from the ham-
let of La Roque two miles off, flowing through meadows. On

the other side of the moat, in the direction of Blancmesnil, lay the steep slope of a meadow known as Le Rouleux, which my mother, a few years after my father's death, had added to the garden. She planted it with two or three clumps of trees and, after long pondering, traced two paths which wound up it in artful curves to the little gate that let one through into the wood. So great was the mystery into which one then plunged that, as the gate closed behind me, my heart would beat with excitement. These woods lay along the crest of the hill and the Blancmesnil woods followed on. In my father's time, there were very few paths through them and their impenetrability made me think them vaster than they were. It was a dreadful disappointment when, on the day mamma allowed me to venture into them by myself, she showed me their boundaries on the ordnance map, and I saw that on their further side the meadows and fields began again. I do not exactly know what I had imagined was on the further side of the woods; nothing at all perhaps; but if I had imagined anything, I should have liked to imagine something different. To know their size and limits lessened their attraction; for at that age I preferred adventure to contemplation and thought nothing worth seeking but the unknown.

My chief occupation at La Roque, however, was not exploring but fishing. O sport of all sports most unjustly decried! Disdained alone by those who know thee not or else are bunglers! It was because I had loved fishing so much that in after days I cared so little for shooting, which, in our parts of the world at any rate, requires scarcely more skill than is necessary to shoot straight. Whereas for trout-fishing what craft, what cunning is needed! Théodomir, the nephew of our old keeper Bocage, had taught me from my earliest childhood to set a rod and bait a hook properly; for as the trout is the greediest of fish, so also he is the most suspicious.

I fished of course without float or lead, and heartily despised those helps for simpletons, which merely serve to scare the fish. On the other hand I used a line of "Florence horsehair," a thread spun from the glands of silkworms; of a slightly bluish colour, it has the advantage of being almost invisible in the water, and is moreover strong enough to be proof even against the moat trout, which were as heavy as salmon. I preferred fishing in the river, however, where the trout are more delicately flavoured, and above all are shyer, which makes them more amusing to catch. My mother was grieved to see me so fond of an amusement she considered gave me too little exercise. And then I would inveigh against the injustice that has labelled fishing as a sport for sluggards, requiring complete immobility; this might be true perhaps of lob-fishing in the larger rivers or in stagnant waters, for sluggish fish; but trout in the little streams I fished had to be surprised in their own haunts from which they hardly ever stirred; as soon as they caught sight of the bait, they rushed at it gluttonously; if they held back, it was because they had seen something besides the fly—a bit of hook, a bit of gut, or the shadow of the fisherman, or perhaps had heard him coming; no good now to wait any longer; the more you waited, the more you spoilt your chances; better to come back later and be more careful, crawling stealthily, making yourself as inconspicuous as you could in the undergrowth, and casting the line from as far off as possible, from as far as the branches of the trees would let you—the willows and hazels that line the river-banks with scarcely a break, except for here and there a huge epilobe or rose-bay—for if once by illluck you caught your line or hook in them, you had a good hour's work disentangling it—not to mention that the fish were scared away for good.

There were a great many visitors' rooms at La Roque; but they were always empty, for the good reason that my father had very little in common with Rouen society, and his Paris colleagues had their own families and habits . . . The only guest I can remember is Monsieur Dorval, who came to La Roque for the first time, I think, in the summer that followed my dismissal from school. He came again once or twice after my father's death, and I suspect my mother considered she was doing something rather daring in continuing to receive him when she was a widow. Nothing could be more *bourgeois* than the society my family moved in, and Monsieur Dorval, though far from being a bohemian, was nevertheless an artist—that is to say he was not in our set at all—a musician, a composer, a friend of other more celebrated musicians, such as Gounod, for instance, or Stephen Heller, whom he sometimes went to visit in Paris. For Monsieur Dorval lived at Rouen, and had succeeded Cavaillé-Coll as head-organist at Saint-Ouen. Being very clerical in his opinions and very religious, he was patronised by the clergy, and his pupils came from the best and most respectable families of Rouen, including our own; in these circles he was greatly admired, if not greatly respected. He had a stern, energetic profile, an abundance of very curly black hair, a square-cut beard, a dreamy expression that suddenly became fiery, a harmonious and even unctuous, though not really sweet voice, a caressing, but masterful manner. In all his words and all his ways, there was something egotistical and domineering. He had particularly beautiful hands—soft and at the same time powerful. At the piano, he was transfigured by an almost celestial fervour; his playing was that of an organist rather than of a pianist and sometimes lacked subtlety, but in *andantes* he was divine, and especially in those of Mozart, for whom he had a passionate predilection. He was accustomed to say laughingly:

63

"I'll say nothing about my *allegros;* but in slow movements, I'm equal to Rubinstein."

This was said so good-humouredly and frankly that one could not take it for boasting; and I really do not think that either Rubinstein (whom I remember perfectly) or any one else in the world could have played Mozart's *Fantasia* in C minor, for instance, or any given *largo* from a Beethoven concerto, with more tragic grandeur, with more warmth and poetry, more power and gravity. Later on, he often gave me reason to be exasperated: he objected to some of Bach's fugues as being too long and monotonous; if he loved good music, he did not sufficiently detest bad; he shared with his friend Gounod a monstrous and obstinate refusal to recognise the merits of César Franck, etc.; but in those days, when I was awakening to the world of sounds, he stood for me as its grand-master, prophet and magician. Every evening after dinner, he gave my ravished ears a feast of sonatas, operas and symphonies; and mamma, who was so inflexible on the point of punctuality and as a rule sent me to bed on the very stroke, on these occasions allowed me to sit up till long past my bedtime.

I have no pretensions to precocity, and I think I must place the intense pleasure I took in those musical evenings chiefly and almost entirely during the time of Monsieur Dorval's last visits, two or three years after my father's death. In the meantime, my mother, in pursuance of his advice, used constantly to take me to concerts, and in order to show I had profited by them, I would sing or whistle scraps of symphonies all day long. Then Monsieur Dorval took over my education. He sat me down to the piano and for every piece he taught me, he invented a kind of running commentary—a verbal accompaniment, which explained and enlivened it; everything was turned into a dialogue or a story. This method, though a little artificial, may not be a bad one for a young child, if the accompanying story is not too foolish or inadequate. It must be remembered that I was barely twelve.

In the afternoon, Monsieur Dorval composed; Anna, whom he had trained to write music from dictation, acted sometimes as secretary; he had recourse to her not only to spare his eyesight, which was beginning to fail, but to have someone to wreak his despotism on—so my mother declared. Anna devoted herself to his service. She escorted him on his morning walks, carried his overcoat, if he was too warm, and held a parasol over him in order to protect his eyes from the sun. My mother objected to these indulgences; Monsieur Dorval's acceptance of them made her indignant; she tried to pay him out for the prestige which even she was obliged to acknowledge, by a shower of small sarcasms, which, however, not being very pointed or well-aimed, he merely laughed at. Long after he had almost lost his eyesight, she, like many other people, cast doubts upon the reality of his growing blindness, or at any rate accused him of making play with it and of not being "as blind as all that." She thought him obsequious, insinuating, cunning, calculating, ferocious; it is true he was something of all this; but he was a musician. Sometimes at meals, an absent look would come into his eyes, half dimmed already behind their spectacles; his great hands, laid on the table as if it were a keyboard, would begin to move; and if anyone spoke to him, he came to himself with a start and said:

"I beg your pardon, I was in E flat."

My cousin Albert Démarest, for whom I was already beginning to feel a great attraction, though he was twenty years older than I, was on especially good terms with "Daddy Dorval," as he used to call him in his cordial way. Albert, the only artist of the family, was passionately fond of music and played the piano himself quite pleasantly; music, in reality, was the only thing they had in common; in every other respect they were at opposite poles. Every defect in "Daddy Dorval's" character was met by a corresponding and contrary trait in Albert's. The latter was as straight and frank as the former was cunning and smooth-tongued, as generous as the other was mercenary, and so on; but Albert, kind and careless to a fault, mismanaged his life; he neglected his own interests and was often unfortunate in his undertakings, so that the family did not take him altogether seriously. Monsieur Dorval always called him "dear old Bertie" with a kind of patronising indulgence, slightly tinged with pity. As for Albert, he admired Monsieur Dorval's talent, but despised him as a man. He told me later that he had one day caught Dorval kissing Anna. He pretended not to have noticed anything at the time out of respect for Anna; but as soon as he was alone with him:

"What did you mean by behaving like that?" cried Albert, very tall and very strong, and pushing the *maestro* up against the wall of the room (it was the drawing-room of the Rue de Crosne).

"My dear old Bertie," stammered Dorval, "don't be such an ass! Can't you see it was nothing but a joke."

"You brute!" cried Albert. "If I ever catch you joking in that way again, I'll . . ."

"I was so indignant," he added, "that if he had said another word, I think I should have wrung his neck."

. . . .

It may have been after the holidays that followed my being sent away from school that Albert Démarest first began to take notice of me. What can he have seen in me to attract his sympathy? I cannot tell; but I think I was all the more grateful for his attention because I felt how little I deserved it. And

I immediately set about trying to deserve it a little more. Sympathy may awaken many dormant qualities; I have often thought that the worst rascals must be those who have had to do without kindness and affection in their youth. It is no doubt strange that my parents did not suffice me; but the fact is I very soon felt more sensitive to Albert's approval or disapproval than to theirs.

I distinctly remember one autumn evening, after dinner, his talking to me apart, in a corner of my father's study, while my parents were playing bezique with my aunt Démarest and Anna. He began by saying in a low voice that he did not quite see what interest I had in life beyond myself; that that was the mark of an egoist, and he had a strong suspicion that that was what I was.

There was nothing of the censor about Albert. He seemed an open-minded, whimsical creature, full of humour and gaiety; there was nothing hostile in his reproof; on the contrary, I felt that if it was sharp, it was because he liked me; that was what drove it home. No one had ever spoken to me in that way before; Albert's words, without a doubt, sank into me more deeply than he ever suspected, or than I myself realised till later. What I generally like least in a friend is indulgence; Albert was not indulgent. If needs were, he could provide one with arms against oneself. And though I was not exactly aware of it, that was what I was looking for.

When my parents sent me back to school, I started again in the ninth class, from which I had been so long absent the year before; this enabled me to take a good place without difficulty; which suddenly gave me a liking for work.

The winter was severe and long that year. My mother had the bright idea of making me learn to skate. Jules and Julien

Jardinier, the sons of a colleague of my father's, (the younger was one of my class-mates) learnt with me; we tried hard to out-do each other and soon acquired a very pretty skill. I was passionately fond of this sport, which we used to practise first on the pool in the Luxembourg Gardens, and then on the pond of Villebon in the Meudon woods, or on the great Versailles canal. The snow fell abundantly and there was such a frost on the top of it that I remember starting from the Rue de Tournon and going the whole way to the Ecole Alsacienne —which was in the Rue d'Assas, that is at the other end of the Luxembourg—without once taking off my skates; and it was more amusing and more strange than I can say to glide thus silently down the paths of the big garden between two high banks of snow. There has never been another winter like it since.

I had no real friendship for either of the two Jardiniers. Jules was too old; Julien an uncommon dunderhead. But our parents, who seemed to have the kind of ideas about friendship that some families have about marriages of convenience, never missed an opportunity of throwing us together. I saw Julien every day at school; I met him again walking and skating. We had the same lessons, the same troubles, the same pleasures; the resemblance stopped there; for the moment that sufficed us. It is true there were other pupils on the benches of the ninth form with whom I might have felt a greater affinity; but their fathers, alas! were not university professors.

Every Tuesday, from 2 o'clock to 5, the pupils of the Ecole Alsacienne (we of the lower school, at any rate) went out in charge of a master to see the sights: the Sainte Chapelle, Notre Dame, the Panthéon and the Musée des Arts et Métiers (here there was a little dark room in which a small mirror, by an ingenious device of looking-glasses, reflected a delightful little moving picture of everything going on in the street, with animated figures, about the size of those in a picture by Teniers, walking about in it; everything else in this museum exuded the most deadly dullness), the Invalides also, the Louvre, and an extraordinary place close by the Parc de Montsouris, called the Universal Georama: it consisted of a wretched garden which the owner, a weird individual dressed in alpaca, had arranged so as to represent a geographical map. The mountains were figured by rockeries; the lakes, in spite of being cemented, had run dry, and a few melancholy goldfish swam about in the basin of the Mediterranean, as if to show up the exiguous proportions of the Italian boot. Our master would tell us to point out where the Carpathians were, while the weird one, with a long stick in his hand, underlined the frontiers, named the towns, pointed out a quantity of grotesque devices, enlarged on the magnificence of his achievement and expatiated on the time it had taken him to carry it out; and when, on going away, our master complimented him on his patience, he answered pompously:

"Patience is nothing without ideas."

I wonder whether this oddity still exists.

Sometimes the head of the lower school, Monsieur Brunig himself, came with us as well as Monsieur Vedel, who then deferentially retired into the background. It was invariably to the Jardin des Plantes that Monsieur Brunig conducted us; and invariably he led us to the dark rooms where the stuffed animals were kept (the new museum had not yet been built), stopping in front of the giant tortoise, which occupied a place of honour in a glass case all to itself; he grouped us round in a circle and said:

"Well, boys! Tell me what you think. How many teeth has the tortoise got?" (I must explain that the tortoise, though stuffed, kept its mouth open and had the most natural and truly life-like expression.) "Count them carefully. Take your time. Now then, are you ready?"

But we were not to be had; we knew his old tortoise. Splitting with laughter as we were however, we pretended to count, and elbowed each other a little to get a better view. Dubled declared obstinately he could only see two teeth—but he was a wag. Big Wenz, with his eyes fixed on the creature, counted out loud without stopping and it was not till he passed sixty that Monsieur Brunig interrupted him with that genial kind of laugh which benevolent people keep specially for children.

"Vous n'en approchez point," said he, quoting La Fontaine. "You're nowhere near. The more you count the more out you are. I had better stop you. You will be exceedingly astonished, but what you take for teeth are merely little cartilaginous protuberances. Tortoises have no teeth at all. Tortoises are like birds—they have beaks."

"O—o—oh!" we all cried politely.

I was present at this absurd performance three times.

Julien's parents and mine gave us each two sous on these weekly outings. They had discussed it together. Mamma would never have consented to giving me more than Madame Jardinier gave Julien; as they were less comfortably off than we were, it was for Madame Jardinier to settle the point.

"What can two children of that age possibly want with fifty centimes?" she had exclaimed. And my mother agreed that two sous were "ample."

The two sous were expended as a rule at old Clément's; Clément's shop was inside the Luxembourg Gardens, right against the railings at the entrance nearest the school. It was just a little wooden stall painted green, exactly the same colour as the benches. Old Clément wore a butcher's blue apron and sold marbles, cockchafers, tops, cocoa-nuts, barley-sugar flavoured with apple, cherry or peppermint, liquorice wound round in coils like watch-springs, and tubes of glass filled with white and pink aniseed and fastened at each end with pink cotton-wool and a cork; the aniseed was only so-so, but when the tubes were empty, they could be used as peashooters. In the same way we used to buy the little bottles labelled cherry brandy, anisette, curaçao, merely for the pleasure of sticking them on to our lips afterwards, like cupping glasses or leeches. Julien and I generally shared the things we bought; and so neither of us ever bought anything without consulting the other.

The year after this, Madame Jardinier and my mother thought they might increase their weekly bounty to fifty centimes—which liberality enabled me at last to keep silk-worms; they were not as expensive as the mulberry leaves they had to be fed on, and which I had to get twice a week from a herbalist's in the Rue Saint-Sulpice. Julien was disgusted by caterpillars, and declared that for the future he would buy what he pleased without consulting me. This produced a coolness between us and on the Tuesday outings, when we had to walk two and two, we each looked out for another companion.

There was one boy for whom I had conceived an absolute passion. He was a Russian. I must look for his name some day in the school books. How I wish someone would tell me what became of him! He was delicate and extraordinarily pale; he had very fair, rather long hair and very blue eyes; his voice was musical and his slight accent gave it the quality of singing. Poetry of a kind breathed from his whole person; the reason of it was, I think, that he felt he was weak and wanted to be loved. The other boys looked down on him and he rarely took part in any games; as for me, one glance from him made me feel ashamed of playing with the others and I remember some recreations in which I suddenly caught his eye and then and there left the game to join him. The boys used to chaff me about it. I longed for someone to attack him so that I might fly to his defence. During the drawing-lessons, when we were allowed to talk a little in a whisper, we sat beside each other; he told me his father was a celebrated man of science; I did not dare question him about his mother nor ask him how he came to be in Paris. One fine day he stopped coming to school and no one was able to tell me whether he had fallen ill or gone back to Russia; some kind of shyness or shame prevented me from asking the masters, who might perhaps have given me news of him; and I shut away in my secret heart one of the first and deepest griefs of my life.

My mother was very careful not to let me know by anything she spent on me that we were considerably better off than the Jardiniers. My clothes were exactly like Julien's and were bought like his, ready made, at the *Belle Jardinière's*. I was extremely sensitive about my clothes and could not bear being always hideously dressed. In a sailor suit, with a beret, or all in velvet, I should have been in a seventh heaven of delight. But Madame Jardinier would have none of sailor suits or velvet. So I was obliged to wear a scrubby little coat, knickers tight at the knee and striped socks—socks that were too short and either drooped disconsolately like wilting tulips or sank abashed into the recesses of my boots. I have kept the most horrible of all for the end—a starched shirt. I had to wait till I was almost grown up before I was allowed to wear shirt fronts that were not starched. They were the custom, the fashion, and there was nothing to be done about it. And if at last I have managed to get my own way, it is simply because the fashion has changed. Imagine an unfortunate child who has to wear year in and year out, at games as well as at lessons, unknown to the world and hidden under his coat, a kind of white breastplate ending in a cast-iron collar; for the washerwoman starched the neckband to which the collar is fastened, as well as the rest of the shirt—and for the same price, no doubt; if it was the tiniest shade too large or too small and did not exactly fit the shirt (which nine times out of ten was the case) it made excruciating creases, and if one happened to perspire, the shirt front became horrible. Think of playing games in such a get-up! A ridiculous little bowler hat completed the whole . . . Ah! the children of to-day don't know their happiness!

And yet I was fond of running; and next to Adrien Monod, I was the champion of my class. In the gymnastic lesson, I was even better than he at climbing a pole or a rope; I was first-rate at the rings, the horizontal bar and the parallel bars; but no good at the trapeze, which made me giddy. On fine summer evenings, I used to join a few of my schoolfellows in one of the broad walks in the Luxembourg Gardens—the one that had old Clément's shop at one end—and play at ball. Not yet football, unfortunately, though the ball was very like; but there were scarcely any rules in our game and it was forbidden to use one's feet. Even so, we were mad about it.

But I have not yet done with the chapter of clothes. At the *mi-carême* every year, the Gymnase Pascaud used to give a ball for its clients' children—a fancy-dress ball. As soon as I saw my mother would let me go, as soon as I began to look forward to this party, the idea of dressing up put me in a fever. I wonder nowadays what could have been the reason of this delirium? Is it possible such rapture can lie in the mere prospect of depersonalisation? What! at that age already? No: the pleasure consisted rather in being dressed in

73

colours, in being brilliant, in being quaint, in pretending to be something different . . . My delight was terribly dashed, however, when I heard Madame Jardinier declare that as for Julien, he should go as a pastry-cook.

"The important thing for the children," she explained to my mother (and my mother at once agreed), "is that they should dress up, isn't it? It matters very little what as."

From that moment I knew my fate; for the two ladies, after consulting a catalogue of the *Belle Jardinière's,* discovered that the pastry-cook's costume, which was at the very bottom of the list that was headed by "the little marquis," and went on diminuendo to the "cuirassier," "Punch," the "Zouave," and the "Neopolitan"—-the "pastry-cook's," I repeat, cost "next to nothing."

With my calico apron, my calico sleeves and my calico cap, I was more like a pocket-handkerchief than anything else. I looked so sad that mamma kindly allowed me to take one of the kitchen saucepans—a real copper saucepan—and slipped a wooden spoon into my belt, with the idea that these accessories might enliven the flatness of my prosaic costume. And she filled my apron pocket with sweet biscuits, "so that I might hand them round."

As soon as I entered the ball-room, I saw at a glance that there were at least a score of "little pastry-cooks"—in fact a regular school of them. The saucepan was too big and got terribly in my way; and to add to my confusion, I suddenly fell in love—yes, positively in love!—with a small boy a little older than myself, who has left me a dazzling recollection of slimness, grace and volubility.

He was dressed as an imp or a clown, that is, his slender figure was perfectly moulded in black tights covered with steel spangles. As people crowded round to look at him, he jumped and pranced and gambolled, as if success and pleasure had gone to his head; he looked like a sylph; I could not take my eyes off him. I longed to make him look at me, and at the same time feared to, because of my ridiculous get-up; I felt ugly and wretched. He stopped to take breath between two pirouettes, went up to a lady, who must have been his mother, and asked her for a handkerchief, with which he proceeded to mop his forehead—for he was dripping with perspiration—after having first undone the black band with which his two little kid's horns were fastened on to his forehead. I went up to him and awkwardly offered him some of my biscuits. He said "Thank you," took one carelessly and at once turned on his heel. I left the ball soon after with a broken heart, and when I got home, I had such a fit of despair, that my mother promised to let me go next year as a "Neopolitan lazzarone." Yes, I thought, that would be something like a fancy-dress; perhaps the imp would think so too . . . So I went to the next ball as a "lazzarone"—but the imp was not there.

I have given up attempting to fathom for what reason my mother sent me to board at school when I was moved into the eighth class. The Ecole Alsacienne objected on principle to the *lycée* sleeping-in system and had no dormitories; but the masters were each of them encouraged to take in a small number of boarders. I was put into Monsieur Vedel's house, though I was no longer in his class. Monsieur Vedel lived in a house that had belonged to Sainte-Beuve, whose bust stood at the end of a passage and filled me with amazement. This peculiar lady saint was presented to my astonished gaze under the aspect of a paternal old gentleman, wearing a tasselled cap on his head. Monsieur Vedel had indeed told us Sainte-Beuve was "a great critic," but there are limits to a child's credulity.

There were five or six of us boarders, sleeping in two or three rooms. I shared a room on the second floor with a great, apathetic, anaemic creature, incapable of mischief, who was called Roseau. I have no recollection of my other companions. Yes though; there was the American Barnett, who had filled me with admiration, when he made himself ink moustaches on his first day in class. He wore a loose jersey and wide knickerbockers; his face was pock-marked but extraordinarily open and merry; he looked bursting with joy and health, and a kind of inward turbulence set him constantly inventing such perilous eccentricities that he wore a halo of prestige in my eyes, and positively transported me with enthusiasm. He always wiped his pen in his tangled locks. The first day that he arrived at Vedel's, when we were all at recreation in the little garden behind the house, he planted himself right in the middle, and flinging his shoulders proudly back, there, under all our eyes, he peed upwards into the air. We were thunderstruck by his effrontery.

This little garden was the scene of a pugilistic encounter. As a rule I was placid enough, rather too gentle if anything, and I detested scraps, being convinced no doubt that I should always get the worst of it. And here I must recount an adventure, the recollection of which still rankles in me bitterly. One day as I was going home from school through the Luxembourg, I chanced to take the path that skirts the railings opposite the little garden,—not my usual way but hardly any longer. As I went, I crossed a group of boys, belonging, no doubt, to the Communal school, in whose eyes, I suppose, the boys of the Ecole Alsacienne were hateful little aristocrats. I caught their jeers as I passed them, their mocking, spiteful glances, and went on my way looking as dignified as I could; but suddenly the biggest boy of the group left his companions and came up to me. My heart sank into my boots. He planted himself in front of me.

"Wh—wh—at do you want?" I stammered out.

He did not answer but fell into step beside me on my left hand. I kept my eyes fixed on the ground as I walked, but I felt him staring at me, and felt the others staring at me too from behind. I should have liked to sit down.

"There! That's what I want!" he said suddenly and fetched me a great blow in the eye with his fist.

I saw stars and pitched headlong into a horse-chestnut tree, where I fell into the little trench left at its foot for the purpose of watering. I rose covered with mud and confusion. My black eye was very painful, and as I had not yet learnt the wonderful elasticity of the eye, I was convinced it had been put out. As the tears gushed from it, "That's it," thought I, "it's all running away." But what was still more painful to me was to hear the other boys' laughter and jokes and the congratulations they showered on my aggressor.

For that matter, I no more liked giving blows than receiving them. All the same, at Vedel's there was a great big, carrotty-haired boy with a low forehead (his name has fortunately escaped me) who really took too great advantage of my pacifism. Twice, three times, I bore with his sarcasms; but suddenly I was seized with a holy rage; I rushed up and fell upon him while the other boys made a circle round us. He was considerably bigger and stronger than I; but I had the advantage of taking him by surprise; and then, to my own astonishment, my fury multiplied my strength tenfold; I punched him, I shoved him and in a moment I had him down. Then, when he was on the ground, intoxicated by my triumph, I dragged him after the manner of the ancients, or what I thought was such —I dragged him by the hair of his head until a handful of it came off in my hand. I was even slightly disgusted by my victory on account of all the greasy hair he left in my hand, but I was above all amazed at having been victorious; beforehand it had appeared so utterly impossible, that I must really have lost my head to have attempted it. My success secured me my schoolfellows' respect and allowed me to live in peace for a long time to come. It convinced me too that there are many things that seem impossible only as long as one does not attempt them.

We had spent part of September in the neighbourhood of Nîmes, in a place belonging to my uncle Charles Gide's father-in-law. (My uncle had recently married.) From this place my father returned with an ailment which was attributed to eating figs. In reality it was intestinal tuberculosis, and my mother, I think, was aware of it; but tuberculosis in those days was an illness which people hoped to cure by ignoring. The disease, however, had no doubt already advanced too far for my father to have had any chance of getting over it. He passed away quietly on October 28th of that year (1880).

I have no recollection of seeing him dead: but I remember seeing him in bed a few days before the end. A big book lay on the sheet before him; it was open but lay face downwards, so that I could only see its brown leather back. My mother told me afterwards it was a Plato.

I was at Vedel's and someone—I cannot remember who—came to fetch me—Anna perhaps. On the way home the news was broken to me. But my grief did not burst out till I saw my mother dressed in deep mourning. She was not crying; she controlled her grief in my presence, but I felt she had been crying a great deal. I sobbed in her arms. She was afraid the nervous shock might be bad for me and tried to get me to take a little tea. I was sitting on her lap; she held the cup and gave me a spoonful at a time, and I remember she said, as she forced herself to smile:

"Come now, come! Let's see whether this one won't get there safely!"

And I suddenly felt her love enfold me—her love, which henceforth would have no one but me to brood over.

As for my loss, how should I have realised it? I would speak of my grief if I could, but alas! what I was most sensible of was the kind of prestige my bereavement gave me in my schoolfellows' eyes. Imagine! They each of them wrote to me, just as each of his colleagues had written to my father when he was decorated! Then I learnt that my cousins were coming. My mother had decided I was not to attend the funeral ceremony; while my uncles and aunts followed the hearse with mamma, Emmanuèle and Suzanne were to stay at home and keep me company. The happiness of seeing them almost, if not quite, got the better of my grief. The time has come for me to speak of them.

IV

Emmanuèle was my elder by two years; Suzanne barely older than I and Louise came soon after. As for Edouard and Georges, who were called "the boys" in one word, as if to dispose of them both as shortly as possible, we considered them at that time practically negligible—barely out of their cradles. Emmanuèle was too quiet for my taste. As soon as our games became "rough" or even noisy, she would have no more to do with them. She went off by herself with a book—like a deserter, we thought; and after that no appeal succeeded in reaching her; the outside world ceased to exist for her; she lost the notion of where she was to such an extent that she would sometimes fall off her chair. She never quarrelled; it was so natural for her to give up her turn or her place or her share, and always with such a smiling grace, that one wondered whether it was not her pleasure rather than her virtue that made her act so, and whether to have acted otherwise would not have cost her a greater effort.

Suzanne was a more daring character, prompt and thoughtless; every game became lively as soon as she came into it. It was she I preferred playing with, and with Louise too, when she was not in the sulks, for she was less even-tempered than her sisters.

Why should I speak of our games? I do not think they were very different from those of other children of our age—except perhaps that we brought more passion to them.

My uncle and aunt lived with their five children in the Rue Lecat. It was one of those dreary provincial streets without shops or any kind of animation, without character or charm; before reaching the still more dreary quay, it ran past the Hôtel-Dieu or hospital, where Flaubert's parents had lived, and where his brother Achille had practised as a doctor, like his father before him.

My uncle's house was as commonplace and gloomy as the street. I shall say more of it later on. I saw my cousins oftener —at any rate I liked seeing them better—in the Rue de Crosne, and better still in the country, where I used to spend a few weeks with them every summer, either when they came to La Roque or when we went to Cuverville, my uncle's country place. At those times we played together, did our lessons together, grew up together; our lives were interwoven, our plans and wishes all in common, and when, at the end of the day, our parents separated us to take us off to bed, I used to think in my childish way "that's all very well now, because unfortunately we are still small, but the time will come when we shall never be separated, even at night."

The garden at Cuverville where I am writing this has

changed very little. The open space surrounded with clipped yews where we played in our sand-heap is still there; not far off, in the "flower-walk," is the place where our little gardens were laid out; in the shadow of a silver-lime tree, is the gymnastic ground, where Emmanuèle was so timid and Suzanne, on the contrary, so daring; then comes the shady part of the garden—the "dark walk," where my uncle on fine evenings after dinner used sometimes to take refuge; on other evenings he would read aloud to us an interminable novel of Sir Walter Scott's.

The great cedar in front of the house had grown enormous; we used to spend hours perched in its branches, where we had each of us arranged a room of our own and paid each other visits; sometimes, from high up in the branches, we fished with hooks or nooses; Suzanne and I used to climb up to the tip top and call out to the people of the lower regions: "The sea ho! We can see the sea!" And indeed, when the weather was clear, we could catch a glimpse of its narrow silver strip fifteen kilometres away.

No, nothing of it has changed and I can still easily recognise in the depths of my heart the little child I then was. But we are not concerned now to go so far back; when Emmanuèle and Suzanne came to stay with me in Paris at the time of my father's death, the games of early childhood were already beginning to turn into amusements of another kind.

My mother was persuaded by her family to spend the first period of her mourning at Rouen. She had not the heart to leave me by myself at Monsieur Vedel's; and this was how I started on that irregular and unsystematic mode of life and that desultory education which I came to find only too much to my taste.

It was in the Rue de Crosne house, at my uncle Henri Rondeaux', that we passed that winter. I worked a little every day with Monsieur Huart, a professor who also gave my cousin Louise lessons. He used "skeleton" maps in order to teach me geography; I had to find out and fill in the names of the places and go over the discreetly faint outlines in ink. The child's effort was considerably reduced in this way, with the result that he remembered nothing. All I can recollect of these lessons are Monsieur Huart's spatula-shaped fingers, which looked extraordinarily flat, large and square, as they strayed over the maps.

That winter I was given a New Year's present of a kind of copying-press; I cannot remember the name of this rudimentary device; in reality it was nothing but a sheet of metal spread with some gelatinous substance upon which you first laid the piece of paper that had been freshly written on, and afterwards the pages that were to be printed. Was the idea of a newspaper suggested by this present? Or, on the contrary, did the present come as a response to a project we had made of founding a newspaper? No matter; in any case, a little family gazette was started. I do not think I have kept the few numbers that came out; but I remember there were prose and verse contributions from my cousins; as for my own collaboration, it consisted solely in the copying out of a few pages from the best authors; with a modesty I make no comments on, I felt convinced my relations would take more pleasure in reading: "The squirrel is a charming little animal" by Buffon, and fragments of Boileau's Epistles, than anything whatever of my own invention—and that this was just as it should be.

My uncle Henri Rondeaux was at the head of a printed linen factory at Le Houlme, four or five kilometres from the town. We went driving there fairly often. There had originally been a house adjoining the factory—a small, square, unpretentious house, so insignificant that it has left no trace in my memory; my uncle pulled it down and built another, if not exactly on the same spot, a very little way off and facing what afterwards became the garden; it was a prosperous-looking, showy building—a cross between a sea-side villa and a Normandy dwelling-house.

. . . .

My uncle Henri was an excellent person—mild, fatherly, perhaps a little too bland; and his face was not more striking than his character. I have said already, I think, that when he was about eighteen, he turned Roman Catholic; my grandmother, on opening a cupboard one day in her son's room, fell back in a fainting fit—it was an altar to the Virgin.

The Henri Rondeaux' used to take in the *Triboulet*—a comic paper of the ultramontane persuasion, which had been founded for the purpose of upsetting Jules Ferry; this rag was full of vile illustrations, the wit of which consisted in playing tricks with the *Tonkinese* [1] minister's nose by turning it into an elephant's trunk—to the intense delight of my cousin Robert. Numbers of the *Triboulet* lay about aggressively at Le Houlme, side by side with the *Croix*, on the drawing-room and billiard-room tables, to the discomfort of those visitors who were of a different way of thinking from the masters of the house; my uncle and aunt Démarest and my mother pretended not to notice; Albert grumbled indignantly below his breath. In spite of political and religious divergences, my mother was too conciliatory not to get on with her eldest brother, and especially with her sister-in-law, Lucile. An excellent manager, a person of great good sense and great good feeling, my aunt was the exact counterpart of her husband; and yet she was considered his superior; for a man who is on the same level morally as his wife must have great intelligence not to appear much her inferior. It was my aunt and not Robert who took over the management of the factory at uncle Henri's

[1] It was during Ferry's ministry that Tonkin was conquered by the French.

death, the year following the one I have reached in my story, and who held her own against the workmen when on one occasion they went out on strike.

The Le Houlme factory was one of the most important in Rouen, where trade at that time was still flourishing. The cloth was not manufactured on the spot but only printed. But the printing was accompanied by a number of subsidiary operations and employed an army of workmen. In a field a little way off there was a lofty shed used for drying; the air that blew through the lattice-work sides of the building kept the lengths of linen waving about in a constant mysterious flutter and rustle; a shaky zig-zag staircase led you up through a multitude of little landings, passages and gangways till you were lost amidst an infinite tangle of vertical streamers, cool and white, tranquil and quivering. Close to the river, there was another little building always kept shut, where the dyes were secretly manufactured, and from which there emanated a curious smell that ended by growing on one. I would gladly have spent hours in the room watching the stuff as it passed under the shining brass rollers, to emerge again bright with colour and life; but we children were not allowed in by ourselves. On the other hand, we could go into the big warehouse without asking permission, whenever we found the door open. It was a vast building where the pieces of stuff, already printed, rolled up and ready to be delivered to the trade, were arranged in orderly piles. On each floor there were three lines of rails, on which small trucks ran from one room to the other throughout the whole length of the building along three parallel passages, bordered on each side by full or empty shelves. Suzanne, Louise and I, each sitting on a truck, instituted thrilling races. Emmanuèle did not come with us into the warehouse, because there were only three trucks and she did not like adventures—and principally because she was not sure it was allowed.

Hard by the factory lay the extensive farm, with its model poultry yard and an immense barn, where my cousin Robert amused himself by rearing a special breed of rabbits; there were great heaps of cut branches in it which served them as burrows; here in my cousins' absence I used to pass hours on end, sitting or lying on the straw and watching the frolics of these quaint little creatures.

The garden was squeezed into the narrow space between the road-side wall and the river. In the middle of it was a pond which for smallness of size and contortion of shape would have delighted Flaubert's heart. It was crossed by an absurd toy bridge made of iron. The bottom of the pond was cemented, and crawling about on it were quantities of caddis larvae, looking like odds and ends of vegetation, in their queer casings of tiny twigs. I tried to rear some of these creatures in a basin, but was obliged to leave Le Houlme before witnessing their transformation.

I doubt whether I ever extracted as much or as keen joy from anything later on, be it from books, music or painting, as I did in those days from the play of living matter. I had succeeded in getting Suzanne to share my passion for entomology; at any rate she would accompany me on my hunting expeditions and was not too much disgusted at turning up bits of dung and carrion in the search for dung-beetles, burying-beetles and devil's coach-horses. It is to be supposed my family ended by having some respect for my devotion to natural history, for, child as I was, at the death of Félix Archimède Pouchet, a first cousin of my grandmother's, it was to me that his collection of insects was handed over. The obstinate old scientist had had his hour of celebrity when he had upheld the daring theory of *heterogenesis*, or spontaneous generation, in opposition to Pasteur. Not everyone can boast a cousin called Archimedes. How I wish I had known him! I had some acquaintance, as I shall mention later on, with his son George, who was professor at the Natural History Museum.

To have been considered worthy of this gift of twenty-four cork-lined boxes full of beetles, all classified, arranged and labelled, certainly flattered me; but I cannot remember that it gave me enormous pleasure. My own poor little collection seemed humiliated by this treasure; and how much more precious I thought the insects I caught and pinned down myself. It was not collecting I enjoyed—it was hunting. What dreams I had of those happy corners of France, haunts of the capricorn and the stag-beetle—the biggest of all our European beetles—though not to be found at La Roque! But I did discover a colony of rhinoceros *(oryctes nasicornes)* at the foot of an ancient heap of sawdust beside the Blancmesnil sawmill. These handsome insects of varnished mahogany are almost as big as stag-beetles and carry the turned-up horn to which they owe their name between their eyes. I was wild with joy when I saw them for the first time.

By digging into the sawdust, one found their larvae as well —enormous white maggots, like cockchafer grubs. One found too strings or packets of soft, whitish eggs as big as damsons, and all sticking together; I was at first greatly mystified by these; they had no proper shell and it was impossible to break them; it was even rather difficult to tear open their soft parchment-like skin, but when one did—wonder of wonders!—out slipped a slender grass-snake!

I brought back a quantity of *oryctes* larvae with me to La Roque and kept them in a box full of sawdust; but they always died before reaching the chrysalis stage: the reason, I

86

think, being that they need to burrow deep into the earth before they can effect their metamorphosis.

Lionel de R . . . helped me in these hunts too. We were exactly of an age. He and his sister were orphans and lived with their grandfather Ch . . . at Blancmesnil in charge of their uncle who was Ch . . .'s son-in-law. I used to go to Blancmesnil every Sunday. When my cousins were with us, our maids escorted us in a troop; the walk there was pleasant enough, but we were dressed in our Sunday best, and the visit itself was an infliction. The intimacy between Lionel and myself, which later became very close, had not yet developed, and at that time I considered him merely a turbulent, passionate, domineering boy, with legs like a cock's, hair like a fox's brush, a perspiring skin and a countenance that turned beetroot whenever he was the least agitated. His favourite game was to seize my fine brand new panama hat and fling it into a bed of dahlias, which was of course forbidden ground; or else he would get Mousse, the huge Newfoundland, to knock us down. Sometimes we found cousins there, girls rather older than ourselves, and then we used to have great fun; we played a kind of prisoners' base; but after tea, as soon as it began to be really amusing, our maids called us away—it was time to go home. I remember one of these walks in particular.

A terrific thunder-storm suddenly came on; heavy purple clouds covered the sky, and we had visions of lightning, wind, hail and perdition. We hurried on so as to get in before we were overtaken. But the storm gained on us, seemed to be actually pursuing us; we felt it was aimed especially at us; yes, we felt directly threatened. So, as was often our habit, we passed our conduct in review, questioned each other, tried to discover which particular culprit had aroused the anger of this terrific Jove. As we could not find, however, that we had been recently guilty of any especially enormous sins, Suzanne exclaimed at last:

"Why, it must be the maids!"

And we took to our heels and fled, abandoning the sinners to the wrath of Heaven.

At La Roque I had lessons from Monsieur Tabourel, the schoolmaster of Saint-Ouen, in the *commune* of Blancmesnil (Monsieur Ch . . . himself had founded the school). Monsieur Tabourel's teaching was far from exciting. It was during one of his lessons that a privet hawk-moth chose the time for coming out of its chrysalis. I had reared the caterpillar and was keeping the chrysalis carefully in a small narrow uncovered box, in which it lay, looking like a mummy in its sarcophagus. I used to examine it every day, but never perceived the smallest change, and I should perhaps have despaired if it had not been for the little convulsive movements this semblance of a creature made when I tickled its abdomen with the nib of my pen. It was really alive then! Now on that day, as Monsieur Tabourel was correcting my sums, my eyes fell on the box. • O Proteus! What did I see? Wings! Great green and pink wings beginning to stir and quiver!

Overwhelmed with admiration, with joy, dancing with enthusiasm, I could not help seizing, for want of a better divinity, old Tabourel's fat paw.

"Oh, Monsieur Tabourel! Look! Oh, if I had only known . . ."

I stopped short just in time, for what I had been meaning to say was: "If I had only known that while you were explaining those deadly sums, one of the mysteries of life, so great a one, so long expected, was going on at my very elbow! . . ." A resurrection like Lazarus's! A metamorphosis, a miracle I had never yet beheld . . .

Monsieur Tabourel was a man of education; calmly, but with a shade of astonishment or blame or something disapproving in his voice:

"What!" said he; "didn't you know that a chrysalis is the envelope of a butterfly? Every butterfly you see has come out of a chrysalis. It's perfectly natural."

At that I dropped Monsieur Tabourel's hand. Yes indeed, I knew my *natural* history as well, perhaps better than he . . . But because it was natural, could he not see that it was marvellous? Poor creature! From that day, I took a dislike to him and a loathing to his lessons.

In the year 1881, the twelfth of my age, my mother, becoming a little uneasy, I suppose, at the irregularity of my studies, engaged a tutor for me. I do not know who can have recommended her M. Gallin. He was a ridiculous young puppy—a student, I greatly fear, in theology—shortsighted and foolish, and apparently even more bored than I was by the lessons he gave me, which is saying a good deal. He used to come for walks with me in the woods, but he did not conceal how much he disliked the country. I was delighted whenever a branch of hazel knocked off his pince-nez. He was continually humming a tune out of the *Cloches de Corneville* in which the following words kept coming:

> "*Little loves*
> *One doesn't love.*"

The self-satisfied mincing affectation of his voice exasperated me; I ended by declaring I could not understand how anyone could take any pleasure in singing such idiotic stuff.

"*You* think it stuff," he answered in a patronising tone, "because you are too young to understand it. As a matter of fact, it's extremely witty."

He added that it was a much admired air in a very fashionable opera . . . Everything he said increased my contempt for him.

The following winter my mother took me to the South—it is really astonishing that such a piece-meal education should have had any good results at all. No doubt this decision was the upshot of much pondering and patient weighing of pros and cons; all mamma's actions were very carefully thought out. Was she anxious about my state of health? Or was she over-ruled by my aunt Charles Gide, who was very persistent in urging what she thought advisable? I cannot tell. Parents' reasons are unfathomable.

The Charles Gides were at that time living at Montpellier, where they occupied the second and top floors of the Castelneaus' town house at the blind end of the Rue Salle l'Evêque. The Castelneaus reserved the first floor for themselves and also the more spacious ground floor, which gave straight on to the garden. We were kindly allowed to make use of this garden, which, as far as I can remember, was nothing but a wilderness of evergreen oaks and laurels, but admirably situated; it formed a corner terrace overlooking one end of the Esplanade and the suburbs of the town, with a view that stretched as far as the distant peak of Saint-Loup, which my uncle could see too from his study windows.

Was it out of discretion that my mother and I did not lodge with the Charles Gides or simply because they had not room to take us in? For we had Marie with us too. Perhaps my mother preferred solitude on account of her mourning. We stayed to begin with at the Hotel Nevet while we were looking for furnished rooms in the neighbourhood, where we could spend the winter.

Those my mother fixed on were in a steep street which went from the Grand' Place to the other end of the Esplanade, running along the foot of the Esplanade wall, so that there were houses along only one side of it. The street became darker and dirtier the further away you got from the Grand' Place. Our house was about half way down.

The apartment was small, ugly and squalid. The furniture was sordid. My mother's room and the room that served as dining-room looked on to the Esplanade; that is to say one's eyes were brought up sharp by its great foundation walls. Both my room and Marie's looked on to a little garden with neither grass, trees, nor flowers in it, which would have been called a backyard, but for two leafless shrubs which blossomed out once a week with the landlady's washing. A low wall separated this garden from the next-door backyard on to which more windows opened; here there was a continual medley of cries, songs, smells of oil, babies' napkins being dried, carpets being shaken, chamber-pots emptied, squalling children, and birds squawking in their cages. Starving cats were to be seen wandering from yard to yard—miserable beasts which on idle Sundays the landlady's son and his friends—big boys of eighteen or so—would hunt with fragments of broken crockery. We used to dine every two or three days with the Charles Gides; their cooking was excellent and a great contrast to the horrid messes that were sent in to us from a neighbouring restaurant on the days we were at home. The squalor of our lodgings made me think that my father's death had involved our ruin; but I did not dare question mamma. And however lugubrious our apartment, it was Paradise compared to the *lycée*.

I doubt whether this had changed much since the time of Rabelais. The entrance to the class-rooms was so public that the boys amused themselves by enticing dogs in from the street. No; I must be making a mistake; the class-room cannot have opened directly on to the street. In any case I distinctly remember that one day a dog came in by the door, which Monsieur Nadaud liked leaving open; after all it may have been the porter's dog . . . As there were no pegs for us to hang our things on, we used them as cushions to sit upon; they served as footstools too for our neighbours, for we sat on rows of steps, one above the other, and wrote on our knees.

My class, and indeed the whole school, was divided into factions: there was the Catholic party and the Protestant party. When I had first gone to the Ecole Alsacienne, I had learnt I was a Protestant; at the very first break, the boys had crowded round me and asked:

"Are you a Cat or a Prot?"

As I heard these mysterious words for the first time, I was perfectly dumbfounded—for my parents had taken good care not to let me know that all French people might not have the same faith, and the perfect amity that reigned between my relations in Rouen blinded me to their differences of religious belief. So I replied that I had not the least idea what they were talking about. An obliging schoolfellow took it upon himself to explain:

"Catholics are people who believe in the Holy Virgin."

Upon which I exclaimed I was certainly a Protestant. By some miracle there were no Jews among us, but a little whippersnapper, who had not spoken before, suddenly announced:

"*My* father is an atheist." This was said with such an air of superiority as somewhat to perplex the rest of us.

I noted the word to ask my mother what it meant.

"What does *atheist* mean?" I asked.

"It means a horrid foolish man."

This failing to satisfy me, I questioned further; I insisted; mamma at last, wearied out, cut me short, as she often did, with:

"You're not old enough to understand" or "There's no need

92

for you to understand that just yet." (She had a choice of such answers which drove me wild.)

Does it seem curious that children of ten or twelve should concern themselves with such matters? I think not. It shows nothing after all but that all Frenchmen, of whatever age or class of society, have an innate need to take sides, to belong to a party.

A little later, driving one day in the Bois de Boulogne with Lionel de R . . . and Octave Join-Lambert, a cousin of mine, in whose parents' carriage we were, I got hauled over the coals by the other two boys. They had asked me whether I was a royalist or a republican and I had answered:

"Why, a republican, of course," not understanding how one could be anything else as we were living under a republic. Lionel and Octave had thereupon fallen upon me and severely trounced me. As soon as I got home, I asked innocently:

"Wasn't that the right thing to have answered?"

"My dear," my mother said, after pausing to reflect a moment, "when you are asked what you are in future, you must say you are for proper constitutional representation. Will you remember?"

She made me repeat these astonishing words.

"But . . . what does it mean?"

"Why, that's just it, my darling—the others won't understand any more than you do, and then they'll leave you alone."

At Montpellier, the question of belief was not important; but as the Catholic aristocracy sent their children to Jesuit schools, the only boys left for the *lycée* were Protestants (who nearly all called cousins with each other), and little plebeians, who were often highly unpleasant and very obviously filled with feelings of hatred for us.

I say "us", for I almost at once joined the set of my coreligionists, children whose parents were friends of my uncle and aunt's, and to whom I had been introduced. There were the Westphals, the Leenhardts, the Castelneaus and the Baziles, all related to each other and very friendly to me. They were not all in my form, but we used to meet as we came out of school. Dr. Leenhardt's two sons were those I saw most of, frank, open-tempered boys, a little given to teasing, but excellent fellows at heart; in spite of which, I took little pleasure in their society. Something downright in their talk, something offhand in their manner, made me retreat still further into my shell, for I had become shyer than ever, depressed and sulky, and only went with my schoolfellows because I could not do otherwise. Their games were noisy, whereas I should have liked mine to be quiet; my taste was as much for peace as theirs was for war. Not content with coming to fisticuffs when school was over, they talked of nothing but guns, gunpowder, and "squibs"; these were an invention we fortunately knew nothing of in Paris; a little saltpetre, a little sand or fine gravel, wrapped up together in a bit of curl-paper and flung on the pavement between the legs of a passer-by, made a devil of a noise. The first time the Leenhardts gave me some squibs, I hastily drowned them in my washing-basin as soon as I got back to our loathsome lodgings. All the pocket-money they possessed went in buying gunpowder, with which they crammed to bursting some little brass cannons that had been given them as New Year presents, and which positively frightened me out of my senses. Their detonations got on my nerves and I hated them. I could not understand what kind of infernal pleasure the Leenhardts found in them. They instituted file-firing with their armies of tin soldiers; I had tin soldiers too; I too played with them; but *my* game was to melt them. You put them to stand upright on a shovel which you heated, and watched them till they suddenly began to totter;

then they dived forward, head foremost, and soon out would flash from every tarnished uniform a little liberated soul— brilliant glowing, chastened . . . But I must go back to the Montpellier *lycée*.

The Ecole Alsacienne had improved on the ordinary *lycée* régime; but some of their improvements, excellent as they were, turned out to my disadvantage. I had been taught to repeat poetry more or less decently, and this was also my own natural inclination; but at the *lycée* (at any rate at the Montpellier *lycée*), the custom was to gabble either verse or prose as fast as possible in one flat monotone, which robbed the text not only of all attraction, but of all meaning, so that nothing was left of it to show why one had taken such pains to learn it. Nothing more frightful or more grotesque can well be imagined; however well one knew the text, it was impossible to recognise a word of it; one could not even be sure it was French. When my time came to recite (I wish I could remember what), I felt at once that, notwithstanding the best will in the world, I should never be able to fall in with their methods —it went really too much against the grain. So I recited as I should have recited at home.

The very first line caused general stupefaction—the kind of stupefaction that is created by a real scandal; then this gave way to an immense roar of laughter. From one end of the tiers of steps to the other, from top to bottom, the whole class rocked with laughter; every boy laughed as he seldom has a chance of laughing at school; it ceased even to be derision, and so hearty and so irresistible was it, that Monsieur Nadaud himself joined in; at any rate, he smiled, and at the encouragement of his smile, the laughter became more uncontrolled than ever. The master's smile was my inevitable condemnation; I do not know how I had the courage to stick it out to the end of my piece, which—Heaven be praised—I knew thoroughly.

Then to my astonishment and to the utter amazement of the class, Monsieur Nadaud, who was still smiling after the laughter had subsided, Monsieur Nadaud, in a voice that was very calm, and even august, was heard to say:

"Gide, ten." (This was the highest mark possible.) "You think it funny, young gentlemen? Well, let me tell you, that is how you ought all to say your poetry."

I was done for. This compliment, by distinguishing me from my companions, resulted in setting them all against me. Fellow pupils do not easily forgive each other the sudden favours of authority, and if Monsieur Nadaud had deliberately wished to confound me, he would not have acted otherwise. Surely it was quite enough that they should think me affected and my recitation ridiculous. But the finishing stroke was that it became known I took private lessons with Monsieur Nadaud. And this is why I took them.

One of the reforms instituted by the Ecole Alsacienne had to do with the teaching of Latin; in the *lycée*, the boys started droning their *rosa, rosae* in the ninth and lowest class, but the Ecole considered that if their pupils began Latin in the sixth, they would have plenty of time between that and the *baccalauréat* examination to catch up with the boys of the *lycée*. They would start later and arrive as soon. Results had proved it. This was all very well, but I, who had missed so many lessons, was handicapped in the race, and in spite of Monsieur Nadaud's wearisome coaching, I soon lost all hope of catching up the boys who were already translating Virgil. I began to founder in a slough of despond.

This recitation of mine with its stupid success and the reputation it bestowed on me of being affected, gave a loose to my schoolfellows' hostility; the boys who had at first been my friends dropped me; the others grew bolder when they saw I had no one to back me. I was jeered at, beaten, hunted. The torture began when we came out of school; not immediately however, for my former friends would not have allowed me to be bullied under their very eyes—but round the first street corner. How I dreaded the end of school! As soon as I was outside, I slipped off as fast as I could and took to my heels. Fortunately we did not live far off; but my enemies lay in wait for me; then, for fear of ambushes, I contrived immense detours; as soon as the others became aware of this they changed their tactics and the hunt which had begun as a stalk developed into a chase; there might really have been some fun in it, but I felt that what moved them was not so much love of sport as hatred of me—wretched game that I was. The chief among them was the son of a travelling circus manager—a boy called Lopez, or Tropez, or Gomez, a great athletic brute, who was considerably older than any of us and who made it a point of honour to be at the bottom of the form. I can see him now— his horrid expression, his low forehead and plastered hair, shiny with hair-oil, his floating scarlet tie; it was he who was the leader and *he* really wanted my blood. There were days when I got home in a lamentable state, my clothes torn and muddy, my nose bleeding, my teeth chattering, haggard with fright. My poor mother was at her wits' ends. Then at last, by some merciful Providence, I fell seriously ill and my torture came to an end.

The doctor was sent for. I had small-pox. I was saved!

I was well nursed and looked after and in the normal course of things should soon have been about again. But as my convalescence advanced and the moment drew near for resuming my halter, I felt overwhelmed with horror, the unspeakable horror left me by the recollection of my torments. I saw the ferocious Gomez in my dreams; I fled panting from his pack; I felt again the abominable sensation on my cheek of the dead cat which he had one day picked out of the gutter and rubbed against my face, while the others held my arms; I used to wake up bathed in sweat, but only to a renewal of my terror, as I thought of what Dr. Leenhardt had said to my mother—that in a few days I should be well enough to go back to the *lycée;* and my heart quaked within me. But I am not wishing to excuse what follows. I leave it neurologists to disentangle what was real and what was assumed in the nervous malady that followed my small-pox.

This, I think, is how it began. The first day I was allowed to get up, I felt a kind of giddiness which made me totter on my legs, as was only natural after three weeks in bed. If this giddiness got a little worse, thought I to myself, can I imagine what would happen? Oh, yes; I should feel my head sink backwards; my knees would give way (I was in the little passage that led from my room to my mother's) and I should suddenly collapse on to the floor. "Ha!" said I to myself, "suppose I were to imitate what I imagine!" And even in the act of imagining I could feel what a relief, what a respite it would be to yield to this suggestion of my nerves. One glance behind me to make sure of a place where the fall would not hurt too much and . . .

I heard a cry from the next room. It was Marie who came running. I knew my mother was out; some remains of shame or pity restrained me when she was there, but I counted on her being told all about it. After this first trial, encouraged by my success, I grew bolder, cleverer and more decidedly inspired; I ventured on other movements; sometimes I invented jerky and abrupt ones; sometimes, on the contrary, they were long drawn out and rhythmically repeated in a kind of dance. I became extremely expert at these dances and my repertory was soon fairly varied; one consisted in just jumping up and down on the same spot; in another, I went backwards and forwards across the little space between the window and my bed, on to

which I sprang, standing upright, at every return journey—
three jumps in all hit it off exactly; sometimes this lasted an
hour on end. There was another I performed in bed with the
bed-clothes thrown off, consisting of a series of high kicks
done in cadence like those of a Japanese juggler.

I have often reproached myself since that time and wondered how I had the heart to carry on in this way in my
mother's presence. But I must confess that nowadays my
self-reproach seems to me less grounded. These movements of
mine, though perhaps conscious were barely voluntary. That
is to say that at most I might have controlled them a little. But
they gave me the greatest relief. Ah! how often in later days,
when suffering from my nerves, have I regretted that I was
no longer of an age when a pirouette or two . . .

At the first signs of this curious malady, Dr. Leenhardt,
who was sent for, reassured my mother. "Nerves," said he;
"nothing but nerves." But as I still went on jigging and pranc-
ing, he thought it best to call in two fellow practitioners to his
assistance. The consultation took place (I cannot remember
why or when)[1] in a room in the Hotel Nevet. There were
three doctors: Doctors Leenhardt, Theulon and Boissier; the
last named was the doctor of Lamalou-les-Bains, where it was
proposed to send me. My mother was present but said nothing.

I was a little anxious at the turn things had taken. These
old gentlemen (two of them were white-bearded) turned me
about in every direction, sounded me and then talked to each
other in whispers. Were they going to see through me? Would
one of them—the severe-looking one, Monsieur Theulon—
say:

"A good spanking, Madame, that's all this boy wants."

[1] On reflection this consultation must, I think, have taken place between my
two visits to Lamalou-les-Bains, which explains how we came to be at the
hotel.

No; and the more they examined me, the more convinced they seemed that my case was genuine. After all, could I be supposed to know more about myself than these learned gentlemen? It was no doubt I who was wrong in thinking that I was shamming.

The consultation was over.

I began to dress. Theulon bent down in a fatherly way to help me; Boissier stopped him; and as he did so, I saw a glance, a wink, pass between him and Theulon. So a cunning eye was fixed on me and meant to watch me whilst I thought myself unobserved. That same eye was secretly following my fingers as I rebuttoned my coat. "If that old boy comes with me to Lamalou, I shall have to look out," thought I to myself, and with apparent innocence, I flung him in a few extra contortions, as my fingers fumbled with the buttonholes.

One person who absolutely refused to take my illness seriously was my uncle Charles, and as I did not know then that he took nobody's illnesses seriously, I was vexed—I was extremely vexed, and determined to get the better of his indifference by playing my trump cards. Oh! what a wretched business! How much I should like to skip it, if only I had not resolved to omit nothing!

It was in the ante-room of the Charles Gides' apartment in the Rue Salle l'Evêque; my uncle had just left his library and I knew he would soon be coming back; I slipped under a side table and when I heard his step, waited a few moments to see whether he would notice me of his own accord, for the ante-chamber was spacious and my uncle walked slowly; but he was holding a newspaper and reading as he walked; in another second he would have passed me . . . I stirred feebly and uttered a moan. At this, he stopped, slowly removed his eyeglasses, and looking over the top of his newspaper:

"Hullo!" he said. "What are you doing there?"

Wriggling, writhing, contorted, I sobbed out in a voice I took to be irresistibly pathetic:

"Oh! I'm in such pain!"

But I was immediately aware of my fiasco. My uncle put his eyeglasses back on to his nose and his nose back into his paper and went on to his library, the door of which he shut behind him with the utmost unconcern. O shame! There was nothing for me to do but to get up, shake the dust from my clothes and start detesting my uncle—which I did with the best will in the world.

Rheumatic patients stopped at Lower Lamalou, where besides the baths, there was a small town, with a casino, and a few shops.

Four kilometres further up was Upper Lamalou or Old Lamalou, the Lamalou for ataxic patients, with nothing to recommend it but its primitive wildness. The bathing establishment, the hotel, a chapel, three villas, of which one belonged to Dr. Boissier—and that was all. And even the bathing establishment was almost hidden from sight at the bottom of a cleft in the rock, which cut the hotel garden in two and ran shadily, stealthily down to the river. At the age I was then at, it is nearness that lends enchantment to the view; a kind of shortsightedness blinds one to the distance; one prefers the detail to the whole; the secret country that gradually unfolds as one advances, to the country lying open to all.

On the day we arrived, while mamma and Marie were busy unpacking, I escaped. I ran into the garden and made my way on and on into the heart of the narrow gorge; above its steep sides of foliated rock, the tall trees bent into an arch; a steaming rivulet, which passed through the bathing establishment, and whose bed was lined with a thick, flaky rust, ran singing beside me; I was breathless with surprise, and the better to express my rapture, I remember walking along with my arms raised above my head in oriental fashion, like a picture I had seen in my beloved Arabian Nights of Sindbad in the Valley of Diamonds. The gorge led down to the river, which made a bend at this place, and here the schist of the cliff side had been washed into a deep hollow by the force of the current dashing against it; along the top of the cliff the hotel gardens ended in a fringe that had been left to grow wild—evergreen oaks, cistus, arbutus and, weaving its festoons from bush to bush or shaking its loose tresses into the void over the waters, smilax, dear to the Bacchantes. The ferruginous heat of the springs was soon quenched in the cool and limpid river; shoals of sprats played among the fragments of slate that had been washed away from the rocks; it was not till a little lower down, where the water was deeper and ran more slowly, that the rocks diminished in height; further up-stream the river was narrower and its current swifter; here there were eddies, leaps, falls, cool and quiet pools where the imagination fondly bathed; in places, when a projecting piece of rock barred the way, there were great flat stones, so spaced that one could step across to the other bank; in places, the two banks so nearly met that one was obliged to leave the river-side, to leave the shade, and climb up to the top of the cliff, where a little patch of cultivated ground lay parching under a burning sun; further away in the distance, began immense forests of Spanish chestnut-trees, clothing the first slopes of the mountains.

The Upper Lamalou bath claimed, I believe, to date from the Romans; at any rate it was primitive, and I liked it for that; small, but that was of no importance, since one was ordered to remain motionless in it, so that the carbonic acid might take effect. The water, an opaque rust colour, was not hot enough to prevent one from shivering when one first dipped into it; then, if you kept quite still, myriads of little bubbles soon came and settled on you, pricked you, flicked you, imparted a mysterious tingle to the coolness of the water, which at once relieved the nervous centres; the iron in the water worked too, either separately or in conjunction with Heaven knows what other strange and subtle elements, and all these together made up the extraordinary efficacy of the cure. One left the bath with a burning skin and frozen bones. A great fire of brushwood was ready blazing for me, which old Antoine stirred into a fiercer flame and at which he aired my night-shirt; for after the bath, you returned to bed again; a walk through an interminable passage brought you back at last to the hotel, to your room and to your bed, which had been warmed in the meantime by a "monk"—as the warming apparatus was called—a charcoal stove with an ingenious arrangement of hoops to keep it from burning the sheets.

The conclave of doctors, after this first cure, decided that Lamalou had done me good (yes, it must have been this consultation which took place at the Hotel Nevet) and pronounced in favour of another cure in autumn—which was exactly what I wanted. In the meantime I was ordered a treatment of douches at Gérardmer.

I refrain from copying the pages I had begun to write about Gérardmer, its forests and valleys and "*chaumes*",[1] and the idle life I led there. They would add nothing new to my story, and I am impatient to emerge from the dark shades of my childhood.

When, after ten months of lying fallow, my mother brought me back to Paris and sent me to the Ecole Alsacienne once more, I had entirely lost the habit of work. I had not been there a fortnight before I added headaches to my repertory of nervous troubles, as being less startling and easier to manage

[1] A special word used in the Vosges, meaning *upland pastures*.

at school. As these headaches left me completely after the age of twenty, and even earlier, I looked upon them for some time with great severity and accused them of being, if not altogether feigned, at any rate greatly exaggerated. But now that they have begun again, I recognise them, at forty-six years old,[1] as being exactly what they were when I was thirteen, and I admit they might very well have paralysed my efforts to work. In truth, I was not lazy; and I approved with my whole heart, when I heard my uncle Emile say:

"André will always love work."

But it was he too who called me "André the irregular." The fact is, I found great difficulty in working against the grain; even at that age, my steady hard work was done in short bouts—by repeating an effort I could not prolong. I was often overcome by sudden fits of fatigue—fatigue of the mind —interruptions of the current, so to speak; and this condition continued even after the sick headaches had left me, or, to be more accurate, succeeded the sick headaches and lasted for days, weeks, months at a time. Independently of all this, I experienced an unspeakable distaste for everything we did in class, for the class itself, for the whole system of lectures and examinations, even for the play hours; nor could I endure the sitting still, the lack of interest, the stagnation of the school régime. My headaches no doubt came in very conveniently; I cannot say how far I made the most of them.

Brouardel, who had originally been our doctor, was now so celebrated that my mother did not like to call him in, being hindered, I suppose, by the same kind of scruples which I have certainly inherited from her and which paralyse me too in my dealings with people of importance. There was no need to have any such fear regarding Monsieur Lizart, who succeeded him as our family doctor; one could rest assured that he, at any

[1] Written in 1916.

rate, would never be singled out for celebrity, for indeed there was nothing in him to single out. A good-natured creature he was; fair and foolish, with a gentle voice, a kind glance, a limp bearing; apparently harmless too—but nothing is more dangerous than a fool. How can his prescriptions be forgiven him? As soon as I felt *nervy*—bromides; as soon as I slept badly—chloral. And this for a growing child and an unformed brain! All my later weaknesses of will or memory I attribute to him. If one could take action against the dead, I would prosecute him. I remember with fury that for weeks together there was half a glass of a solution of chloral (the bottle of little crystals was put entirely at my own disposal and I could measure out any dose I fancied)—of chloral, I repeat, placed by my bedside at night, in case of sleeplessness; that for weeks, for months together, when I sat down to table, I found beside my plate a bottle of "Sirop Laroze" (peel of bitter oranges and bromide of potassium). At every meal, I had to take one, two, and then three spoonfuls (not tea-spoons but table-spoons) of this mixture, and so on, in a rhythmical series of threes; and this treatment went on indefinitely, nor was there any reason it should ever stop, until it left the poor foolish patient—such as I was—completely stupefied. Especially as the syrup was very good! I cannot understand how I escaped perdition.

Decidedly the devil was on the watch for me; the shades of night were gathering thick and fast and no sign gave warning there was any rift through which a ray of light might reach me. It was then that occurred the angelic intervention that came to snatch me from the Evil One—an event infinitely slight in itself, but as important in my life as revolutions in the history of empires—the first scene of a drama which is not yet played out.

V

It must have been a little before the New Year. We were again at Rouen; not only because it was holiday time, but because, after a month's trial, I had again left the Ecole Alsacienne. My mother resigned herself to treating me as an invalid and to the inevitable necessity of my learning nothing except by accident; this meant another and prolonged interruption to my education.

I could not eat; I could not sleep. My aunt Lucile was all kindness and attention; in the morning, Adèle or Victor came to light the fire in my room; I used to lie in my big bed long after I woke, lazily listening to the great logs as they hissed and spurted their harmless sparks against the fireguard, sinking with a delicious feeling of torpor into the comfort that pervaded the house from top to bottom. I see myself sitting between my mother and aunt in the big, pleasant, stately dining-room, its four corners adorned with white statues of the four seasons; there they stood, decently lascivious, after the style of the Restoration, each statue in its niche, on a pedestal fitted up as a sideboard (winter's being provided with a hot-plate).

Séraphine used to prepare me special little dishes, but nothing tempted my appetite.

"You see, my dear," said my mother to my aunt, "all the saints in the calendar won't get him to eat."

"Juliette," my aunt would suggest, "do you think he might fancy oysters?"

Then Mamma:

"No, no, you're much too kind . . . Well, perhaps, one might try oysters."

I can honestly say that this was not mere fastidiousness on my part. Everything was distasteful to me; I went to table as one might go to the scaffold; it was with the greatest difficulty that I swallowed a morsel or two; in vain my mother begged, scolded, and threatened, and nearly every meal ended in tears. But it is of quite another matter I wanted to speak . . .

I had met my cousins again at Rouen. I have said that my tastes as a child had drawn me more especially to Suzanne and Louise; but even this is not quite accurate; no doubt I played more with them, but it was because they liked playing with me; I preferred Emmanuèle, and more and more as she grew older. I was growing older too, but it was not the same thing; however serious I tried to be when I was with her, I felt I was still a child; I felt that she was one no longer. The sweetness of her expression had now a tinge of sadness in it which drew and held me all the more because I could not fathom it. And I did not actually know that Emmanuèle was sad; for she never spoke of herself, and her sadness was of a sort that no other child could have guessed at. Already I lived with my cousin in a conscious community of tastes and thoughts which I strove with all my heart to make closer and more perfect. This amused her, I think; for instance, when we dined together at the Rue de Crosne, she would make a game of forcing me to refuse the sweets I liked best, by refusing them herself; for she knew I would not touch any dish she had not helped herself to first. Does all this sound childish? Alas! There is nothing childish in what follows.

The secrets of a soul are as a rule only to be discovered by degrees, but it was not by degrees that I discovered the secret grief that had so precociously matured my friend and cousin. It was the total and abrupt revelation of an unsuspected world to which my eyes were suddenly opened, like the eyes of the blind man after the Saviour had touched them.

I had left my cousins in the evening to go back to the Rue de Crosne, where I thought my mother was expecting me, but I had found the house empty. I hesitated a little and then determined to return to the Rue Lecat; this seemed to me a specially good idea because I knew I was not expected there. I have already spoken of my childish mania for crowding whatever space and time lay beyond my ken with mysterious happenings. I was extremely preoccupied with what went on behind my back, and sometimes felt that if only I could turn round quick enough I should see . . . Heaven knows what!

I went then at an undue hour to Rue Lecat, bent on surprising. That evening my taste for the clandestine was gratified.

On the very threshold I scented something unusual. Contrary to custom, the *porte-cochère* was open, so that I did not have to ring. I was slipping in stealthily, when Alice, a detestable maidservant of my aunt's, suddenly appeared from behind the hall door, where she was apparently lying in wait, and in her most disagreeable voice:

"You, is it?" she asked. "What are you doing here at this time of day?"

It was evidently not I who was expected.

I made my way in, however, without answering.

My uncle Emile's office was on the ground floor; it was a dreary little room smelling of cigars, where he used to shut himself up half the day, and where, I think, he was much more occupied with his worries than with his business; he used to come out from it looking careworn and aged. He had certainly aged a good deal lately; I don't know whether I should have noticed it by myself, but after I overheard my mother saying to aunt Lucile one day: "Poor Emile! How he has changed!" I was immediately struck by the painful knitting of his brows and the anxious, and sometimes harassed expression of his eyes. My uncle was not at Rouen that day.

The stairs were in darkness and I went up noiselessly. The children's rooms were at the top of the house; below them my aunt's and uncle's, and on the first floor the drawing-room and dining-room, which I passed quickly. I meant to make a dash past the second floor too, but the door of my aunt's room was wide open; the room was brightly lighted and the light shone out on to the landing. I only gave one rapid glance and caught sight of my aunt stretched languidly on a sofa; Suzanne and Louise were bending over her and fanning her, and I think giving her salts to smell. I did not see Emmanuèle, or rather, a sort of instinct told me she could not be there. Fearing I should be seen and caught, I ran quickly past.

Her sisters' room, which I had first to go through, was dark, or, at any rate there was nothing to guide me but a dim twilight from the two windows, the curtains of which had not yet been drawn. I reached my cousin's door and knocked gently; as there was no answer, I was going to knock again, when the door yielded, for it had not been closed. In this room it was darker still; the bed was at the further end; I did not see Emmanuèle by it at first, for she was kneeling. I was going away, thinking the room was empty, when she called me:

"What have you come for? You ought not to have come back."

She had not risen. I did not realise at once that she was unhappy. It was when I felt her tears on my cheek that my eyes were suddenly opened.

I do not choose here to speak of the details of her wretchedness, nor to say much of the abominable secret that was the cause of her suffering, which moreover I was then too young to do more than guess at. To-day I cannot imagine anything more cruel for a young girl all purity, love and sweetness, than to have to judge and condemn her own mother's conduct; and what increased her unhappiness was that she was obliged to keep to herself and hide from a father she loved and revered a secret she had accidentally discovered and which was now crushing her—a secret which was the talk of the town, which the servants laughed over, and which took advantage of her two sisters' unheeding innocence. No, I was unable to understand any of this till later; but I felt that this little creature, already so dear to me, was possessed by a great, an intolerable grief—a grief that not all my love and all my life would be enough to cure. What more can I say? . . . Till that day, I had been wandering at random; now all at once, my mark was fixed, the mystic lodestar of my life discovered.

To all appearances nothing was changed. I shall return to the story of the small events that occupied me; the only change was that they no longer occupied me entirely. I kept hidden away in the depths of my heart the secret of my destiny. Had that destiny been less crossed and thwarted, I should not be writing these memoirs.

It was on the Riviera that we spent the rest of the winter. Anna was with us. Some unlucky inspiration made us first try Hyères, where the country inland is difficult of access and where the sea, which we thought would be close at hand, was only visible, like a deceitful mirage, in the distance, on the other side of a wide tract of market gardens; we thought it a deadly place; moreover Anna and I both fell ill. A certain doctor (I shall remember his name to-morrow), a child-specialist, persuaded my mother that all my ills, nervous and otherwise, came from flatulence; he discovered on sounding me that my abdomen was full of alarming cavities and had a tendency to swell; he even pointed out in a masterly manner the portion of the intestine in which the peccant vapours formed, and prescribed an orthopaedic bandage, price 150 francs, to be supplied by his cousin the surgical-instrument maker, which, he said, was a sure preventive of wind. I wore this ridiculous apparatus for some time; it hampered all my movements and had all the more difficulty in flattening my stomach, inasmuch as I was already as thin as a lath.

The palm-trees at Hyères delighted me less than the eucalyptus-trees which were in flower. The first one I saw sent me into transports; I was alone, but I ran off at once to announce the event to my mother and Anna, and as I had not been able to bring them back the smallest sample, for the flowering branches were out of my reach, I did not rest satisfied till I had dragged Anna to the spot where the tree of wonders grew. She said then:

"It's a eucalyptus—a tree imported from Australia." And she bade me observe the hang of the leaves, the way the branches grew, the deciduous bark . . .

Just then a cart passed by; a small boy perched up on the top of some sacks, picked and threw us a twig covered with the curious flowers I was longing to examine at close quarters. The buds, which were verdigris colour, were covered with a kind of resinous bloom, and looked like little closed caskets; one might have thought them seeds, but for their look of freshness, and suddenly the lid of one of the caskets would burst open under the tumultuous pressure of the stamens; then, when the lid fell to the ground, the released stamens would stand out in an aureole; from a little way off, among the tangle of long sickle-shaped, drooping leaves, the white, petal-less flower looked like a sea-anemone.

My first meeting with the eucalyptus and the discovery of a little hooded arum in the hedges by the roadside on the way to Costebelle were the great events of this stay.

While we were kicking our heels at Hyères, mamma, refusing to accept defeat, went on a voyage of discovery as far as the Esterel and beyond, came back in ecstasies and carried us off to Cannes next day. Though we were very indifferently lodged, near the station and in the least pleasant part of the town, I have kept an enchanting recollection of Cannes. At that time not a single hotel and hardly a villa had sprung up in the direction of Grasse; the Cannet road passed through groves of olives; the country began at once where the town ended; narcissus, anemones, tulips grew in abundance in the shadow of the olive-trees, and in profusion further afield.

But it was a different order of flowers that chiefly aroused my admiration; I mean the submarine flora, which I was able to study once or twice a week, on the days that Marie took me to the islands of Lêrins. There was no need to walk much further than our favourite landing-stage at Saint-Honorat, in order to find recesses sheltered from the surf, deep creeks, which had been subdivided into innumerable little pools by the erosion of the rocks, where shells, sea-weed and madrepores displayed their splendour with oriental magnificence. The first glance was an enchantment, but the passer-by who was satisfied with the first glance had really seen nothing : I had only to remain motionless for a little, leaning like Narcissus over the surface of the water, and from a thousand holes, from a thousand crannies in the rocks, there slowly emerged before my admiring eyes all the wonders my approach had put to flight. All around began to breathe and palpitate; the rock itself seemed to come to life and what had appeared inanimate began timidly to move; strange translucid creatures with ghostly motions rose from the tangle of weeds; the water became populous; the pale sand that carpeted the floor stirred here and there, and from the tip of some dull tube that might have been a withered reed-stalk, there would begin to flower, in little nervous jerks, as though half fearful still, a lovely frail corolla.

While Marie read or knitted at a little distance, I would stay for hours, regardless of the sun, gazing indefatigably at the slow rotatory work of an urchin digging itself a cell, at the changing colours of an octopus, at the groping progress of an anemone, at hunts and pursuits and ambushes, at many a mysterious drama which made my heart beat. I used to get up from this entranced contemplation utterly stupefied and with a violent headache. How could there be any question of working?

During this whole winter, I cannot remember having opened a single book, written a letter or learnt a lesson. My mind was as completely idle as my body. I think to-day that my mother might have taken this opportunity to make me learn English, for instance; but that language my parents had reserved for their own use in order to be able to say things before me they did not want me to understand; and besides, I was so stupid at picking up the little German Marie taught me, that it was thought prudent not to trouble me further. There was a piano indeed, though a very poor one, in the drawing-room, on which I might have practised a little every day; alas! my mother had been recommended carefully to avoid anything that might cost me an effort . . . I am furious, like Monsieur Jourdain, when I think what a pianist I might have become, if only I had had a little encouragement in those days.

When we got back to Paris at the beginning of spring, mamma began to look out for a new apartment, for it was generally admitted that ours in the Rue de Tournon was no longer suitable. Evidently, thought I, remembering the sordid furnished lodgings of Montpelier, evidently papa's death has ruined us, and in any case the Rue de Tournon apartment is much too big for us now. Who knows what we shall have to put up with in the future?

My anxiety did not last long. I soon heard my aunt Démarest and my mother discussing questions of rent, situation and floor, and it did not at all sound as if our style of living was to be reduced. Since papa's death, my aunt Claire had acquired great influence over my mother. (She was very much older.) She used to say in a decided voice and with a particular little pout of her own:

"Yes, you might manage on that floor. It doesn't so much matter being high up. But as for the other point, no, Juliette; certainly not." And she made a little sharp peremptory gesture with the flat of her hand, which cut short the discussion with a snap.

The other point was the *porte-cochère*. It might occur to a child that if one did not give parties or drive in a coach oneself, a *porte-cochère* was a thing one might do without. But the child upon this occasion had no voice in the matter, and besides what could one find to say when my aunt declared:

"It's not a question of convenience but of decency."

Then, seeing that my mother kept silent, she went on more gently but with no less insistence:

"You owe it to yourself; you owe it to your son." Then, very quickly, thrown in as an extra:

"It's perfectly simple, my dear; if you haven't a *porte-cochère*, I can tell you straight off the people who won't come to see you."

And she immediately reeled out a list of names such as to terrify the stoutest heart. But my mother looked at her sister and smiled rather sadly:

"And you, Claire," she said; "would you stop coming to see me?"

Upon which, my aunt would purse up her lips and return to her embroidery.

These conversations only took place when Albert was not there. Albert, no doubt, was not a man of the world. My mother, however, liked to hear what he had to say, remembering that she herself had once been something of a rebel; but my aunt preferred him not to give his opinion.

In short, the new apartment was decidedly larger, finer, more pleasant, more luxurious than the old one. I will describe it later on.

Before leaving the Rue de Tournon, however, let me have one last look at the past connected with it and at what I have so far written. It seems to me that I have made the shadows in which my childhood lingered so long, too dark; or rather, I have failed to speak of two flashes, two strange thrills which momentarily stirred the darkness of my night. If I had described them before and in the proper place chronologically, it would no doubt have been easier to understand the overwhelming agitation that shook me that autumn evening in the Rue Lecat, when I came into contact with the invisible reality of life.

The first takes me back into the dim distance; I wish I could say the exact year, but all I know is that my father was still alive. We were at table; Anna was lunching with us. My parents were sad because they had heard that morning of the death of a little child of four, the son of some cousins called Widmer; I had not heard the news, but I gathered it from a word or two my mother said to Nana. I had only seen little Emile Widmer two or three times, and had no particular feeling for him; but I no sooner understood he was dead, than a very ocean of grief rolled over my heart. Mamma took me on to her lap and tried to quiet my sobs; she told me that we must all die; that little Emile had gone to Heaven where there were no more tears or suffering, in short, all the most consoling things a tender mother can think of; nothing was of any avail, for I was not exactly weeping for my little cousin's death, but for something I could not understand, an indefinable anguish or terror, which it was not surprising I could not explain to my mother, for I am incapable of explaining it any better to-day. Ridiculous though it may seem to some of my readers, I must say however, that in later life, on reading certain pages of Schopenhauer, I suddenly seemed to recognise my own particular anguish. Yes, it is a fact that in order to understand [1]. . . . .

. . . .
. . . . . it was the recollection of my first *schaudern* that I quite unconsciously and quite irresistibly evoked.

The second of these tremors was still more peculiar: it was a few years later, a little after my father's death; that is to say I must have been about eleven. The scene again took place at table, but this time my mother and I were alone. I had been at school that morning. What had happened? Possibly nothing. . . . Then why did I suddenly break down? Why did I again feel, as I fell convulsively sobbing into mamma's arms, that indefinable anguish, the very same exactly that I had felt at my little cousin's death? It was as though the special sluice-gate of some unknown, unbounded, mystic sea had suddenly been opened and an overwhelming flood poured into my heart. I was not so much unhappy as terrified; but how was I to explain it to my mother? All she could distinguish through my sobs were, repeated again and again, these blind despairing words:

"I'm not like other people . . . not like other people!"

Two other recollections are also connected with the Rue de Tournon: I must tell them quickly before making the move. I had managed to get myself given as a New Year's present Troost's big book on Chemistry. It was aunt Lucile who gave it me; aunt Claire, whom I had asked first, thought it would be absurd to give me a lesson book; I insisted, however, so

[1] Too long to quote.

violently that no other book would give me as much pleasure, that aunt Lucile was persuaded. She had this excellent thing about her, that she consulted my tastes rather than her own when she wanted to please me, and it was to her I owed some years later the collection of Sainte-Beuve's *Lundis* and Balzac's *Comédie humaine*. But I must return to my chemistry.

I was only thirteen, but I protest that no student could ever have plunged more eagerly into this book than I. It goes without saying, however, that part of the interest I took in it depended on the experiments I proposed to make. My mother consented to my using the little backroom which was at the further end of the apartment, next door to my bedroom, and in which I also kept my guinea-pigs. There I installed a small spirit stove, my matrasses and the rest of my paraphernalia. I am still astonished that my mother should have allowed it; either she did not fully realise what risks the walls, the floor and myself were running, or perhaps she thought it was worth while running them, if it were to be of any benefit to me; in any case she made over to me weekly a tidy little sum which I immediately laid out in the Place de la Sorbonne or the Rue de l'Ancienne-Comédie on tubes, retorts, crucibles, salts, metalloids and metals—and on acids too, some of which I now wonder the shops consented to sell me; but no doubt the shopmen took me for a mere errand-boy. The inevitable result was that one fine morning the receptacle in which I was making hydrogen exploded in my face. I remember, I was making the experiment called "the chemical harmonica," which is performed with a lamp-chimney. I made the hydrogen with perfect success; I had fixed the long thin tube by which the gas was to come out and was preparing to set fire to it; in one hand, I held the match and in the other the lamp chimney in which the flame was supposed to come and sing; but I no sooner applied the match than the flame flashed into the inside of the apparatus and sent the whole concern—glass, tubes, corks—flying. At the noise of the explosion, the guinea-pigs leapt sky-high and the lamp-chimney dropped from my hands. I realised with terror that if the receptacle had been corked a little tighter the glass itself would have burst in my face. This made me more reserved in my dealings with chemicals. From that day I studied my chemistry book with a different eye. As God divides the just from the unjust, I marked with a blue pencil the quiet well-behaved bodies, those there is some pleasure in cultivating, and with a red pencil those that comport themselves in a suspicious or alarming manner.

A short time ago, I happened to open one of my young nieces' chemistry books. I found myself completely at sea; everything was changed—formulae, laws, the classification of bodies, their names, their places in the book, and even their properties . . . And I who had believed so entirely in their constancy! My nieces laugh at my dismay; but in the face of such revolutions a secret melancholy overtakes me; it is like meeting an old crony one had always thought of as a confirmed bachelor and finding him a married man and the father of a family.

The second recollection is of a conversation with Albert Démarest. When we were in Paris, he and his mother used to come and dine with us once a week. After dinner, aunt Claire and mamma would play a game of cards or backgammon together; Albert and I as a rule sat down to the piano. But that evening conversation took the place of music. I must have said something—I cannot remember what—during dinner, which Albert thought deserved reproof. He said nothing before the others and waited till the meal was over; but immediately after it he took me on one side . . .

At that time I had a kind of adoration for Albert; I have

already said how eagerly I used to drink in his words—above all when they ran counter to my own natural bent—especially as this was rarely the case, and I found him as a rule extraordinarily anxious to understand the very things about me that were likely to be least understood by my mother and the rest of the family. Albert was very tall, very strong, and at the same time very gentle; his slightest remarks amused me inexpressibly, perhaps because he said the very things I did not dare say, or even did not dare think; the mere sound of his voice enchanted me. I knew he had been first-rate at every kind of sport, especially swimming and rowing, and now, after having experienced the exhilaration of an open-air life and the delights of physical development, he was devoting himself almost entirely to painting, music and poetry. But on that particular evening, we discussed none of these matters. On that particular evening, Albert explained to me the meaning of patriotism.

I must own I had much to learn on that subject; for neither my father nor my mother, good French people as they were, had ever instilled into me any very definite sense of the frontiers of our territories or of our minds. I cannot swear they possessed any themselves; and for myself, being inclined, like my father, to attach less importance to realities than to ideas, I reasoned at thirteen years old like an idealist, a child and a fool. I must have declared during dinner that in '70, "if I had been France, I should not have defended myself," or some nonsense of the kind; and that moreover, I had a horror of everything military. This was what Albert had thought it necessary to reprove.

He did it without protestations or fine phrases, but simply by telling me about the invasion and his own recollections as a soldier. He told me that his horror of the power that provokes was as great as mine, but for that very reason, he admired the power that defends, and that the beauty of the soldier's life came from the fact that it was not himself he was defending, but those weaker than himself whom he knew to be in danger. And as he spoke, his voice trembled and grew grave.

"Then you think one can coolly allow one's parents to be insulted, one's sisters raped, one's goods plundered? . . ." And no doubt an image of the war he had been through passed before his eyes, for I saw them fill with tears, though his face was in the shadow. He was in a low armchair, beside my father's big writing-table, on which I was perched, swinging my legs, and a little embarrassed by what he was saying and at being seated above him. At the other end of the room, my aunt and mother were intent on a game of cribbage or bezique with Anna, who had come to dinner that night. Albert spoke in a low voice so that the ladies should not hear him; after he had finished, I took his big hand in both of mine and remained silent, more moved, I know, by the beauty of his nature than convinced by his arguments. But I was to remember his words later on, when I was better fitted to understand them.

I was immensely amused and excited by the idea of changing houses and by the prospect of arranging the furniture in our new home; but the move took place without me. When we came back from Cannes, mamma sent me to board with a new professor; this plan, she hoped, would be of advantage to me and give her more freedom.

Monsieur Richard, into whose charge I was put, had had the good taste to settle at Auteuil; or perhaps it was because he had settled at Auteuil that mamma thought of sending me to him. He lived at No. 12, I think, Rue Raynouard, in a little two-storied old-world house, with a garden attached, of no great size, but forming a terrace from which one could see over half Paris. The house and garden still exist, though they will not do so for long, no doubt, for the time has gone by when a small professor, from motives of economy, was able to set up his modest establishment in the Rue Raynouard. At that time M. Richard gave lessons only to his boarders, that is to say, to me and to two English spinsters, who paid, I think, chiefly for the air and the view. M. Richard was a professor *in partibus;* it was not till later that he obtained a German lectureship at some *lycée.* He had at first intended to go into the ministry, and it was for this, I think, that he had pursued his studies pretty far, for he was neither lazy nor stupid; then doubts or scruples (both most likely) had stopped him on the threshold. His first vocation had given a kind of unction to his look and voice; the latter was by nature pastoral—by which I mean that it had a soul-stirring quality; but a half-sad, half-amused, and I think an almost involuntary smile tempered his austerest sayings and made one realise he did not take himself very seriously. He had all sorts of good qualities, virtues even, but nothing about him seemed quite sterling or established on a solid basis; he was inconsistent, desultory, ready to laugh at serious things, and take trifles seriously—faults which, young as I was, I was very sensible of and which I judged at that time with perhaps even more severity than I do now. I think his sister-in-law, the widow of General Bertrand, who lived with us too, did not have a very high opinion of him, which raised her greatly in mine. A woman of excellent sense, who had known better times, she was, I now think, the only sensible person in the house; added to which, she had plenty of heart as well, though she only showed it on rare occasions. Madame Richard had no doubt as much heart as she; she even appeared to have more, for as she had no sense, it was always her heart that spoke. She had poor health, and was thin, pale and drawn-looking; being very gentle, she always effaced herself before her husband and sister, which is no doubt the reason I have kept such a very indistinct impression of her; whereas Madame Bertrand, who was on the contrary solid, affirmative and decided, managed to imprint her personality on my memory. She had a daughter a few years younger than myself, who was always carefully kept apart from us all, and who, I thought, suffered a little under her mother's excessively authoritative rule. Yvonne Bertrand was a delicate, almost puny child, as if the life had been crushed out of her by discipline; even when she smiled she always looked as if she had been crying. She hardly ever appeared except at meals.

The Richards had two children; a little girl about eighteen months old, whom I regarded with awe ever since the day I saw her eating earth in the garden, to the great amusement of her small brother Blaise, who was in charge of her, though he was only five himself.

I used to work, sometimes by myself and sometimes with M. Richard, in a small orangery, if I can give such a name to a glazed lean-to placed against the blank wall of a large house at the end of the garden.

On a little shelf beside the desk at which I worked, grew a gladiolus, whose growth I had planned to watch. I had bought the bulb at the Saint-Sulpice market and planted it in its pot myself. A green blade had soon risen out of the soil and its growth from day to day filled me with wonder; in order to measure it exactly, I stuck into the pot a white label on which I marked its progress every day. I calculated that the leaf grew three-fifths of a millimetre per hour, which really with a little attention ought to be visible to the naked eye. Now I was tormented by curiosity to know at which end the growth took place, but reluctantly came to the conclusion that the plant must do all its growing by night, for in vain I sat with my eyes glued to the leaf . . . The study of mice was infinitely more repaying. I had not been five minutes in front of my book or my gladiolus when they came running out in the most charming fashion to entertain me; every day I brought them some little dainties to eat, and finally they got tame enough to come and nibble the crumbs on the very table where I was working. There were only two of them, but I persuaded myself that one was going to breed, so that every morning with a beating heart I expected the appearance of a family of baby mice. There was a hole into which they ran when Monsieur Richard approached; this was their nest, and I watched it out of the corner of my eye while I said my lessons; naturally I said them very badly; finally, Monsieur Richard asked me why I was so inattentive. So far, I had kept the presence of my playfellows a secret. That day I told him all about them.

I knew that girls were afraid of mice; I understood how it was that housewives disliked them; but Monsieur Richard was a man. He seemed keenly interested in my tale. He made me show him the hole; then he went out without a word, leaving me puzzled. A few minutes later, I saw him come back with a steaming kettle in his hand. I did not dare take his meaning and with a trembling voice:

"What have you got there, Monsieur Richard?" I asked.

"Boiling water."

"What for?"

"To scald out your horrid creatures."

"Oh, Monsieur Richard, please, I beg, I implore you not to. I think they've just had little ones."

"All the more reason."

And it was I who had betrayed them! I ought to have asked him first if he was fond of animals . . . Tears, supplications were of no avail. Oh, what a wicked man! I think he chuckled as he emptied the kettle into the hole; but I had turned away my eyes.

I found it difficult to forgive him. To tell the truth, he seemed a little astonished afterwards at the violence of my grief; he did not exactly excuse himself, but I felt he was a little abashed, from the effort he made to prove to me how ridiculous I was, and what horrid little animals they were, and how unpleasant they smelt, and how much harm they did; and in particular, they prevented me from working. And Monsieur Richard was not without compunction; he tried to make amends a little later by offering to present me with any animals I liked, provided they were harmless.

I chose a pair of turtle-doves. After all, did he present me with them or did he merely tolerate them? My ungrateful memory forsakes me at this point . . . Their wicker cage was hung up in a rather dilapidated aviary, which made a pendant to the orangery; it was the home of one or two screaming, bad-tempered stupid fowls, in which I took no interest whatever.

During the first day or two I listened enthusiastically to my doves' cooing; I had never heard anything so delicious; they cooed like burbling springs, all day long without stopping; the noise, from being delightful, became maddening; Miss Elvin, one of the two English boarders, was particularly irritated and persuaded me to make the birds a nest. I had no sooner done this, than the female dove began to lay and the cooing became less incessant.

She laid two eggs; such is their custom; but as I did not know how long she would take to hatch them, I made continual incursions into the hen-house; there, perched on an old stool, I could look down on to the nest; but as I did not want to disturb the sitter, I waited and watched interminably until she should be kind enough to get up and show me that the eggs were still unhatched. Then, one morning, even before going in, I caught sight of fragments of faintly bloody egg-shell lying on the floor of the cage, on a level with my nose. At last! But when I tried to get into the aviary, I found to my profound amazement that the door was shut and secured by a small padlock, which I recognised as one which Monsieur Richard had bought with me a day or two before in a neighbouring shop.

"Is it any good?" he had asked the shopman.

"As good as a big one," had been the answer.

Monsieur Richard and Madame Bertrand, irritated at seeing me spend so much time with my birds, had resolved to put an obstacle in the way; they told me at lunch that the padlock would remain fastened and that Madame Bertrand would keep the key, and only let me have it once a day, at four o'clock, during the tea hour. Madame Bertrand always came to the fore when it was necessary to take an initiative or apply a punishment. She spoke at such times calmly, and even gently, but very firmly. As she informed me of this terrible decision she was almost smiling. I took care not to object; but it was because I had a plan of my own. Those little cheap padlocks all have the same keys; I had noticed that fact the day Monsieur Richard was buying his. With the few pennies that were jingling in my pocket I could . . . Off I ran to the shop directly after lunch.

I declare there was not the slightest feeling of revolt in my heart. Neither then, nor ever, have I taken any pleasure in deceiving. I meant to have a game with Madame Bertrand, not to take her in. How could the fun I hoped to get out of this childish prank have blinded me to the possibility that Madame Bertrand might look at it in a different way? I liked and respected her, and, as I have said, I was even particularly anxious for her esteem; any slight annoyance I may have felt came chiefly from the fact that she had adopted material means when all she had to do was to appeal to my obedience; for when I came to think of it, she had not actually forbidden me to go into the aviary; she had simply put an obstacle in the way, as if . . . Well! She should see what her padlock was worth! Naturally I should not go into the cage on the sly; it would be no fun unless she saw me; I should not open the door until she was in the drawing-room, the windows of which faced the aviary (I laughed at the thought of her astonishment), and afterwards I should hand her my double key and assure her of my good intentions. I turned all this over in my mind on my way back from the shop; it would be no use, however, to look for any logic in this account of my reasoning; I give it in the rough, just as it occurred to me, without any further attempt at arranging it.

As I went into the hen-house, I was thinking more of Madame Bertrand than of my turtle-doves. I knew she was in the drawing-room and I watched the windows, but there was nothing to be seen; it almost looked as if it were she who was hiding. What a sell! Still I could not very well call her. I waited and waited, but in the end I had to come out. I had hardly glanced at the brood. Without taking the key from the padlock, I returned to the orangery, where a piece of translation from Quintus Curtius was awaiting me and set to work, vaguely uneasy, and wondering what I should do when the tea-bell rang.

Little Blaise came to fetch me a few minutes before four o'clock—his aunt wanted to speak to me. Madame Bertrand was waiting for me in the drawing-room. She rose as I entered, with the evident intention of being more impressive, allowed me to take a few steps towards her and then:

"I see I have been mistaken in you," she said; "I hoped you

126

were an honest little boy . . . You thought I didn't see you just now."

"But . . ."

"You kept looking at the house for fear . . ."

"Yes, because . . ."

"No, I won't allow you to say a word. What you have done is very wrong. Where did you get that key?"

"I . . ."

"I forbid you to answer. Do you know where people go to who break open locks? To prison. I shall not tell your mother of your conduct, it would make her too unhappy; if you had only given her one thought you would never have dared do such a thing."

I realised as she was speaking that it would be utterly impossible to make her understand the secret motives of my conduct; and to tell the truth, they were no longer very clear to myself; now that my excitement had subsided, my trick struck me in another light and seemed mere foolishness. And besides, the impossibility of defending myself had at once produced in me a kind of disdainful resignation which enabled me to bear the brunt of Madame Bertrand's sermon without a blush. I think that after she had forbidden me to speak, she was irritated by my silence, which forced her to go on talking when she had nothing left to say. I put all the eloquence that was denied my tongue into my eyes.

"I don't care what you think now," they said; "since you have been so very unfair to me, I cease to respect you."

And to emphasise my disdain, I refrained for a whole fortnight from going near my birds—with excellent results for my work.

Monsieur Richard was a good professor; he took more pleasure in teaching than in learning; he had a quiet way with him and a kind of gaiety which prevented his lessons from being dull. As I still had everything to learn, we drew up an elaborate time-table, which, however, was constantly being upset by my persistent headaches. I must also say that my mind easily went off at a tangent; Monsieur Richard lent himself to this, both because he was afraid of tiring me and because he was inclined that way himself, and the lesson degenerated into a conversation. This is a common failing in private tutors.

Monsieur Richard had a taste for letters, but was not sufficiently cultivated for his taste to be good. He did not conceal from me that the classics bored him; he was obliged to follow the curriculum, but after an analysis of *Cinna*, he would take a rest by reading me *Le Roi s'amuse*.[1] Triboulet's apostrophes to the courtiers brought the tears to my eyes, and with sobs in my voice I would declaim:

> *"For see! This poor hand, rough and brown with toil,*
> *Hand of a peasant serf, son of the soil,*
> *This unarmed hand that makes you laugh, my lord.*
> *It still has nails, if it has not a sword!"*

To-day, I think these lines intolerably pompous and empty but at thirteen, they seemed to me magnificent and infinitely more moving than the celebrated speech in Corneille's *Cinna*,

> *"Embrassons-nous, Cinna . . ."*

which I was asked to admire. I used to repeat after Monsieur Richard the Marquis de Saint-Vallier's famous tirade [2]:

[1] *"Oh! voyez! Cette main, main qui n'a rien d'illustre,*
Main d'un homme du peuple, et d'un serf et d'un rustre,
Cette main qui paraît désarmée aux rieurs
Et qui n'a pas d'épée, a des ongles, Messieurs!"
                                    Le Roi s'amuse : VICTOR HUGO

[2]   *"Dans votre lit, tombeau de la vertu des femmes,*
Vous avez froidement, sous vos baisers infâmes
Terni, flétri, souillé, déshonoré, brisé,
Diane de Poitiers, Comtesse de Brézé.
                                    Le Roi s'amuse : VICTOR HUGO

"For in your bed, where women's virtue lies
As in a tomb, you have, as cold as ice,
Tarnished, dishonoured, soiled in lustful play
Diane de Poitiers, Countess of Brézé."

That anyone should venture to write such things—and in verse too! I was rapt in amazement. For what I chiefly admired in these lines was, no doubt, their daring. But the daring thing was to read them at thirteen.

Seeing my emotion and that I vibrated as responsively as a violin, Monsieur Richard resolved to put my sensibility to more exquisite tests. He produced Richepin's *Blasphèmes*, and then Rollinat's *Névroses*, which for the moment were his bedside books, and began to read them to me. A peculiar education!

What enables me to give the exact date of my reading these works is that I can remember the place where I read them. Monsieur Richard, with whom I worked for three years, moved to the centre of Paris the following winter; the scene of *Le Roi s'amuse*, *Les Névroses* and *Les Blasphèmes* was the little orangery of Passy.

Monsieur Richard had two brothers. Edmond, the second one, was a tall, slim young man, of distinguished intelligence and manners. He had succeeded Gallin, the dandy, as my tutor, the summer before. I have not seen him since; he was delicate and could not live in Paris. (I have heard recently that he had a brilliant career in the banking world.)

I had only been a short time with Monsieur Richard when the third and youngest brother, who was only five years older than I, came to stay with him. He had been living till then at Guéret with a sister of whom I had already heard, because Edmond Richard had spoken of her to my mother the summer before. On the first night he arrived at La Roque:

"You have no sisters, have you?" she asked affably.

"Yes," he had answered. Then, thinking, like a well-bred man, that his monosyllable had been rather abrupt, he had added:

"I have one sister; she lives at Guéret."

"Really!" said mamma; "at Guéret? . . . And what does she do?"

"She's a pastry-cook."

This conversation took place at dinner; my cousins were there; we were hanging on the lips of the new tutor—the stranger, who had been imported into our life and who, if he happened to be affected or silly or disagreeable, might spoil our holidays for us.

Edmond Richard seemed charming, but we were on the look-out for his first remarks in order to pronounce our collective judgment on them—the implacable, irrevocable judgment which young people ignorant of the world are so prone to pass. We were not given to making fun of our neighbours, but when we heard the words "She's a pastry-cook," we were overcome by laughter, which, though there was nothing at all ill-natured in it, was quite uncontrollable. And yet Edmond Richard had spoken very simply, straightforwardly, and courageously too, if he had any suspicion of the effect it might have on us. We stifled our laughter as well as we could, for we felt how improper and vile it was; the thought that he may have heard it is still very painful to me.

Abel Richard, if not exactly weak-minded, was, to say the least, considerably less intelligent than his two elder brothers, and on this account his education had been very much neglected. He was a tall, limp youth, with a gentle expression, a flabby hand, a plaintive voice; he was anxious and even eager to be agreeable, but not very tactful, so that he often got more snubs than thanks for his pains. Though he was always hanging round me, we did not talk much; I had nothing to say to him, and as for him, it was as much as he could do to get out three sentences together without gasping for breath. One summer evening—one of those fine hot evenings when the weary day sinks to rest in quiet adoration—we were all sitting up late on the terrace. Abel came up to me as he often did, and I, as I often did, pretended not to see him. I was sitting apart from the others on the children's swing (but they had gone to bed long before), steadying it with the tip of my toe, so as to keep it motionless. I felt Abel standing beside me, motionless too; he was leaning against one of the supports of the swing and shaking it slightly without meaning to. But I would not look at him; I kept my face turned away and fixed my eyes on the lights of the town shining their response to the stars of Heaven. We stayed a long time like this, until at a little movement he made, I at last looked at him. He had no doubt only been waiting for my look. Stammering and choking, in a voice I could hardly hear:

"Will you be my friend?" he said.

Now I felt for Abel nothing but the most ordinary affection; but it would have needed hatred to repulse this offer of his heart.

"Yes, of course," or "All right," I answered awkwardly and vaguely.

"Then," said he, without the slightest hesitation, "I will show you my secrets."

I followed him. In the hall, he tried to light a candle; he was trembling so that he broke several matches without succeeding. Just then, Monsieur Richard's voice was heard calling:

"André! Where are you? It's time to go to bed."

Abel took my hand in the dark.

"Then it must be to-morrow," he said in a tone of resignation.

The next day, he took me up to his room. There were two beds in it, but one had been left unoccupied since Edmond Richard's departure. Abel, without a word, went up to a small doll's cupboard standing on a table, and opened it with a key he wore hanging from his watch-chain; he took out a bundle of about a dozen letters, tied round with a pink ribbon, which he undid, and handing me the packet:

"There!" he said, in a burst of generosity, "you may read them all!"

To tell the truth, I had not the smallest wish to do so. The handwriting of all the letters was the same; a woman's handwriting, running, even, commonplace, like a clerk's or a shopkeeper's, and the mere sight of it froze one's curiosity. But there was no help for it; I had to read or cruelly mortify Abel.

I had thought they were love-letters; but nothing of the kind; they were from his sister, the Guéret pastry-cook; poor, woebegone, lamentable letters, full of nothing but bills falling due, liabilities, "arrears" (it was the first time I came across that sinister expression), and I realised from allusions and reticences that Abel had generously made over to his sister a portion of the money which should have come to him from his parents; I remember in particular a phrase which said that what he had given would unfortunately not be enough to "cover the arrears" . . .

Abel had moved away to let me read; I was sitting in front of a deal table, beside the tiny cupboard out of which he had taken the letters; he had not shut it again, and as I read I gave it an uneasy glance now and then, fearing there might be more letters to come out of it; but the cupboard was empty. Abel was standing at the open window; he certainly knew the pages by heart; I felt him following me as I read. He was no doubt expecting some words of sympathy, and I hardly knew what to say, for I shrank from showing more emotion than I felt. Money troubles are not those in which a child can easily find beauty; I could have sworn they had none, and beauty of some kind I had to have before feeling moved. I thought at last of asking Abel if he had a photograph of his sister; it spared me the necessity of lying and might pass for a mark of interest. He pulled a photograph out of his pocket-book with twittering haste.

"How like you she is!" I exclaimed.

"Oh! isn't she?" said he rapturously. I had said the words without thinking, but he found more comfort in them than in a protestation of friendship.

"Now you know all my secrets," he went on, after I had given him back the photograph, "you'll tell me yours, won't you?"

Already while I was reading his sister's letters, I had vaguely thought of Emmanuèle. From what a halo of brightness my cousin's fair face shone out beside these sordid miseries! The vow I had made to devote my whole life's love to her gave wings to my heart and brimmed it full of joy; a thousand unformed ambitions, a thousand mingled impulses were already stirring deep within me; songs and laughter and leaping harmonies danced round my love in a festal train . . . I, with my overflowing riches, felt my heart stick in my throat at Abel's question. And could I decently spread out my treasures in face of his penury, thought I? Should I detach a tiny fragment of them to show him? But no! My immense fortune was one single solid block—an ingot it was impossible to coin. I looked again at the packet of letters which Abel was now carefully tying up with the pink ribbon, at the little empty cupboard, and when once more he asked me:

"Tell me your secrets, won't you?"

"I haven't any," I answered.

VI

The Rue de Commaille was a new street leading out of the Rue du Bac; it had been cut through a number of gardens which had long lain hidden behind the façade of tall houses in that portion of the old street. If the *porte-cochère* of one of those houses happened to be open, a curious and admiring eye could plunge through it into the unsuspected, secluded, mysterious depths of garden after garden—gardens of private houses, gardens of public ministries, gardens of embassies—gardens like Fortunio's, jealously guarded, but which the windows of the more modern houses in the vicinity sometimes had the expensive privilege of overlooking.

The two windows of the drawing-room, that of the library, those of my mother's room and of mine, looked over one of these marvellous gardens, from which we were separated by the width of the street alone. This street had houses along one side of it only; there was nothing on the other but a low wall which interfered with the view of the lower floors; but we were on the fourth.

It was in my mother's room that she and I usually sat. It was there we took our tea in the morning. I am speaking now of the second year when Monsieur Richard, having settled in the centre of Paris, I was only a day-boarder, and came home every evening to dine and sleep. I left in the morning again just as Marie began to do my mother's hair, and so it was only on holidays that I had the privilege of assisting at this performance which lasted half an hour.

Mamma, dressed in a morning wrapper, sat well in the light, facing the window. Marie set up a standing oval mirror in front of her, so that she could see herself. It was jointed and mounted on a three-legged metal rod, which could be raised or lowered at will; there was a tiny circular tray fixed round the rod, on which the brushes and comb were laid. My mother sat with the *Temps* newspaper in her hand, alternately reading three lines and looking at herself in the glass, in which she could see the top of her head and Marie's hand brandishing the brush or comb; whatever Marie did, it was with the appearance of being infuriated.

"Oh, Marie! You're hurting me," my mother would moan.

I used to read while this was going on, lolling in one of the two big armchairs that stood right and left of the fireplace and blocked up the approach to it—two leviathan armchairs, whose frame-work and very shape were lost to view under the bloated volume of their padding. I raised my eyes now and then to look at my mother's handsome profile; her features were naturally grave and gentle, but on such occasions a little hardened by the dead white of her wrapper and by her resistance to Marie tugging her hair back.

"Marie, you don't brush, you bang!"

Marie stopped a moment and then started again with renewed vigour. Then mamma would let the paper slip off her knees and fold her hands in a way she had to mark her resignation, with her fingers exactly crossed, except for the two fore-fingers, which were joined in an arch and pointed outwards.

"Madame had better do her hair herself; then she won't complain."

But mamma's hairdressing needed some little artifice and she would have had great difficulty in doing without Marie's assistance. Her hair was parted in the middle and smoothly brushed down on either side of her face, below a low crown of plaits, and it was only with the help of certain extraneous adjuncts that it could be made to puff out becomingly above her temples. In those days such things were stuffed into all sorts of places; it was the hideous period of "bustles."

Marie was not allowed to have absolute freedom of speech —mamma would not have tolerated it—she confined herself to an occasional bluster, when a few words would come hissing out under the pressure of internal fury. Mamma was a little frightened of her; when Marie was waiting at table, it was not till she had left the room that mamma ventured to say :

"It's no use talking to Désirée (this was addressed to aunt Claire), she *will* put too much vinegar in the mayonnaise."

Désirée had succeeded Delphine, Marie's ex-flame; but whoever the cook was, Marie would always have taken her part. Then the next day, when I went out with her:

"You know, Marie," I would begin, horrid little tell-tale that I was, "if Désirée won't listen to what mamma says we shan't be able to keep her." (This was to give myself an air of importance.) "Her mayonnaise yesterday . . ."

"Had too much vinegar in it again, I know," interrupted Marie, with an air of vengeance. She pursed up her lips, kept her wrath down for a moment, and then, as the strain became too much for her, out shot:

"Oh, you're a dainty lot, you are!"

Marie was not impervious to the æsthetic emotions; but with her, as with a great many Swiss people, the sense of beauty was inextricably mixed with that of altitude; and in the same way, her musical tastes were strictly confined to the singing of hymns. One day, however, when I was at the piano, she suddenly marched into the drawing-room; I was playing one of the *Songs without Words*—rather a sickly, sentimental one.

"*There's* music for you!" she said with a melancholy toss of her head; then, "I ask you now," she added furiously, "if that isn't better worth listening to than all those tirra-lirras of yours?"

She called any music she didn't understand "tirra-lirras" indiscriminately.

Mademoiselle de Goecklin's lessons being now considered inadequate, I was handed over to a male professor, who, unfortunately was very little better. Monsieur Merriman showed pianos in Pleyel's shop; he had adopted the profession of pianist without having the smallest vocation for it; nevertheless, by dint of hard work, he had succeeded, if I remember right, in carrying off a first prize at the Conservatoire. His playing was correct, polished, icy, and more like arithmetic than art; when he sat down to the piano, it was like a cashier sitting down to his desk; his fingers added up the notes—the minims and crotchets and quavers—as if they were figures; he *proved* the piece as if it were a sum. He might certainly have given me some mechanical training; but he took no pleasure in teaching. Music with him became the driest of tasks; his favourite composers were Cramer, Steibel, Dusseck —at any rate it was under their rod of iron he thought fit to place me. He considered Beethoven libidinous. Twice a week, he made his appearance, punctual to the minute; the lessons consisted in the monotonous repetition of a few exercises (and even these were not really useful for finger work, but just dull routine), a few scales, a few arpeggios; then I would drum out "the eight last bars" of the piece I was learning, that is to say the last bars I had practised; after that, he made a pencil mark —a kind of large V—eight bars further on, to show the next piece of work that had to be got through, much as one marks the trees that have to come down when a wood is being thinned; then, getting up as the clock struck the hour:

"For next time, practise the eight following bars," he would say.

Never the smallest explanation. Never the slightest appeal, I will not say to my musical taste or feeling (how could there be any question of such things?) but to my memory or judgment. At that age, when a child is all growth and pliability and receptiveness, what progress I might have made, if my mother had confided me in the beginning to Monsieur de la Nux, the incomparable master I had later on—too late, alas! But no! after two years' mortal droning, I was only delivered from Merriman to fall into the hands of Schifmacker.

It was not, I admit, as easy then as it is now, to find good music-masters; the Schola had not yet begun to turn them out, and the musical education of the whole of France was still far to seek; moreover the people in my mother's set knew practically nothing about music. My mother unquestionably made great efforts to educate herself as well as me; but her efforts were ill-directed. Schifmacker had been warmly recommended to her by a lady friend.

"Would you believe it?" she said to my mother; "he has actually made me take a liking to it—to music! An extraordinary man! Try him."

The first day he came to the house he expounded his system. He was a stout fiery old man who puffed and panted, who was as red as a furnace, who whistled and stuttered and spluttered as he spoke like a locomotive letting off steam. He had white hair, cut *en brosse*, and white whiskers, and it all looked like a mass of driven snow melting on his face, which he was continually mopping.

"What do most music-masters tell you?" said he. "You must do exercises! Exercises here! And exercises there! But look at me! Do you suppose I ever did exercises? Never in the world! One learns by playing. Like speaking. Come, Madame, a sensible lady like you, what would you say if your son was to do tongue exercises every morning, because, forsooth, he will have to use his tongue during the day: *ra, ra, ra, ra, gla, gla, gla, gla.*" (Here, my mother, positively out of her wits with terror at Schifmacker's moist explosiveness, drew back her armchair, while he pulled his so much the nearer.) "However fast or slow your tongue wags, you can only say what you have to say, and at the piano you always have fingers enough to express what you feel. Ah! if you feel nothing, you might have ten fingers on each hand and be none the better for it!" Then he went off into a loud laugh, caught his breath, coughed, choked for a few moments, turned up the whites of his eyes, then mopped himself, then fanned himself with his handkerchief. My mother offered to fetch him a glass of water, but he made a sign that it was nothing, fluttered his little arms and short legs in a final spasm, explained he had wanted to laugh and cough at the same moment, gave a resounding "H—h—m" and turned to me:

"So, my boy, that's an understood thing, eh? No more exercises. Look, Ma'am. Look how pleased the little rascal is! He's thinking, 'We shall have fun with old Schifmacker.' And he's quite right too."

My mother, completely overwhelmed and bewildered by all these tomfooleries, and amused by them too, no doubt, was still more alarmed; for she, who never spared herself pains and brought unrelaxing diligence to all she did, could not altogether approve of a method that did away with all compulsion and effort; she tried in vain, however, to get in a completed sentence through all this spattering of words and saliva.

"Yes, provided he . . ." "But he doesn't want . . ." "Evidently . . ." "On condition you . . ."

And suddenly Schifmacker got up:

"Now I'll play you something, so that you mayn't think I can do nothing but talk."

He opened the piano, struck a chord or two, and then dashed with a triumphant flourish into a little study of Stephen Heller's which he played diabolically fast and with amazing brio.

He had little short red hands with which he seemed positively to knead the piano almost without moving his fingers. His playing was like nothing I have ever heard before or since; he was totally lacking in what is called "mechanism," and I think he would have come to grief over a simple scale; it was never in fact the actual piece as it was written that he played, but an approximation, full of spirit, flavour and strangeness.

I was not particularly delighted at having my exercises cut off; I was already fond of practising; if I changed masters, it was in order to get on and I wondered whether this devil of a fellow . . . ? He had peculiar theories; as, for instance, that the finger on the note should never be motionless; his idea was that the finger should continue dealing with the note like the finger or bow of a violinist which is directly applied to the vibrating string itself; in this way he fancied himself able to increase or lessen the sound, and mould it as he pleased, according as he weighed with his finger on the key, or lightened his pressure on it. This is what gave his playing the strange, swaying motion which made him really look as if he were *kneading* the melody.

His lessons came to an abrupt end with a frightful scene. This is what happened. Schifmacker, as I have said, was corpulent. My mother, fearing that the delicate constitution of the little drawing-room chairs would be incapable of supporting such a weight, had fetched in out of the hall a stout and hideous seat covered with American cloth and strangely at odds with the drawing-room furniture. She put this seat by the piano and moved the others some distance away, "so that he should understand where he was to sit," said she. At the first lesson, all went well; the chair bore up under the oppression and agitation of his ponderous bulk. But the next time something appalling happened—the American cloth, which had no doubt been softened during the previous lesson, began to stick

140

to the seat of his trousers. We didn't notice it, alas! till the end of the hour, when he tried to get up! In vain! He stuck to the chair and the chair stuck to him. His trousers were thin (it was in summer) and if the stuff had been ever so little worn, it would have given way to a certainty; there were a few moments of agonising suspense . . . But no! One last effort and it was the American cloth that yielded, very, very gently, and not without relinquishing something of its own, as if in a spirit of conciliation. I was holding the chair down, not as yet daring to laugh, so great was my consternation, while he kept exclaiming as he pulled:

"Good God! Good God! What's this hellish invention?" while all the time he was trying to look over his shoulder backwards at the unsticking process, so that his face grew redder than ever.

Fortunately, however, it was managed without any serious damage being done except to the American cloth, which was left limp and draggled, with an effigy of Monsieur Schifmacker's voluminous behind imprinted on it.

The curious thing is that it was not till the following lesson that his wrath broke out. I don't know what upset him that day, but when I went with him into the hall to see him out, he suddenly burst into the most violent invective, declared that he saw quite clearly what I was up to, that I was a sly, deceitful little wretch, and that he would never again set foot inside a house where he was treated with such ignominy.

And as a matter of fact, he never came back; we learnt from the papers a little later that he had been drowned in a boating party.

I rarely went into the drawing-room except for the sake of the piano. The room was usually kept half shut up; and the furniture carefully protected by loose covers of white dimity, finely striped with bright red. These covers so exactly fitted the chairs and sofas, that it was a pleasure putting them on again every Thursday morning after Wednesday's ceremonial —for Wednesday was my mother's "at home" day; the covers were cunningly shaped and adjusted, and there were little hooks which kept them in place and well stretched over the chair-backs. I am not sure that I did not like the drawing-room better when it was dressed in its dimity uniform, looking so decent and modest and, in summer, so deliciously cool behind the closed shutters, than when it shone forth in all its dreary, inharmonious glory. There were various tapestry chairs, and imitation Louis XVI armchairs, upholstered in blue and gold damask, of the same stuff as the curtains; these armchairs were arranged along the walls, or else in two rows starting from the middle of the room and ending up on either side of the fireplace with two still larger chairs, whose grandeur was absolutely dazzling; I knew they were covered in "Genoese velvet," but on what complicated loom, I wondered, could such a stuff have been woven—a snuff-coloured stuff in a combination of velvet, guipure and embroidery; the woodwork of these chairs was in black and gilt; I was not allowed to sit on them. On the chimney-piece was a bronze-gilt set of candelabra and clock, the latter with a subject-piece representing Pradier's Sappho—all propriety. What shall be said of the chandelier and the sconces? I took a great step towards emancipation on the day I first ventured to say to myself that it was not necessary for all chandeliers in all respectable drawing-rooms to have cut-glass pendants like ours.

In front of the fireplace was a screen in silk cross-stitch; it represented a kind of Chinese bridge (I still have a vivid recollection of the blues in it) in a bower of wild roses; the bamboo framework was adorned on either side with danglers from which swung silk tassels of the same blue as the cross-stitch;

they hung in pairs from the heads and tails of mother-of-pearl fishes, to which they were fastened by gold threads. I was told afterwards that my mother had worked it secretly in the early days of her married life; entering the study on his birthday one morning, my father had been met by the startling sight. Gentle as he was and adoring my mother, he had almost lost his temper:

"No, Juliette," he had cried; "no, I beg of you. This is my study. Let me arrange this room at any rate in my own way."

Then, recovering his good-humour, he had persuaded my mother that though he liked the screen very much, he preferred seeing it in the drawing-room.

After my father's death, we used to dine every Sunday with aunt Claire and Albert; they came to us and we went to them turn and turn about; it was not necessary to take the chair-covers off for them. After the meal, while Albert and I sat down to the piano, my aunt and mother drew up their chairs to the big table which was lighted by an oil-lamp; the lamp-shade was one of those complicated affairs which were then the fashion; I don't think they exist nowadays; once a year, at a fixed date, mamma and I used to go and choose a new one at the stationer's shop in the Rue de Tournon, where there was a great choice to be had; the cardboard they were made of was cunningly embossed and perforated, so that the rays of light came filtered through variously coloured layers of very thin paper. It was absolutely ravishing!

The drawing-room table was covered with a thick velvet table-cloth, which had a very wide border of silk and wool cross-stitch—the product, I believe, of my mother's and Anna's patient labours at the time they had lived in the Rue de Crosne. The cloth hung straight down over the edge of the table so that it could only be properly admired from a distance.

The border, which represented a twist of peonies and ribbons, or at any rate, something yellow and convoluted which might pass for such, had made an effort to adapt itself to the velvet; that is to say, along its upper edge there was a regular indentation of points of imitation velvet which were meant to look as if they were prolongations of the velvet and to act as connecting links between the border and it. Unfortunately the velvet had made no similar attempt to harmonise with the border, preferring to match the Genoese velvet chairs, and adopt their snuff-colour, while the connecting links remained pea-green.

So while my aunt and mother played their game of cards, Albert and I plunged with frenzy into the trios, quintets and symphonies of Mozart, Beethoven and Schumann, reading at sight any arrangement for four hands we could get hold of, either in French or German editions.

I was now about as good as he at the piano—which was not saying much, but it enabled us to share with the same pleasure in what I now recall as some of the liveliest and most profound musical pleasures I have ever known.

All the time we were playing, the ladies went on chatting; their voices rose under cover of our fortissimos; but I grieve to say were not much lowered for our pianissimos, and we were greatly distressed by this lack of proper feeling. Only twice did it happen that we were able to play in silence, and then it was rapture. Mamma had gone away for a few days and Albert had been charming enough to come two nights running to keep me company at dinner. If I have made it clear what my cousin was to me, it will be understood how great a treat it was to have him all to myself and to feel he had come for me alone. We sat up very late playing, and so beautifully that the angels themselves must have heard us.

It was to La Roque mamma had gone; an epidemic of typhoid fever had broken out on one of our farms, and mamma no sooner heard of it than she went off to look after the patients, as she considered it her duty to do, seeing that they were her tenants. Aunt Claire tried in vain to prevent her by saying that her first duty was to her son and not to her tenants; that she was running a great risk in order to be of very little service; and my aunt might have added too that they were comparatively new to the farm, and pig-headed, grasping folk, who were utterly incapable of appreciating a disinterested action like my mother's. Albert and I joined our entreaties to hers, for we were very much alarmed as two of the farm people had already died. Advice, entreaties, reproaches, however, were of no avail; what mamma recognised to be her duty, that she did in the teeth of wind and weather. If this was not always very obvious, it was because she had encumbered her life with so many adventitious cares, that her idea of duty was often splintered up into quantities of trifling obligations.

As I have constantly to speak of my mother, I had hoped that my recollections of her as we went along would give a sufficiently good picture of her; but I am afraid I have not succeeded in showing how full of "good will" she was (I use this expression in the scriptural sense). She was always striving after what was good—after what was better, and was never content to rest in a state of self-satisfaction. It was not enough for her to be modest; she was continually trying to diminish her imperfections, or the imperfections she discovered in others, to correct herself or others, to *improve*. During my father's life-time, all this had been subordinated to, had been swallowed up in a great love. Her love for me, no doubt, was scarcely less, but she now exacted from me all the submission she had formerly shown my father, with the result that conflicts arose which helped to convince me that my only likeness was to my father; the deepest seated ancestral resemblances do not show themselves till late in life.

In the meantime, my mother, who was very anxious to cultivate herself and me, and full of respect for music, painting, and generally speaking, for everything that was beyond her, did what she could to enlighten my taste and judgment and her own at the same time. If we went to see an exhibition of pictures—and we never missed one which the *Temps* was kind enough to recommend—we always took with us the number of the paper that had reviewed it, and read the appreciation of the critic when we were on the spot, for fear of admiring the wrong thing or of not admiring at all. As for concerts, the narrowness, timidity and monotony displayed in the programmes of the day left little scope for error; there was nothing to do but to listen, to approve and to applaud.

Mamma took me to the Pasdeloup concerts nearly every Sunday. A little later we had a season ticket for the Conservatoire concerts, and for two years running we attended them every other Sunday. Some of these concerts made a profound impression on me, and even the music I was not old enough to understand (it was in '79 that mamma began taking me to them) helped no less to fashion my sensibility. I admired almost everything indiscriminately, as is right at that age, almost without preference, from an urgent need to admire: the *Symphony in C Minor* and the *Hebrides Symphony*, Mozart's concertos, the whole series of which Ritter (or Risler) played on consecutive Sundays, and Félicien David's *Désert*, which I heard several times, for Pasdeloup and the public had a particular liking for this agreeable work, though nowadays it would no doubt be considered old-fashioned and slight; I was charmed with it at the time, just as I was charmed with an oriental landscape of Tournemine's I had seen when I first went to the Luxembourg with Marie, and which I thought the finest picture in the world; there was a background of crimson and orange sunset sky, reflected in still waters, a herd of elephants or camels stretching out their long necks or trunks to drink, and in the distance the minarets of a mosque pointing their long fingers up to the sky.

But lively as are my recollections of these first "musical moments," there are others beside which they seem pale. In 1883 Rubinstein gave a series of concerts in the Erard concert room; the programmes were designed to illustrate piano-music from the earliest days down to the present time. I did not attend all these concerts, for the seats, mamma said, were unconscionably dear—but only three of them; and yet the memory they have left me is so luminous, so distinct, that I sometimes doubt whether it is really a memory of Rubinstein himself I have kept, or only of the pieces he played—pieces I have so often played and practised myself since then. But no; it is his very self I can still hear; and I have never been able to listen to some of the things he played without remembering his playing of them: some of Couperin, for instance, Beethoven's sonata in C sharp (op. 53) the rondo of the sonata in E (op. 90) and Schumann's *Vogel als Prophet*.

His prestige was enormous. In person, he was like Beethoven and was sometimes said to be his son (I have not looked up the dates to see whether this is possible); he had a flat face with high cheek-bones, a wide forehead, half swamped in a thick mane of hair, shaggy eyebrows, eyes that were sometimes vague and sometimes imperious, an obstinate jaw, and something ill-tempered in the expression of his fleshy mouth. He did not charm—he subdued. Something wild in his eyes made him look drunk, and rumour had it that he often was. He played with his eyes shut as though unconscious of the public. He seemed to be not so much presenting a piece to them as to be searching for it, discovering or composing it as he went along—not like an improvisation, but, as it were, in a glowing inward vision, a progressive revelation, which filled even himself with astonishment and rapture.

The three concerts I went to were devoted, the first to old music, the other two to Beethoven and Schumann. There was another I very much wished to hear, at which he played nothing but Chopin, but my mother considered Chopin's music "morbid" and refused to take me.

The following year, I went less often to concerts and more often to the play—the Odéon and the Théâtre Français; and especially to the Opéra-Comique, where I heard almost the whole of the old-fashioned repertory of those days—Grétry, Boieldieu, Hérold; their melodious grace which delighted me then, would certainly seem mortally dull to me to-day. No, I have nothing to say against any of these composers, it is musical drama—the theatre in general that I dislike. Perhaps because I saw too much of it in my youth. If by some accident I still venture into a theatre, unless I have a friend at my side to keep me there, I have the greatest difficulty in sitting out the first act, so as to disappear more or less decently at the end of it. It took the Vieux Colombier a short while ago and all Copeau's art and zeal to reconcile me somewhat to the pleasures of the stage. But enough of comments! I return to my memories.

For the last two years, a boy of my own age had come to spend the holidays with us; mamma, who took great trouble to find me this playmate, thought the plan a good one in two ways—it gave the benefit of a change of air to a boy in poor circumstances, who would otherwise not have been able to leave Paris all the summer, and it snatched me from the too contemplative pleasures of the rod. Armand Bavretel's function was to go out walking with me. A pastor's son, of course.

The first year he came with Edmond Richard, and the second with the eldest Richard, with whom I was already boarding. He was a rather fragile-looking boy, with delicate, almost pretty features; his very bright eyes and shy looks reminded me of a squirrel; he was mischievous and full of fun as soon as he was at ease, but the first evening in the big drawing-room at La Roque, he must have felt himself lost, in spite of Anna's and my mother's affectionate welcome, for the poor little fellow burst into tears. I too had received him as affectionately as I could, and I was more than astonished, I was almost shocked by his tears; I thought he did not properly appreciate my mother's kindness; I was within an ace of thinking him disrespectful to her. I was too young to understand how offensive the appearance of wealth may be in the eyes of poverty; not that the La Roque drawing-room had anything very luxurious about it, but one felt sheltered in it and free from all the pack of hounding cares that bark at poverty's heels. It was the first time too that Armand had left home, and I think his was a nature easily hurt by contact with the unfamiliar. The unhappy impression of the first evening, however, did not last long; he soon let himself be petted by my mother and by Anna, who had every reason to be even more sympathetic. As for me, I was delighted to have a playfellow and to lay by my rod.

What most amused us was to strike across the woods in the manner of Gustave Aimard's *Arkansas Trappers*, scorning paths, never sticking at thickets or bogs, and enchanted on the contrary when the copsewood was so thick that we were compelled to crawl on our hands and knees, or even go flat on our faces, for we would have thought shame to turn aside for any obstacle.

We spent Sunday afternoons at Blancmesnil; and then there were epic games of hide and seek, with all their multitude of peripetiae, for we played in the big farm, amongst its barns and stables and sheds and any other buildings we could find. And after we had exhausted the mysteries of Blanc-mesnil, we went in search of fresh ones at La Roque; Lionel and his sister Blandine came to play with us there; we went up to Cour Vesque (the farm my parents used to call Cour L'Évêque) where our games were carried on with redoubled vigour amidst the unexpectedness of these new surroundings. Blandine used to pair off with Armand while I stayed with Lionel, one pair seeking and the other hiding; we crouched under faggots and litters of straw and bundles of hay; we climbed on to the roofs, crawled into all the openings and all the trap-doors we could find, and into the dangerous hole above the cider-press, through which the apples are tumbled; what acrobatic feats we were put to when pursued! . . . But thrilling as was the chase, perhaps our greatest pleasure came from our contact with the fruits of the earth—diving into the thick of the harvest, bathing in all the varied odours of the farm. O perfume of dried clover, pungent smells of pig-sty and stable and cowshed! Heady fumes of the cider-press, and from further back where the great casks stood, those draughts of icy air in which a little spice of mouldiness mingled with the sickly smell of the barrels. Yes, I afterwards came to know the intoxicating vapours of the vintage, but like the Shulamite who begged to be comforted with apples, it is that fruit's exquisite ether I breathe in preference to the blunted sweetness of the must. When Lionel and I came upon the enormous heap of golden corn that flowed down in gentle slopes to the clean floor of the barn, we would take off our coats and with our shirt-sleeves rolled up as far as they would go, plunge our arms in shoulder high and feel the small cool grains slip through our open fingers.

It was settled among us one day that we were each singly

and secretly to set up a sort of private residence of our own, to which we should invite the others who would come bringing refreshments with them. The lot fell to me to begin. I selected a huge limestone rock to be my place of reception; it was white, smooth and extremely handsome, but surrounded by a sea of nettles, which I could only cross by taking a prodigious leap with the help of a pole and an immense run. I christened my magnificent dwelling the "Why not?". Then, seated on my rock as on a throne, I awaited my guests. They arrived at last, but when they saw the rampart of nettles that divided us, they set up a loud clamour. I passed them the pole I had used, so that they could take the leap in the same way; but they had no sooner got hold of it than they ran off in fits of laughter, taking with them both pole and refreshments, and abandoning me to my fate in this fiendish retreat, from which I had the greatest difficulty in extricating myself.

Armand Bavretel spent only two summers with us. In the summer of '84, my cousins did not visit us either, or for a very short time, so that as I was alone at La Roque I spent a great deal more time with Lionel. Not content with meeting openly on Sundays, the day on which it was arranged for me to take tea at Blancmesnil, we made regular lovers' trysts, to which we hastened with beating hearts and agitated thoughts. We agreed to have a post office in a hiding place of our own; in order to settle the times and places of our meetings, we exchanged odd, mysterious letters in cypher, which could only be read with the help of a key or a grille. The letter was put in a closed box hidden in the moss at the foot of an old apple-tree, in a meadow on the skirts of the wood and equidistant from our two houses. No doubt there was a good deal of absurdity, although no hypocrisy, in the exaggerated expression of our feelings, and after we had sworn eternal friendship, I think we would have gone through fire and water to get to each other. Lionel persuaded me that such a solemn pact necessitated a pledge; he broke a cluster of clematis in two, gave me one half and kept the other himself, swearing to wear it as a talisman. I put my half in a little embroidered sachet which I hung round my neck like a scapulary and wore next my heart until my first communion.

Passionate as our friendship was, there was not the slightest tinge of sensuality in it. Lionel in the first place was powerfully ugly; and no doubt I already felt that fundamental incapacity for mixing the spirit with the senses, which is, I believe, somewhat peculiar to me, and which was soon to become one of the cardinal repulsions of my life. On his side, Lionel, worthy grandson of Ch . . ., affected the bearing of Corneille's heroes. One day when I was going away, I went up to give him a fraternal embrace, but he waved me aside.

"No," he said solemnly; "men never kiss."

He had a friendly wish to introduce me more intimately into his family life. As I have said, he was an orphan; Blancmesnil at that time belonged to his uncle, who was also Ch . . .'s son-in-law, the two brothers de R . . . having married two sisters. Monsieur de R . . . was a member of the Chamber of Deputies, and would have remained one to the end of his life, if at the beginning of the Dreyfus case, he had not had the exceptional courage to vote against his party—that is to say the Right. He was an excellent and honourable man, but a little wanting in backbone, in solidity or in something or other which would have enabled him to take the head of the table with more real authority than that bestowed merely by age; for the younger members of the numerous family that sat round it were not always very orderly. But the worthy man had as much as he could do already to keep his head up beside his wife, whose superiority completely overshadowed him. Madame de R . . ., however, was very calm, very gentle

152

and sufficiently amiable; there was nothing domineering in her voice or manners; without perhaps saying anything very original or very deep, she never spoke for the mere sake of speaking and what she said was always to the point (my childish recollections are borne out by other later ones), so that the ascendency she exercised over everyone as by a natural right of sovereignty was a very real one. I do not think her features recalled Monsieur Ch . . .'s, but she had been his secretary and confidante, and certainly her prestige was enhanced by the memories of the weighty past attaching to it.

The whole family, as well as Monsieur de R . . . were more or less interested in politics. When I saw Lionel in his room, he made me take my hat off to a photograph of the Duke of Orleans (I had not the slightest idea at the time who he was). His elder brother, who was canvassing a constituency in the South, had been defeated at the polls again and again. The postman used to bring in the mail-bag from Lisieux every day while the family were still at table; everyone, old and young, immediately fastened on a paper and for a long time, I, their guest, was unable to see a single face all round the table.

On Sunday mornings, Madame de R . . . read prayers in the drawing-room, which parents, children and servants attended. By Lionel's orders, I sat next him; and during prayers, when we were on our knees, he took my hand and held it tightly in his, as though he were offering our friendship to God.

Lionel, however, did not always breathe sublimity. Next the room where prayers were read (the drawing-room, as I have said) was the library—a spacious square room lined with books, where the great French Encyclopædia stood beside the works of Corneille, within easy reach of a boy's hand and a boy's curiosity; as soon as Lionel knew the room was disengaged, he would rummage feverishly among its pages. One article led to another; everything was written in a lively, agreeable and vigorous style; these XVIII century writers, impertinent *esprits forts*, had their own inimitable and entertaining way of combining instruction with amusement.

When we went through the room, Lionel used to nudge me with his elbow (there were always people about on Sundays) and show me the naughty volumes with a wink, but I never had the good fortune to handle them. For that matter, my mind was slower than Lionel's, or else otherwise occupied, and I was much less curious than he about such things— needless to say what things I am alluding to; and when he afterwards related his explorations of the dictionary and told me of his discoveries, I listened, but more bewildered than excited; I listened, but I did not question. I never understood anything unless all the i's were dotted, and even a year later, when Lionel told me with the superior and knowing air he sometimes put on, that he had found a book in his brother's room with the suggestive title of *Memoirs of a Sporting Dog*, I thought it was about shooting. The novelty of the Encyclopædia, however, eventually wore off, and the time came when Lionel had nothing more to learn from it. By the most singular reversal we then, but this time together, took to really serious reading; we read Bossuet, we read Fénelon, we read Pascal. By dint of saying "next year," I have now reached the sixteenth of my age. I was being prepared for confirmation, and the correspondence I had begun with my cousin was also having its effect on me. After the summer of that year, Lionel and I continued to meet in Paris and used to visit each other alternately. Whatever profit we may have got out of them eventually, our conversations at this time were inconceivably pretentious; we were presumptuous enough to *study* the aforesaid great writers; we outdid each other in commentaries on philosophical passages, taking for choice the thorniest and most abstruse, and portioning out for discussion such treatises as *Of Concupiscence, Of the Knowledge of God and of Oneself*, etc. So enamoured were we of grandiloquence that every step that did not take us out of our depths we despised as hum-drum; the learned glosses and paraphrases we elaborated would make me blush if I read them again to-day, but they nevertheless helped to strengthen the intellect and were chiefly ridiculous because of the self-satisfaction we found in them.

I must finish up with Lionel, for all our fine friendship came to nothing and there will be no occasion to return to it. We still went on meeting for several years, but with less and less pleasure. He disliked my tastes, my opinions, and my writings; he began by trying to improve me and finally ceased seeing me. He was one of those people, I think, who are only capable of friendships with inferiors—friendships they can accompany with condescension and patronage. Even at the height of our passion, he made me feel that my birth was not equal to his. The correspondence of the Comte de Montalembert with his friend Cornudet had just come out; the book (the new edition of 1884) lay on the drawing-room tables at La Roque and Blancmesnil; Lionel and I followed the fashion and were enthusiastic over these letters, in which Montalembert figures as a great man; we thought his friendship with Cornudet touching; in Lionel's fancy, it was like ours; needless to say I was Cornudet.

This, no doubt, was also the reason why he could not endure to be told anything; he always knew everything before you did, and sometimes he repeated your opinion to you as if it were his own, having forgotten meanwhile that it was from you he had taken it; or else, in a patronising way he would give you a piece of information which *you* had already given *him*. In general, he served up things he had poached in other people's preserves as though they came from his own. I was highly amused to recognise in some review or other the phrase—an absurd one—dropped loftily as a fruit of his own reflections, at the time we were discovering Musset: "A hairdresser's assistant with a musical box in his heart." (I should not have mentioned this weakness perhaps, if I had not read in Sainte-Beuve's *Cahiers* that Ch . . . was also subject to it.)

And Armand?

For some time, I continued at long intervals going to see him in Paris. He lived in the Rue de l'A . . ., near the central markets, with his family—his mother, a good, gentle, reserved woman, and his two sisters; one of them was a good deal older than the other and used deliberately to efface herself (a common enough case), out of a kind and unselfish consideration for her younger sister, undertaking, as far as I could see, all the hardest and most disagreeable jobs of the household, in order to spare her. This second sister was about the same age as Armand, and a charming girl; she seemed to be consciously filling the rôle of grace and poetry in this sombre household; it was obvious the whole family adored her, and particularly Armand, though he showed his affection in a very peculiar way, as I shall explain.

Armand had also an elder brother who had taken a medical degree and was beginning to set up in practice; I do not remember ever having seen him. As for Pastor Bavretel, the father, he was no doubt completely taken up by good works, and I had never met him, when suddenly one afternoon on which Madame Bavretel had invited a few of Armand's friends to tea, he made a sensational entry into the dining-room, where we were cutting up a Twelfth Night cake. Great God, how ugly he was! He was a short, square-shouldered man, with arms and hands like a gorilla's; the dignity of his parsonical black coat only accentuated his ungainly appearance. And oh, his face! His greasy greyish hair hung in lank locks over his shiny collar; eyes like boiled gooseberries rolled under his thick eyelids; his nose was a shapeless and cumbersome protuberance, and his pendulous, swollen, lower lip was flabby, purplish and slobbering. We were all struck dumb at the sight of him. He stayed only a moment, pronounced an insignificant word or two, such as: "Bless you, my children!" or "God be with you!" and went out with Madame Bavretel to whom he wished to speak.

Next year exactly the same thing happened. He made the same apparition in exactly the same circumstances, said the same or an exactly equivalent sentence, and was going out again in the same way, followed by his wife, when she suddenly had the unfortunate idea of calling me up to be introduced. The pastor, who so far only knew me by name, drew me towards him and—horror of horrors!—before I was able to escape, embraced me.

I only saw him on those two occasions, but the impression he made on me was so great that he never ceased to haunt my imagination; I even began to give him a place in a book I was planning to write (there is no saying I may not still write it) into which I intended infusing some of the murky atmosphere I had breathed at the Bavretels'. Poverty here was not merely privative, as rich people are too apt to think; one felt it to be something actual, aggressive, attentive; it exercised its frightful sway over hearts and minds, crept into every corner, touched whatever was most secret and sensitive, threw out of gear all the delicate springs of life. I was not at that time experienced enough to understand many things that have since become clear to me; many anomalies in the Bavretel family I no doubt thought strange only because I was unable to discern their origin and failed to attribute them to the constant and ever present pinch of poverty, which they took such pains to hide. I was not exactly a spoilt child; I have already said how careful my mother was not to give me more indulgences than other less happily circumstanced children; but she never proposed I should make any change in my habits or break the magic circle of my good fortune. I was well off without knowing it, just as I was French and Protestant without knowing it; outside this magic circle everything seemed foreign to me. And just as the house we lived in had to have a *porte-cochère*—or rather, just as we owed it to ourselves to have a *porte-cochère*, as aunt Claire said, so we owed it to ourselves always to travel first-class, for instance, and at the theatre I could not imagine self-respecting people sitting anywhere but in the dress-circle. What a variety of shocks such an education had in store for me it would be premature to say here. I am still at the period when I took Armand one day to a matinée at the Opéra-Comique; my mother had booked two seats for us in the upper circle—we were going for the first time by ourselves and she had thought these places good enough for two schoolboys of our age—but when I got there, I was completely upset by finding myself so much higher up than usual, and surrounded too by people who appeared to belong to the lower orders; so, rushing down to the booking-office, I emptied the whole of my pockets to pay the extra price which would enable me to get back to my proper level. I must say too that having Armand for my guest for once in a way, it was painful to me not to offer him the best.

So on Twelfth Night, Madame Bavretel used to invite Armand's friends to come and "draw kings." I attended this little party several times; not every year though, for at that season we were usually at Rouen or in the South; but I must have gone there again a little after 1891, for I remember the excellent Madame Bavretel's introducing me as a celebrated author to the other young men present, all of them more or less celebrated too. Evidently a secret concern for the young sister's problematical future was not entirely absent from these gatherings. Madame Bavretel thought that there might be a possible husband for her among these celebrities; but this preoccupation of hers, which she would have liked to conceal, and even to disown, was brutally laid bare by Armand's cynical and embarrassing allusions; it was he who cut the cake and as he knew where the bean was, he managed so that it should fall to his sister or to the possible suitor, who, as there were no other young girls present, was obliged of course, to choose her as "queen." And then what jokes! Armand was certainly already suffering from the strange malady which led him some years later to commit suicide. The cruel persistence of his teasing seems otherwise inexplicable; nothing would satisfy him till his sister was in tears, and if words were not enough, I have seen him go up to her and actually pinch her. Did he really detest her then? No, on the contrary, I think he adored her and felt all her sufferings acutely, even the mortifications he himself inflicted, for he was tenderhearted by nature and far from cruel; but some obscure demon in him took a wicked pleasure in spoiling his love. With us, Armand was lively and sparkling, but that same caustic temper which he was always turning against himself and his people and everything he cared for, made him continually harp upon their poverty; he made his mother miserable and all the guests uncomfortable by drawing attention to everything she would have liked to conceal—stains, rents or things that didn't match. Then Madame Bavretel would get flurried, half admit her deficiencies, try to make the best of a bad job, and finally ruin everything by apologising: "Of course, in Monsieur Gide's home a Twelfth Night cake would never be served on a chipped plate." And then Armand would

emphasise the awkwardness of this by bursting into an insolent laugh or by calling out: "There now, I've put my foot
into it again!" or "Knocked out by that, old chap, aren't
you?" exclamations which escaped him nervously and for
which he seemed barely responsible. And in the midst of all
this—Armand gibing, his mother protesting, his sister crying, the guests not knowing which way to look, imagine to
crown it all—the solemn entry of the pastor!

I have explained how sensitive my education had made me
to the exotic atmosphere of poverty, but here there was an
added element of strangeness, at once so stilted, so forced, so
courteous and so grotesque that it affected my head, and after
a little I completely lost all sense of reality; everything about
me began to float in a haze, to lose consistency, to approach
the borderland of the fantastic, and not only the place, the
people, the talk, but I myself, and the sound of my own voice,
which seemed to come from a long way off and was strangely
unfamiliar. Sometimes I thought Armand himself was not
unaware of all this queerness, and was even trying to add to it
—the acid note he contributed to the concert was so exactly
attuned, so exactly, as it were, the right thing, and, more
than this, I even went so far as to think that Madame Bavretel herself became slightly elevated by this distracting harmony, when she introduced the author of the *Cahiers d'André
Walter*, "that very remarkable book, you have of course read,"
to Monsieur Dehelly, "first prize for elocution at the Conservatoire, whose praises are being sung in all the papers," and
every one of the other guests in the same fashion, so that very
soon Dehelly and I and the rest of us, were all talking and
gesticulating like fantastic puppets, under the compulsion of
an atmosphere we had ourselves created. When one left the
house, it was amazing to find oneself in the street again.

I saw Armand once more . . . It was his eldest sister who

received me that day. She was alone in the apartment and told me I should find Armand in his room two stories higher up, for he had sent word to say he was not coming down. I knew where his room was, though I had never been into it. It gave directly on to the staircase opposite his brother's consulting-room. It was a fair-sized room, but very dark, as it looked on to a little courtyard; a dismal leaden light was cast into it by a hideous reflector of corrugated zinc. Armand was lying in his clothes on the bed, which had not been made; he had not changed his night-shirt, nor shaved, nor put on a tie. He got up when I came in and pressed me in his arms, which was unlike him. I cannot remember the beginning of our conversation. No doubt I was more taken up with the appearance of the room than with what he was saying. There was not the smallest object anywhere on which the eye could rest with any pleasure; its poverty, ugliness and darkness were so stifling that I asked him whether he would not come out with me.

"I never go out now," he said briefly.

"Why not?"

"I can't go out like this."

I insisted, telling him he could easily put on a collar and that his not being shaved didn't matter.

"I'm not washed either," he objected. Then, with a painful kind of snigger, he told me that he had given up washing, and that was why the room smelt so; that he never left it except for meals and that he had not been out of doors for three weeks.

"What do you do?"

"Nothing."

As he saw I was trying to read the titles of the few books lying on the corner of a table near his bed:

"You want to know what I'm reading?" he said.

And he handed me Voltaire's *Pucelle*, which I had long known was one of his bedside books, Pigault-Lebrun's *Citateur* and Paul de Kock's *Cocu*. Then, becoming confidential, he explained in a queer sort of way that he shut himself up because he was only capable of doing harm, that he knew he was objectionable and that other people disliked and loathed him; that besides, he was not nearly so clever as he seemed and that even the little cleverness he had he didn't know how to make use of.

I think now that I ought not to have abandoned him in this state; that at any rate I ought to have talked to him more; it is certain that Armand's appearance and conversation did not make as much impression on me then as they would have done later. There is one thing more I must add: I seem to remember his suddenly asking me what I thought of suicide, and that I looked him in the face and answered that I thought in certain cases suicide might be a praiseworthy action—a cynicism of which in those days I was perfectly capable—but after all, I am not quite sure whether the whole thing may not be imaginary, a result of turning our last conversation over in my head with an idea of putting it into a book, together with a portrait of the pastor.

It came back to my mind more particularly when some years later—having in the interval lost sight of him—I received the news of Armand's death. I was travelling and unable to go to his funeral. When I saw his unfortunate mother a little later, I did not dare question her. I only learnt indirectly that Armand had thrown himself into the Seine.

VII

On the threshold of this year (1884), I had an extraordinary adventure. On the morning of New Year's Day, I had been to wish Anna, who lived, as I have said, in the Rue de Vaugirard, a happy New Year. I was coming back in high spirits, pleased with myself, with Heaven and with all mankind, interested by everything, amused by anything and blessed with all the unbounded wealth of the future. That day, why I cannot tell, instead of going along the Rue Placide, as I usually did, I went down a little street on the left, parallel to it—just for fun, for the mere pleasure of changing. It was near noon; the air was clear and the sun, which was almost hot, shone straight across the street, so that one pavement was bright and the other dark.

Half way down, I left the sunny side, thinking I would try the shady. I was feeling so joyful that I went along singing and skipping, my eyes turned up to Heaven. And then, all at once, I saw coming down to me, as though in answer to my happiness, a little, fluttering, golden thing, falling through the shade like a bit of sunshine. Nearer and nearer it came, hovered for a moment, and then settled on my cap, Holy Ghostwise. I put up my hand and a charming little canary-bird nestled into it; the little creature was palpitating like my own heart, which was as light in my bosom and as winged as any bird. Surely the excess of my joy had become visible, though perhaps not to the dull senses of man; surely, for eyes of any discernment, my whole being must be shining with the brightness of a decoy mirror, and it was my radiance that had drawn this creature down from Heaven.

I ran home in delight to my mother, carrying my canary with me; but what chiefly excited and uplifted me was the thrilling assurance that the bird had been sent by Heaven especially in order to mark me out. I was already more than inclined to think I had a vocation of a mystic nature; henceforth I felt I was bound by a kind of secret pact, and when I heard my mother making plans for my future, wishing, for instance, that I might enter the Forestry Department, which she thought particularly suited to my tastes, I would acquiesce half-heartedly, for politeness' sake, as one lends oneself to a game, but knowing all the while that the vital interest lies elsewhere. I was on the verge of saying to my mother: "How can I possibly dispose of my future? Don't you know I haven't the right to? Don't you realise I am one of the elect?" I think indeed, that one day when my mother spoke to me about the choice of a profession, I did say something of the kind.

The canary, which was a hen, was put into a large cage along with a family of finches which I had brought from La Roque, and lived on very good terms with them. But the most surprising part of the story remains to be told. A few days later, as I was on my way to Batignolles, where Monsieur Richard now lived, just as I was going to cross the Boulevard Saint-Germain, what should I suddenly see drop slantwise down into the middle of the roadway—had I gone crazy?— but another canary! I darted after it; but this bird (it had no doubt escaped from the same cage) was a little wilder than the first and flew away to avoid me, not in a single steady flight indeed, but with little pauses, skimming along the ground like a bird accustomed to a cage and bewildered by its liberty. I ran after it for some time along the tram-lines and it escaped me three times, but at last I managed to clap my cap over it, just as a tram was on the point of running over us both.

This chase made me late for my lesson; wild with joy, in a state of delirium, I ran all the way to my professor's, holding my canary fast in my hands. I had no difficulty with Monsieur Richard, who was easily distracted; the lesson hour was delightfully spent in looking for a tiny cage in which to carry my bird back to the Rue de Commaille. As for me, I had been longing for a mate for my canary, and to see one drop again from Heaven was nothing short of a miracle. That such exquisite adventures should befall me of all people in the world filled me with more frantic pride than if I had accomplished some wonderful feat myself. There was no doubt about it, I was predestined. I walked about now with my head in the air, expecting, like Elijah, my pleasure and my food to fall from Heaven.

My canaries bred, and a few weeks later, the cage, big as it was, was crowded with my pensioners. On Sundays, when my cousin Edouard was allowed out of school, we used to let them fly about my room together; there they disported themselves, letting their droppings fall wherever they felt inclined, and perching on our heads, on the furniture, on the branches we had brought home for them from the Bois de Boulogne or the forest of Meudon, and which we fastened in the drawers and stuck horizontally into key-holes or vertically into pots. On the ground floor, I had a family of white mice which gambolled in a labyrinthine heap of ingeniously disposed carpets. I will spare you my bowls of fish.

Various reasons had brought the Richards to Paris: the fact that rents had been raised in the neighbourhood of Passy; the wish to be near a *lycée* for little Blaise; the hope of getting private pupils among the boys attending the *lycée*. Added to this Madame Bertrand had decided to set up for herself with her daughter, which certainly brought about a considerable reduction in the family budget. Lastly, the two misses had departed again across the Channel. Edmond Richard had returned to Guéret. I myself no longer slept at Monsieur Richard's; I arrived every morning about nine o'clock, had lunch there and went home again in time for dinner. At the beginning of the autumn term this year, I had indeed made another attempt at the Ecole Alsacienne, and had hung on there for a month or two, but again the most troublesome headaches had continually disabled me and I had been obliged to revert to the former system—the system, that is, of desultory, indulgent education, with as little drudgery as possible. Monsieur Richard was an excellent hand at this, having somewhat of a loafing disposition himself. How often the lesson turned into a walk! If the sun shone, our industry evaporated and: "It's a sin to stop indoors this fine weather!" we would cry. At first, we merely loitered through the streets, observing, discussing, discoursing; but this year our walks had an object. For some reason or other, Monsieur Richard again took it into his head to move; the lodging he had was not to his liking; he had to find something better . . . So, as much for amusement's sake as anything else, we went round searching for rooms and visiting everything that was marked "To let".

What countless stairs we climbed! What luxurious abodes and wretched dens we visited! Our favourite time for hunting was the morning. It often happened that we came upon the inmates before they had left their lairs, while they were at their morning toilets. These voyages of discovery were more instructive to me than the reading of many novels. Our hunting ground lay round about the Lycée Condorcet, the Saint-Lazare railway-station and in the district known as Europe. I leave to the imagination what kind of game it was we sometimes started. It amused Monsieur Richard too; he took care to go first for decency's sake and sometimes he would turn round and call out suddenly: "Don't come in!" I managed, nevertheless, to see a good deal and I came away from these domiciliary visits feeling absolutely flabbergasted. For a nature other than mine, this indirect initiation might have offered considerable dangers; but the amusement I took in it caused me no disturbance and excited nothing but my mind; more than that, it induced in me a feeling of reprobation for the debauchery of which I caught glimpses and against which my instinct was in secret revolt. Some particularly shady episode may finally have enlightened Monsieur Richard as to the unsuitability of these visits, for he called an abrupt halt —unless he simply ended by finding a lodging to his taste. In any case, our search came to an end.

Outside my lessons I read a great deal. It was the time when Amiel's *Journal Intime* was all the rage; Monsieur Richard drew my attention to it and read me aloud long passages; he found in it a flattering picture of his own indecisions, relapses and doubts—an excuse for them, so to speak, and even an authorisation; as for me, I could not help feeling the ambiguous charm of all this moral preciosity, though nowadays Amiel's scruples and probings and highfalutin complexities only exasperate me. I was influenced too by Monsieur Richard and admired out of sympathy, or rather, as so often happens, in order not to feel out of it; but at the same time, with perfect sincerity.

There were two other boarders at the Richards' table; one a little older than I, the other two years younger. Adrien Giffard, the elder, was an orphan without either brothers or sisters, a kind of foundling; I do not know what series of adventures had finally landed him on the Richards' doorstep. He was one of those minor characters, whose part in life seems to be merely to act as "supers" and eke out the numbers on the stage. He was neither good nor bad, neither grave nor gay, and was never more than half interested in anything. He came to La Roque the year that Armand stopped coming. For the first few days, he was very unhappy because he did not dare smoke his fill out of respect for my mother; he almost fell ill in consequence; when this was discovered, he was given as much tobacco as he wanted and then smoked without stopping, like a chimney.

When I was practising, he would come and stand with his ear glued to the side of the piano, in a state of bliss, as long as I was playing my scales, but as soon as I began a piece, he walked off again. He used to say:

"I don't so much care for music; it's your exercises I like."

He himself practised the penny whistle.

My mother frightened him. In his eyes, I imagine she represented a pitch of civilisation which made him dizzy. It happened one day, when he was out walking, that he tore the seat of his trousers on a bramble as he was going through a hedge—for he was rather clumsy. The idea of having to appear before my mother in this state terrified him to such a degree, that he ran away and disappeared for two days, during which time no one ever knew where he slept or what he ate . . .

"The thing that made me come back," he confided to me afterwards, "was the tobacco. I can do without everything else."

Bernard Tissandier was a big, cheery, talkative boy, down-right, fresh-coloured, and with black hair cut *en brosse;* he had plenty of good sense, liked talking, and I felt a good deal drawn to him. At the end of the day, when we left Monsieur Richard's—for we were both day-boarders—we used to walk home part of the way together, chattering as we went; one of our favourite subjects was the education of children. We agreed perfectly in thinking that the Richards brought theirs up deplorably, and we launched out together on an ocean of theories—for I did not know then how much stronger innate qualities are than acquired ones, and that in spite of every kind of starching, dressing, pressing and folding, the natural stuff persists and remains unchanged—stiff or limp, as it was originally woven. I purposed at that time writing a treatise on education which I promised to dedicate to Bernard.

Adrien Giffard attended lectures at the Lycée Lakanal, and Bernard Tissandier at the Lycée Condorcet. Now it happened that one evening as my mother was reading one of the articles in the *Temps*, she uttered an exclamation:

"I hope," said she, in a tone of enquiry, "your friend Tissandier doesn't go through the Passage du Havre, when he comes out of the *lycée?*" (Let me say for the sake of the uninformed that this passage is within a few steps of the *lycée*.)

As I had never enquired into my friend Tissandier's itinerary, the question remained unanswered.

"You ought to tell him to avoid it," mamma went on.

Mamma's voice was grave and she knitted her brows like the captain of a boat I once saw during a rough crossing between the Havre and Honfleur.

"Why?"

"Because I see in the paper that the Passage du Havre is extremely disreputable."

She said no more, but I was disturbed by these enigmatical words. I understood more or less what the word "disreputable" was supposed to mean, but my imagination was uncontrolled by any notion of laws or customs, and I immediately figured the Passage du Havre (I had never been down it) as a place of lechery and abomination, a gehenna, a battlefield where all decency lay slaughtered. Notwithstanding my excursions through the apartments of *cocottes*, I had remained, for the age of fifteen, astonishingly ignorant of the surroundings of debauchery; nothing I imagined had any foundation in reality; my extravagant fancies were woven of the indecent, the charming and the horrible—the horrible especially, because of the instinctive reprobation of which I have just spoken; for

169

instance, I had a vision of my poor Tissandier being orgiastically torn to pieces by hetairae. And as I sat thinking of all this at Monsieur Richard's, looking at the big kindly boy, with his plump rosy cheeks and his calm cheerful simple ways, my heart failed me altogether. We were alone in the room, Adrien Giffard, he and I, doing our preparation. At last I could bear it no longer, and in a voice choking with emotion:

"Bernard," I asked, "when you leave the *lycée*, you don't go down the Passage du Havre, do you?"

He answered at first neither "yes" nor "no", but replied to my question by another which my unexpected query made natural.

"Why do you ask that?" said he, opening his eyes in astonishment.

Suddenly I felt overwhelmed by some enormous presence —a religious, a panic terror took hold of me—the same that had come upon me at the time of little Emile's death and on the day I had felt myself cut off from humanity. Shaken by sobs, I flung myself down before my schoolfellow.

"Bernard!" I cried; "oh, I implore you, don't, don't!"

My voice, my vehemence, my tears were those of a madman. Adrien drew back his chair, his eyes starting out of his head. But Bernard Tissandier, who had been brought up in a Puritan family like myself, did not for a moment misunderstand the nature of my emotion.

"Do you suppose then," he said very naturally and in the tone of voice best fitted to calm me, "that I don't know all about the profession?"

Those were his very words. I can swear to them.

My excitement subsided abruptly. I realised at once that he knew as much as I did or more about such matters; and his straightforward way of looking at them, firm and even a little ironical, was certainly in reassuring contrast with my dismay;

but that was exactly what astounded me—that *it*—this dragon of my imagination—could be considered so coolly, without a shudder of terror. The word *profession* sounded painfully in my ears; it introduced a practical and vulgar element into what I had hitherto only seen as a dramatic mixture of the hideous and the poetical; I really believe it had never occurred to me that the question of money had anything to do with debauchery, or that pleasure could be financed; or perhaps (for all the same, I had read a certain amount and don't want to make myself out more of a simpleton than I was) it was seeing someone younger and, so to say, tenderer than myself, aware of it, that upset me so. The mere knowledge of such things seemed to me blighting. Some sort of affection mingled with it too, and perhaps, unknown to myself, a little flutter of the senses, some wish to give brotherly protection —and the vexation of seeing it uncalled for . . .

In the meantime, as, after Tissandier's rejoinder, I had remained rooted to the ground, overcome by the sense of my own absurdity, he patted me on the shoulder and with a jolly, frank, matter-of-fact laugh, which set everything straight again:

"It's all right," said he; "there's no need for you to bother about me."

I have done my best to describe the kind of overpowering suffocation, accompanied by tears and sobs, to which I was subject, and which, in its first three manifestations surprised me so greatly. But to those who have never experienced anything of the kind, I am afraid it will remain utterly incomprehensible. Since those days I have become acclimatised to the attacks of this strange aura; they are far from being less frequent, but are tempered now, controlled, and so to speak *tamed*, so that I have learnt to be as little afraid of them as Socrates of his demon. Drunkenness without wine, as I was soon to realise, was no other than the true lyric ecstasy, and the happy moment in which I was shaken by that divine madness was the very one in which Dionysus visited me. But, alas, for him who has once known the god, how forlorn, how despairing are the languid hours in which he withholds his presence!

If Bernard Tissandier had been very little moved by my pathetic outburst, I, on the contrary, had been very much so by his smiling, good-natured reply. It was some time after this conversation, I think, that I began to notice some of the sights of the streets. My aunt Démarest lived in the Boulevard Saint-Germain, almost opposite the Théâtre Cluny, or, to be more accurate, in the steep street that goes up to the Collège de France, whose façade could be seen from the balcony of her apartment on the fourth floor. The house, to be sure, had a *porte-cochère;* but how could my aunt, with her tastes and principles, have chosen such a neighbourhood? At nightfall, between the *Boul' Mich* and the *Place Maub',*[1] the streetwalkers began to prowl. Albert had warned my mother:

"I think, Aunt," he had said to her in my presence, "that it would be better for this big boy here to go home with you in the evenings, when you come to dine with us." (This we did once a fortnight.) "And I think, on your way back, you had better walk in the middle of the road, as far as the tram stopping-place."

I cannot say whether I altogether understood. But one evening, contrary to my custom, which was to run without stopping from the Rue du Bac to my aunt's house, making it a point of honour to get there before the tram, into which I had first seen my mother—one evening then—a fine spring evening—as my mother had spent the afternoon at aunt Claire's,

[1] Paris students' way of speaking of the Boulevard Saint-Michel and the Place Maubert.

172

I started earlier than usual and was walking slowly, in order to enjoy the first warm weather of the season. I had almost reached my destination, when I noticed the curious appearance of some women in the street; they were not wearing hats and were walking vaguely up and down, as if they were undecided where to go, and just at the very place where I should have to pass close by them. The word *profession* which Tissandier had used flashed into my mind; I hesitated for a second as to whether I should not step off the pavement to avoid going too near them; but there is something in my nature that nearly always predominates over fear——namely, the fear of being cowardly; I went on therefore. Suddenly, another such woman, whom I had not noticed at first, or who had sprung out from behind a door, came up and stared me full in the face, as she stood barring my way. I had to make an abrupt détour, and how my legs shook beneath me, and how I hurried! She had been singing to begin with, but now she left off.

"There's no need to be so frightened, my pretty lad!" she exclaimed in a voice at once threatening, mocking, coaxing and playful.

The blood rushed to my face. I was as agitated as if I had escaped with my life.

Many years later, these questing creatures still inspired me with as much terror as vitriol-throwers. My Puritan education encouraged to excess a natural reserve about which I was simple enough to have no misgivings. My lack of curiosity about the other sex was absolute; if I could have discovered the whole mystery of womankind with a single gesture, it was a gesture I should not have made; I indulged myself in the flattering thought that my repugnance was disapproval, and set my aversion down to the score of virtue. I lived withdrawn and constrained, and made resistance my ideal; if I ever gave way, it was to my early vice; no outside provocation had any effect on me. At that age, moreover, and on those questions, how generously one cheats oneself! On the days on which it occurs to me to believe in the Devil, as I think of my saintly repulsions, my noble shudderings, I seem to hear the Adversary laughing and rubbing his hands in his lurking-place. But how could I have foreseen what snares—but this is not the place in which to speak of them ...

In describing our apartment, I have not spoken of the library. The fact is that after my father's death, my mother refused to allow me into it. The room was kept locked up; but though it was at the further end of the apartment, it always seemed to me its centre; my thoughts, my ambitions, my desires gravitated round it. In my mother's eyes, it was a kind of sanctuary, in which the beloved memory of my father still lingered; she would no doubt have thought it sacrilege if I had taken his place too soon; I also think she did her best to remove out of my way anything likely to increase my importance in my own eyes; and lastly, I may say she did not consider it prudent to put so many books within reach of my devouring appetite. As my sixteenth year approached, however, Albert began to intercede in my favour; I overheard fragments of a discussion between him and mamma.

"But he'll be ransacking the whole library!" exclaimed she.

Albert replied gently that my taste for reading deserved to be encouraged.

"He has plenty of books in the passage and his own room. We can wait till he has read all those," rejoined my mother.

"Aren't you afraid of giving the library books the attraction of forbidden fruit?"

My mother protested that "in that case, one ought never to forbid anything." She resisted in this way for some time and then ended by giving in, as she almost always did when it was Albert who opposed her, because she had a great deal of affection and esteem for him, and because in the end common sense always prevailed with her.

But no, I can truthfully say that the fact of the room's being forbidden added nothing to its attraction—or only a touch of mystery. I am not one of those people whose first impulse is to rebel; on the contrary, I have always been glad to obey, to submit to rules, to give way; and moreover, I had a particular horror of doing anything on the sly; if it sometimes happened afterwards—and only too often, alas!—that I found myself obliged to hide the truth, it has never been except for the passing purpose of protecting myself, and always with the constant hope, and indeed, the fixed determination of shortly bringing everything to light. And why else should I be writing these memoirs? . . . To return to the subject of my reading, I may say that I cannot remember ever to have read a single book behind my mother's back; I made it a point of honour not to deceive her. What was there so special about the library books then? First of all, their fine appearance. And besides, the books in my room and the passage were almost all works of history, exegesis or criticism, while in my father's study, I discovered the authors themselves that these works spoke of.

Albert had almost convinced my mother, but nevertheless, she did not give in at once and altogether; she compounded. It was decided I should be allowed into the room, but only accompanied by her; I might choose this or that book as I pleased and be allowed to read it, but it must be aloud and to her. The first book my choice lighted on was the first volume of Gautier's poems.

I liked reading aloud to my mother, but her desire to form her taste and her mistrust of her own judgment inclined her to

175

favour books of a very different kind. Paul Albert's flat and tedious essays, for instance; Saint-Marc-Girardin's lectures *On Dramatic Literature*, whose five volumes, at the rate of one chapter a day, we had just got through. It is a wonder to me that I was not disgusted by such fare. But no, on the contrary, I liked it, and my appetite was so keen, that my preference went to what was most instructive, most stodgy and most arduous. I think to-day that my mother was not wrong in attaching so much importance to works of criticism; her mistake lay in not choosing them better; but she had no one to advise her. And then, even if I had read Sainte-Beuve's *Lundis* or Taine's *Littérature Anglaise* at that early age, should I have profited by them as I did later? The important thing was to occupy my mind.

If it is thought surprising that my mother did not rather or at any rate, *also*, encourage me to read history, my answer is that that study was particularly uncongenial to my cast of mind. I must say something about this infirmity of mine. A good teacher might perhaps have succeeded in arousing my interest, if he could have brought out the play of character that underlies events; but as ill-luck would have it, I never had anyone to teach me history but the driest of schoolmasters. Many a time since then have I tried to force my inclination and apply myself to the best of my abilities; but my brain refuses its allegiance and however brilliantly the story is told, I can remember nothing but what lies outside the actual events —the glosses in the margin, so to speak, and the conclusions a moralist may draw from them. How gratefully I came across (it was in my last year at school) the passage in which Schopenhauer tries to establish the difference between the historian's mind and the poet's. "That is why I can make nothing of history!" I said to myself with rapture. "It is because I am a poet! It is a poet I want to be! It is a poet I am!"

"Was sich nie und nirgends hat begeben
Das allein veraltet nie." [1]

And I repeated to myself the sentence he quotes from Aristotle: "Philosophy is a more important thing and poetry a more beautiful one than history." But I must return to my reading of Gautier.

Imagine me then one evening, sitting with my mother in her room, in my hand the book she had allowed me to take out of the little glazed bookshelf specially reserved for the poets. Off I start reading *Albertus* aloud. *Albertus* or the *Soul and Sin* . . . What a halo of prestige still shone round the name of Gautier at that time! And then the impertinent sub-title *Theological Poem* attracted me. Gautier, for me and for numbers of schoolboys in those days, stood for scorn of conventionality, for emancipation, for license. No doubt, there was a little bravado in my choice too. Mamma wanted to read with me! Very well! We would see which of the two would cry for mercy first. But the bravado was directed chiefly against myself; as when a few months before, I had forced myself, so painfully too, with such an air of false assurance, to go into a loathsome little shop in the Rue Saint-Placide, where they sold all sorts of things, including songs, and buy the silliest and vulgarest song among them: "Oh, how nice Matilda smells!" And with what object? I repeat it was purely out of bravado, for most certainly, I had not the slightest desire for the song. Yes, out of a wish to coerce myself, and because the day before I had said to myself as I passed the shop: "At any rate, *that's* a thing you wouldn't dare do." I had done it.

I read on without looking at mamma, who was sitting in one of the huge armchairs, doing her cross-stitch. I had

1 "That which ne'er and nowhere has befallen,
That alone it is which cannot age."

started off gaily enough, but as the text became more ribald, my voice became less confident. One of the two characters in this so-called "Gothic poem" is a witch who, in order to attract Albertus, assumes the form of a lovely young damsel—a pretext this for endless descriptions . . . Mamma plied her needle more and more feverishly; as I read, I caught the flash of its moving point out of the corner of my eye. I had reached verse CI:

> "*The holiest saint, so beautiful the dame,*
> *Would for her sake have risked the fires of Hell,*
> *Oh, lovely sight! A rosy blush of shame . . .*"

"Pass me the book a moment," said my mother, suddenly interrupting me, to my immense relief. Then, and not till then, I looked at her; she held the book up to the lamp, and with the compressed lips and frowning brow of a judge *in camera*, listening to indecorous evidence, she glanced over the stanzas that followed. I waited. She turned the page, then looked back and hesitated, then turned again and read on; at last she handed me back the book and pointed to a place where I could take up the thread:

"Yes . . . Here! . . 'a whole seraglio in herself'," said she, quoting the line which she thought would best sum up the verses she had censored—and which I became acquainted with long after, to my considerable disappointment.

This painful and ludicrous attempt was, I am glad to say, not repeated. I refrained for some time from making any allusion to the library, and when at last my mother allowed me into it again, there was no more talk of her accompanying me.

My father's library was composed for the most part of Greek and Latin books, of law-books too, of course; though these were not in the place of honour. This was occupied by Euripides, in the great Glasgow edition, by Lucretius, Aeschylus, Tacitus, Heyne's fine edition of Virgil, and the three Latin elegiac poets. I think this choice had been determined not so much by my father's preferences as by a harmonious combination of bindings and formats. A number of these books were clothed in white vellum and stood out without too harsh a contrast against the sombre, glowing, many-coloured richness of the general effect. The immense bookcase was deep enough to admit of a second rather taller row at the back; and there was something exquisite in the sight of the collection of Greek elegiac poets, standing between a Horace and a Thucydides, their blue morocco humbly lowered before the ivory white of Burmann's Ovid and a Livy in seven volumes, also bound in vellum. In the middle of the bookcase, under the Virgils, was a cupboard in which were kept albums of various sorts; between the cupboard and the bookshelf immediately above it was a shelf which served as a desk on which you could rest the book you were studying; on each side of the cupboard stood the lower rows of big folios—the Greek Anthology, a Plutarch, a Plato, Justinian's Digest. But in spite of the attraction these handsome books had for me, my preference went to those in the small glazed bookcase.

Here, there were nothing but French books; and almost nothing but poets . . . I had long been in the habit of taking with me on my walks one of Hugo's early volumes in a charming little edition belonging to my mother, which had been given her, I think, by Anna; in this way, I had learnt numbers of pieces out of the *Voix Intérieures*, the *Chants du Crépuscule*, and the *Feuilles d'Automne*, which I never wearied of saying over to myself and which I looked forward to repeating to Emmanuèle. At that time I had a passionate predilection for poetry; poetry, I considered was the flower and fulfilment of life. It took me a long time to recognise—I think it is better not to recognise too early—the greater excellence of fine prose, and its greater rarity. I confused, as is natural at that age, art with poetry; I abandoned my soul to the swinging alternation of the rhymes and their enforced recurrence; I revelled in feeling their rhythmic beat in my heart, like the spreading of two wings which raised me with them in their flight . . . And yet the most thrilling discovery I made in the little bookcase was, I think, Heine's poems. (I am speaking of the French translation.) No doubt the absence of rhyme and metre lent them an added though deceitful allurement; for what appealed to me in these poems, besides the charm of their emotion, was what I tried to believe I should soon be able to imitate.

I can see myself, in this spring-time of my sixteenth year, sitting on the carpet Etruscanwise at the foot of the little glazed bookcase; trembling at the discovery, the feeling, that in my heart too the riches of spring were awakening, were responding to Heine's call. But how can one describe the impression made by a book? This is the fatal defect of my story, and indeed of all memoirs; one sets out the most apparent, but the things that matter most, having no contours, elude one's grasp. So far I have enjoyed lingering over all these trifling facts. But the time has come when I was beginning to awake to life.

My headaches, which the year before had been worse than ever and had forced me to give up working almost entirely, or at any rate working at all consecutively, now became less frequent. I had left Monsieur Richard's, my mother being doubtless of opinion that his teaching was no longer adequate; she sent me this year to the Pension Keller in the Rue de Chevreuse, close to the Ecole Alsacienne, to which there was still some hope of my returning.

180

There were a great many boys at the Pension Keller, but I was the only one among them who did not attend a *lycée*. I arrived, morning and evening, precisely at the hours when the Pension was deserted. Deep silence reigned in the empty class-rooms, and I took my lessons sometimes in one and sometimes in another; the one I preferred was quite a small room, more propitious to work, where contact with the blackboard was more neighbourly; propitious too to the undermasters' confidences; I have always had a sweet tooth for confidences; I flattered myself I was particularly good at listening to them, and there was nothing I felt prouder of. It was long before I realised that as a rule the confider is merely indulging in that desire to talk of himself that is inherent in the heart of man, and cares very little whether the ear into which he pours his story is really fitted to hear it.

And so it was that M. de Bouvy imparted his sorrows to me. M. de Bouvy, the principal usher of the school, never began a lesson without a preliminary sigh. He was a flabby little man, black and bearded. I cannot exactly remember what he taught me, and I hardly suppose I learnt much, for the lesson had barely begun before Monsieur de Bouvy's eyes would grow dim; his sighs became more frequent and his words soon ceased to follow them. While I was repeating my lesson, he would wag his head pensively, murmur a series of melancholy "oh's" and "ah's" and then suddenly interrupt me:

"She locked me out again last night."

Monsieur de Bouvy's sorrows were of the conjugal order.

"What!" cried I, more, I fear, in amusement than pity; "you spent the night on the staircase again?"

"Oh, so *you* think it's intolerable too, do you?"

He gazed into the distance. I think he had ceased to see me and forgotten he was talking to a child.

"Especially," he went on, "as it makes me the laughing-stock of the other people in the house. They don't understand the situation."

"Couldn't you force your way in?"

"When I do that, she beats me. Put yourself in my place."

"In your place, I should beat *her*."

He gave a deep sigh, raised his cow-like eyes to the ceiling and said solemnly:

"The man who lifts his hand against a woman . . ." and then muttered below his breath: "Especially when she isn't alone". . .

M. de Bouvy was soon succeeded by a M. Daniel, who was a dirty, ignorant, boozy individual reeking of the pot-house and the brothel, but who at any rate did not confide in me; he was followed by someone else I have totally forgotten. The ignorance and vulgarity of these successive undermasters greatly distressed M. Keller, who was a man of real merit and who took great pains to keep his school up to its original reputation, which had been, and I believe justifiably, considerable. It was soon arranged that I was to take all my lessons with him, except mathematics, which I did with M. Simonnet. These two were both excellent teachers—of that kind of born teachers who, far from overtasking a child's brain, devote themselves instead to delivering it, and wear themselves out in the effort; so that they seem in their dealings with their pupils to be putting into practice the words of the Baptist: "He must increase, but I must decrease." These two then coached me so successfully, that in little more than eighteen months I made up my wasted years and was able in October 1887 to take up work again at the Ecole Alsacienne in the highest class but one; and here I once more came across my old schoolfellows, whom I had lost sight of for so long.[1]

[1] I think I must be making a mistake here and that it was the boys who had been in the class below me whom I now joined. My first class-mates were by now a year ahead of me.

VIII

In my case, it is always the feeling of joy that gets the upper hand; for which reason my arrivals are more sincere than my departures. At the moment of leaving, there are often occasions when it would be scarcely decorous to show the joy I am feeling. I was delighted to quit the Pension Keller, but I did not wish to make it too apparent lest M. Jacob, of whom I was very fond, should have his feelings hurt. We used always to call our professor, M. Keller, by his Christian name, or rather, it was he who insisted on being so called out of respect for his old father, the founder and head of the school. Like Wemmick in *Great Expectations*, M. Jacob had a quasi-religious and absolutely paralysing veneration for his parents—for his mother was also living. Though he himself was getting on in years, he subordinated his thoughts, his plans, his life to this *Aged*, who was almost unknown to the pupils, for he only appeared on the most solemn occasions; his authority however, weighed heavily on the whole household and M. Jacob returned clothed in it, when (like Moses coming down from the mountain with the Tables of the Law) he came down from the room on the second floor, where the Old Man lived in seclusion. Into this sacred abode I was only allowed to enter very rarely, and then accompanied by my mother—for I never should have dared to go alone—but I can answer for it that the *Aged* really did exist. You were shown into a small Evangelical-looking room, where the old man sat installed for the whole day in a large green rep armchair, beside a window overlooking the playground, so that he was able to keep his eye on the boys at their games. He used to begin by apologising for not being able to get up to receive you; his right elbow rested slantwise on a mahogany bureau, covered with papers; on a little table at his left I noticed an enormous

183

Bible and a little blue bowl he used as a spittoon, for he suffered from catarrh. In spite of his great height, the weight of years had bowed him over much. His glance was unswerving, his voice severe, and it was impossible not to understand, not to feel, that the orders transmitted by M. Jacob to the rest of the school, had been received by *him* straight from God.

As for old Madame Keller, who resigned herself to leaving this world before her husband, my only recollection of her is that she was more shrivelled and withered than any other creature I had ever set eyes on, except my grandmother. She was even smaller than my grandmother, though not quite so wrinkled.

M. Jacob himself was married and the father of three children about my own age. They were submerged in the rest of the school and I only came into the most fleeting contact with them. M. Jacob tried in vain to look stern and unapproachable and to hide his natural kindness from his pupils; for at heart he was the mildest of men—debonair is perhaps the word I should use—a word which in my mind implies something child-like in the way of talking. As he was gay by nature but not very witty, he was in the habit of making puns rather than epigrams, and was never tired of repeating the same jokes over and over again, as if to make it clear that all he wanted was to show he was in a good temper, and also, no doubt, because his daily cares prevented him from attempting to do better. But what an excellent fellow he was! Switzerland is the home of beings like him. They come straight out of the pages of Topfer.

On Sunday mornings, he played the harmonium at the Protestant chapel in the Rue Madame, where M. Hollard and M. de Pressensé took it in turns to preach. The latter, who was the father of the editor of the *Temps*, was an old pastor and senator, and nearly as ugly as Monsieur Bavretel himself;

he was fairly eloquent as a preacher, but harped too much on the same string, and was afflicted besides with a chronic cold in the head which sometimes spoilt his most pathetic passages. Before the hymn began, M. Jacob at the harmonium would improvise washy little preludes, which displayed the whiteness of his soul. As for me, being entirely without musical imagination myself, I was struck with admiration by his powers of invention.

Accordingly, before leaving the Pension Keller for the Ecole Alsacienne, I looked about for some delicate way of showing M. Jacob the gratitude I felt for his kindness and attention. I might, of course, have kept in touch with him by paying him an occasional visit, as his school was on the way to the Ecole. But I should have found nothing to say to him, and besides I did not think it enough. Inspired by the absurd delicacy of my feelings, or more strictly speaking, by the desire to show how delicate my feelings were, I was constantly attempting to "gild refinèd gold," sometimes tormented by foolish scruples and sometimes driven into offering attentions that were totally incomprehensible to the receivers of them. Upon this occasion, the idea suggested itself to me of going to the Kellers' once a week for a meal. I had a fancy too that I should like to have a taste—just a taste—of life in a boarding school. So it was settled that I should lunch at the Pension Keller every Wednesday. It was veal day. I thought I should be put to sit with the other boys; but M. Jacob insisted on treating me like a distinguished guest and embarrassed me exceedingly by the place of honour he gave me. About fifteen boys took their meals at one end of an enormous table; Monsieur and Madame Keller sat at the head at the other end. I sat beside M. Keller, separated from the other boys by a long empty stretch, so that I seemed to be presiding with him. The worst of it was that the Keller boys themselves sat at a distance from their parents amongst the common herd. So that this attempt of mine to submit myself to discipline only resulted in differentiating me more than ever, as has always happened indeed, whenever I have tried to take my place with the rank and file.

The extreme interest I took in everything from this time forward arose chiefly from the fact that Emmanuèle was everywhere my companion. I never made a discovery but my first desire was to impart it to her, and my joy was never perfect unless she shared it with me. In every book I read, against every sentence that seemed to call for our admiration, wonder or love, I set her initials in the margin. Life had no value for me save with her, and I dreamed she would always be with me, as she was on those summer mornings at La Roque when we used to roam the woods together. The house still slept when we left it. The grass was heavy with dew; the air was cool; the rose of dawn had long since faded from the sky, but the slanting sunbeams laughed their early greeting to us with delightful freshness. We went along together hand in hand, or, where the path narrowed, I a few paces ahead of her. We stepped lightfooted and silent, for fear of startling god or game, rabbit or squirrel or roe-deer, at their play in the glad confidence of the innocent hour, when every morning they create their Paradise anew, before man is awake and the day grows drowsy. Pure and dazzling light, in the hour of death, may your remembrance vanquish the shades! How often in the dust and heat of noon has my soul found refreshment in your dews . . .

When we were apart, we wrote to each other. A regular correspondence had sprung up between us . . . A little while ago, I thought I would re-read my letters, but their tone is unbearable and I seem to myself odious in them. I try to persuade myself to-day that it is only the simple-minded who can be naturally natural. As for me, I had to disengage my line from among a multitude of curves; and even so, I was not as yet conscious of the intricacy of the tangle through which I had to find my way. I felt my pen held up, but by what I could not say; and without the skill as yet to unravel the knots that hampered me, I dictatorially cut them.

It was about this time that I began to discover the Greeks, who have had such a decisive influence on my mind. Leconte de Lisle's translations had just finished coming out. There was a great deal of talk about them and my aunt Lucile (I think) gave them to me. Their sharp definition of line, their unfamiliar glitter, their exotic and sonorous phraseology were the very things to enchant me; and even their very roughness was grateful and that little surface difficulty which kept off the profane by requiring from the reader an increase of attention and sympathy. It was through them that I first beheld Olympus, and man's suffering and the smiling severity of the gods; I began to learn mythology; fervently I caught and pressed Beauty to my heart.

My cousin, on her side, read the Iliad and the tragic poets; her admiration raised mine to a still higher pitch and was one with it; I doubt whether our communion was closer even at the paschal feast of Easter. Strange! This brave pagan fervour flared so brightly in me at the very time I was being prepared for confirmation in the Christian faith. To-day it is a wonder to me that the one interfered so little with the other; there might have been some explanation if I had been luke-warm as a catechumen; but no! and I shall soon have to tell of my zeal and the lengths to which I pushed it. In truth the temple of our hearts was like those mosques which stand open to the East, so that light and music and perfumes may divinely flood them. Exclusion seemed impiety; whatever was beautiful found in us a welcome.

Pastor Couve, who prepared me for confirmation, was certainly the worthiest of men; but, good Heavens, how tedious his lessons were! About a dozen of us, girls as well as boys, attended them; but I have not kept the smallest recollection of any of my fellow-pupils. The class was held in the dining-room of M. Couve's apartment in the Boulevard Saint-Michel, opposite the Luxembourg. We sat round a big oval table, and after we had repeated the Scripture texts M. Couve had given us to learn the time before, he began his lesson, always preceding and winding it up by a prayer. The first year was spent in studying the Holy Book, and during all that year I kept hoping that in the next the lessons would be more lively; but M. Couve brought to the study of dogma and to the historical exposition of the Christian doctrine the same impassive gravity—it was part, I think, of his orthodoxy. And all the while, as his monotonous voice flowed on, we took note upon note for the résumé we had to hand in at the next class. Wearisome lessons, followed at home by work more wearisome still! M. Couve was orthodox even in the very tone of his voice, which was as even and as steady as his soul; and nothing could have been more repellent to my tremulous anxiety than his imperturbability. At the same time he had the tenderest of hearts, but this was not the place in which to show it . . . I was bitterly disappointed; for I advanced towards the sacred mysteries as the Greeks of old approached Eleusis. How I trembled as I questioned! And for only answer I learnt the number of the Prophets or the itinerary of St. Paul's voyages. I was disappointed to my heart's core; and as my questioning remained unanswered, I began to wonder whether the faith in which I was being instructed—the Protestant faith, I mean—was really that which responded to my needs; I could have wished to know something too of the Catholic; for I was by no means insensible to all the art that surrounds it, and M. Couve's teaching had never awakened in me any of the emotion that stirred me as I read Bossuet, Fénelon or Pascal.

I was simple enough to open myself on the matter to M. Couve himself; I even went so far as to tell him in a private interview that I was not sure to which altar my heart felt most drawn in its search for God . . . And so, excellent man that he was, he gave me a book in which the Catholic doctrine was very honestly set forth; it was of course not an apology; but nothing could have been less of an attack—nothing more fit to damp me. It was as bare as an inventory, as dreary as one of M. Couve's own expositions; so that, upon my word! I thought, there as here, my thirst is doomed to remain unquenched—unless indeed, I slake it myself at the very source; and this I proceeded to do passionately. That is to say, I began to read the Bible more thoroughly than I had ever done before. I read the Bible eagerly, greedily, but methodically too. I began at the beginning and read on, but starting in several places at once. Every evening, as I sat with my mother, in her room, I read one or more chapters of the historical books, one or more chapters of the poetical, one or more of the prophets. In this way, I soon went through the Scriptures from end to end; then I began again to re-read them in parts, more steadily, but still with unappeased appetite. I immersed myself in the text of the Old Covenant with piety and reverence, but the emotion I felt was no doubt not purely religious in its character, just as that with which I read the Iliad and the Oresteia was not purely literary. Or rather art and religion were devoutly wedded in my heart and I tasted my most perfect ecstasy there where they most melted into one.

But the Gospels . . . Ah! At last I found the reason, the occupation, the inexhaustible spring of love. The feeling I had

189

here made clear to me and at the same time strengthened the feeling I had for Emmanuèle; it did not differ from it; it seemed merely to deepen it and give it its true place in my heart. I fed upon the Bible as a whole only in the evenings, but in the mornings, I turned with deeper intimacy to the Gospels; I turned to them again and again in the course of the day. I carried a New Testament in my pocket; it never left me; I took it out every moment, and not only when I was alone, but when I was in company with the very people who were most likely to laugh at me, and whose laughter would be most disagreeable to me—in the tram, for instance, and during recreation hours at the Pension Keller, or later, at the Ecole Alsacienne; and when my schoolfellows jeered at me, I offered my confusion and my blushes to God. The ceremony of my first Communion made very little difference in my habits; the Eucharist did not bring me any fresh ecstasy, nor even perceptibly increase that which I already felt; I was shocked, on the contrary, by the kind of official parade with which people surround themselves on that day and which almost profaned it in my eyes. But as there had been no lukewarmness before the day, so there was no slackening after it; on the contrary, after my confirmation, my fervour continued to increase and reached its culminating point in the following year.

For months on end now, I lived in a kind of seraphic state —the state, I suppose, attained by saintliness. It was summertime. I had almost entirely given up going to classes, having been allowed as an extraordinary favour to attend only those which I found really profitable, that is to say, very few. I drew up a time-table, and followed it strictly, for its very rigour was a source of the deepest satisfaction to me, and I put my pride in keeping to it exactly. I rose at dawn and plunged into a tub of icy water which I had prepared over night; then, before beginning my work, I read a few verses of the Scriptures, or rather I re-read those I had marked the evening before as the proper food for the morrow's meditation; then I prayed. My prayer was like a perceptible motion of the soul towards a deeper penetration into the intimacy of God; and from hour to hour I renewed that motion; such were the breaks in my studies, and I never changed the subject of them without dedicating it afresh to God. Out of self-mortification I slept on the boards; in the middle of the night, I got up again, and again knelt down, not so much for self-mortification as in the impatience of joy. I felt then that I had attained the very apex of happiness.

What more can I say? . . . Ah! would that I could express to exhaustion the ardour and the radiance of those memories! There lies the snare of this kind of tale: the most futile and the most meaningless events, and all that can be put into words perpetually usurp the place of all the rest. Alas! what can be told here? All that so filled my swelling heart can be put into three words and in vain I lengthen and inflate them. O cumbersome radiance! O careless heart, unheedful of the shadows that radiance cast on the other side of my flesh! Perhaps, in imitation of the love of God, my love for my cousin was too easily content with absence. The most marked traits of a character are formed and accentuated before one is conscious of them. But could I possibly have understood so early the signification of what was shaping within me? . . .

And yet it was not the New Testament that Pierre Louis [1] found in my hands during the recreation hour that evening, but Heine's *Buch der Lieder*, which I was reading now in the original. We had been writing a French composition. Pierre Louis had remained at the Ecole Alsacienne all the time I was away from it, and when I returned, I came across him again

[1] It was not till the publication of his first book that he spelt his name Louÿs.

in *Rhétorique*.[1] He was more than a brilliant pupil; a kind of genius dwelt in him, and what he did best he did most gracefully. In French composition, he was always easily first; the rest were nowhere. Dietz, our professor, with a smile of amusement, would announce what the professors of the other classes had so often announced before him: "First, Louis." It was a place no one dared dispute; no one dreamt of it; I assuredly no more than the others, accustomed as I had been for years to working by myself, nervous as I was, and much less stimulated than hampered by the presence of twenty-five other boys. And suddenly, without my thinking I had particularly deserved it by that composition:

"First, Gide," began Dietz, with the list of marks before him.

He said it in his loudest voice, as if flinging down a challenge, and brought his fist down with a great thump on to his desk, while an amused glance round the class trickled over his spectacles. Dietz, with his class before him, was like an organist at his keyboard—a maestro who drew from us at will the most unexpected sounds—sounds that we ourselves had never even hoped for. Sometimes he seemed to be almost too much amused by his power, as is often the case with a virtuoso. But how delightful his lessons were! I came out from them full to bursting. And how much I liked the warmth of his voice, and the affectation of indolence with which he lolled back in his chair, with one leg over its arm, and his knee on a level with his nose!

"First, Gide!"

I felt all eyes turn towards me. I made an immense effort

[1] In those days the two highest classes in French *lycées* (except for boys going in for science) were called *Rhétorique* and *Philosophie*. The former prepared boys for the first part of the *baccalauréat* examination, the latter for the second part. The *baccalauréat* is the preliminary examination before entering upon University studies—more or less equivalent to the English *matriculation*.

not to blush and blushed all the more; my head swam; but I was not so much pleased with my place as dismayed at the thought of vexing Pierre Louis. How would he take this affront? Supposing he were to hate me? In class I had eyes for no one but him, though he certainly had no suspicion of it; up to that day, I had barely exchanged twenty words with him; he was all exuberance, and on very easy terms with his school-fellows, while I was lamentably shy, crippled by reserve, paralysed by scruples. Lately, however, I had made up my mind: I would go up to him; I would say: "Louis, you and I must have a talk. If anyone can understand you here, it is I" . . . Yes, truly, I felt I was on the verge of speaking to him. And all of a sudden, the catastrophe:

"Second, Louis."

And I watched him from afar—from farther off than ever, I said to myself—where he sat sharpening his pencil, looking as if he had heard nothing, but all the same, a little strained, I thought, a little pale. I watched him through my fingers, for I had put my hand over my eyes when I had felt myself blush.

During the recreation hour that followed, I went, as was my habit, into a glazed corridor which led to the playground, where the others played noisily; there I was alone; there I was safe. I took the *Buch der Lieder* out of my pocket and began to read:

> *"Das Meer hat seine Perlen,*
> *Der Himmel hat seine Sterne,"*

consoling with its love my heart athirst for friendship.

> *"Aber mein Herz, mein Herz,*
> *Mein Herz hat seine Liebe."*

Steps came up behind me. I turned round. It was Pierre Louis. He wore a black and white check coat with sleeves that were too short; a torn collar, for he was given to fighting; a tie with flowing ends . . . I can still see him so distinctly! Lithe, delicate, with the long, rather ungainly limbs of an overgrown child; his handsome brow half hidden by his ruffled hair. He was close upon me before I had time to recover myself.

"What are you reading there?" he began at once.

Incapable of speech, I held out my book. He turned over its pages for a moment or two.

"You're fond of poetry then?" he went on, with a voice and smile I did not know were his.

So then it was not as an enemy he had come. My heart melted within me.

"Yes, I know those verses," he continued, giving me back the book. "But in German, I prefer Goethe's."

"I know you write poetry too," I ventured timidly.

There had recently gone round the class a burlesque poem which Dietz had ordered Louis to write as an imposition for having grumbled in class.

"Monsieur Pierre Louis, you will write me thirty lines *On Grumbling* for next Monday," Dietz had said.

I had learnt the piece by heart (I believe I know it still); it was schoolboy's work, but wonderfully well pulled off. I began to repeat it. He stopped me with a laugh:

"Oh, that's only fun. If you like, I'll show you some others. Real ones."

There was an exquisite youthfulness about him; it was as though a sort of boiling agitation inside him were shaking the lid of his reserve in a kind of passionate stammer. I thought it the most charming thing in the world.

Just then, the lesson-bell rang and put an end to our talk.

I had had my fill of joy for that day. But on the following days there was a sad falling off. What had happened? Louis did not speak to me; he seemed to have forgotten me. I think it was a kind of lover-like bashfulness that made him want to keep our budding friendship a secret from the others. But I did not understand it so; I was jealous of Glatron, Gouvy, Brocchi, to whom I saw him talking; but I would not go near them; it was not so much timidity that kept me back as pride; I disliked mixing with the others and could not brook that Louis should treat me as one of them. I watched for a chance of catching him alone; one soon turned up.

I have said already that Louis was fond of fighting; as however, though hot-tempered he was not very strong, he often got the worst of it. The sparring matches between the boys at the Ecole Alsacienne had nothing very ferocious about them; they were very different from the brutal ragging that went on at the Montpellier *lycée*. But Louis was a tease, inclined to be provoking, and as soon as he was touched, fighting like a wild-cat; and his clothes were sometimes very much the worse for it. On that particular day, he had lost his cap in the fray; it flew off into the distance and landed near me; I picked it up surreptitiously and hid it under my coat with the intention of taking it back to him after school. (He lived almost next door.)

"He will certainly be touched by my attention," I thought to myself; "I expect he will ask me in. I shall begin by refusing. And then I shall go in after all. We shall talk. Perhaps he will read me some of his verses."

All this was when lessons were over. I let the others go off and went out last. Louis was walking ahead of me, without looking round; and as soon as he got into the street, he quickened his pace; I did the same. He reached his door. I saw him disappear into a dark passage, and when I followed him in, I heard his footstep on the stairs. He lived on the second floor. He reached the landing, rang the bell . . . Then, quick, before the door should open and shut again between us, I called out in a voice I struggled to make friendly, but which was choking with emotion:

"Hullo, Louis! I've brought you your cap."

But from the top of the stairs, two stories high, these crushing words dropped down on to my poor little hopes:

"All right. Leave it with the concierge."

My disappointment did not last long. Two days later a heart to heart talk put an end to it; this was followed by many others, and it was not long before I had fallen into the habit of going to Louis' house after afternoon school as often and for as long a time as our home work permitted. My mother had asked to know the new friend whose praises I was always singing. How I trembled when I took him for the first time to the Rue de Commaille. Supposing he did not find favour!

Louis' good manners, however, his tact and his politeness reassured me as soon as I had introduced him, and I had the immense pleasure of hearing my mother say after he had gone:

"Your friend has excellent manners." Then, sotto voce, as if to herself: "which surprises me," she added.

"Why?" I asked nervously.

"Didn't you tell me he had lost both his parents early and that he lived with his elder brother?"

"That seems to show his good manners come naturally."

But mamma was set on education. She made a little gesture with her hand (something like her sister's) which meant: "I know very well what I could answer, but I prefer not to discuss the matter." Then in order to be conciliatory, she added:

"At any rate, his manners are certainly very distinguished."

Shortly after this presentation, Louis invited me to spend a Sunday with him in the country. We might go to the Meudon woods, for instance; it is true they were already as familiar to me as the Luxembourg Gardens, but our youthful friendship, would somehow make them seem as full of mysterious windings as the Labyrinth. The only dark spot in this plan was that I had promised to bring some of my own verses to show Louis. My verses! It was considerably stretching a point to speak of them as existing; a desire for poetry, indeed, never ceased tormenting me, but no muse ever wore heavier shackles than mine. In reality, my whole effort was centred upon translating into verse thoughts to which I attached far too much importance—in the style of Sully Prudhomme, about whom I was besotted at that time, and whose example and teaching were the very most pernicious a sentimental schoolboy like myself could follow. I was horribly hampered by the rhymes. Instead of letting them escort, guide and support me, I exhausted all my emotion searching for them, and so far had never made a success of a single piece. The Saturday before our expedition, I struggled in vain—how despairingly!—to get beyond the second verse of a poem that began in this way:

> *"I tried to speak—he would not understand.*
> *I told him that I loved him and he smiled . . ."*

The rest of it was no good and this enraged me. But in order to account for my failure to Louis, I told him that my whole heart was taken up by a book—the idea of a book— which entirely absorbed me to the neglect of everything else. This was *André Walter* which I had already begun to write, and into which I poured all my questionings, all the thoughts and feelings that divided and disturbed and perplexed me— and above all my love, which was the very pivot of the book and round which I made everything else gravitate.

This book rose before me blocking out my view of the future so utterly that it was impossible for me to conceive I should ever get past it. I could not somehow think of it as my first book, but as my only one, and imagined nothing beyond it; I felt it would consume my substance utterly; after it, lay death, madness, some kind of dreadful void towards which I was myself rushing as well as precipitating my hero. And soon I no longer knew which of us two was leading the other; there was nothing in him indeed which I had not first felt myself, nothing, so to speak, I had not made trial of on my own person; but often too it was I who drove my double before me and rashly followed after; and it was *his* madness in which I was preparing to founder.

It was not till a year later that I was able really to harness myself to this book; but I got into the habit of keeping a diary, from a desire to give some form to my vague agitation; and many pages of this diary were copied straight into the *Cahiers*. The very serious drawback to the state of preoccupation in which I then lived was that all my attentive faculties were absorbed by introspection; I wrote, and wished to write, nothing that was not intimate; I disdained history and considered events impertinent and disturbing intruders. To-day, when there is perhaps nothing that I admire more than a good narrative, I am filled with irritation as I re-read my *André Walter;* but at that time, far from understanding that art can only live and have its being in the particular, I held that it should be removed from all contingencies, considered any definition of outline to be contingent and aspired only after the quintessential.

If Pierre Louis had encouraged me in this sense, I should have been lost. Fortunately, he took good care not to, being as much an artist as I was a musician. It is impossible to imagine two natures more dissimilar, and it was for this reason I found his company so extraordinarily profitable. But we had not as yet learnt how unlike we were. An equal love for art and letters united us; we thought (were we wrong?) that this love was the only thing that mattered.

The following year parted us. Georges Louis settled at Passy. My friend Pierre went to the Lycée Janson for his last year's schooling. As for me, I decided, I don't exactly know why, to leave the Ecole Alsacienne for the Lycée Henri IV. Or rather I decided to attend no more lectures, but to prepare my examination by myself, with the help of some private coaching. I wished and intended that the *Philosophy* class should be my initiation to wisdom, and in my opinion this necessitated solitude. No sooner was my first term over than I cut the *lycée*.

IX

My story has so carried me along that I have failed to speak of Anna's death in its proper place. It was in May 1884 that she left us. My mother and I had taken her ten days before to the nursing-home in the Rue de Chalgrin, where she was to be operated on for a tumour that had been disfiguring and oppressing her for some time past. I left her in a little clean, bare, cheerless room, and never saw her again. The operation, it is true, was successful, but left her too weak to recover; Anna took leave of life in her own modest way, so quietly and unobtrusively that no one noticed she was dying, but only that she was dead. I was extremely affected by the thought that neither my mother nor I was with her at the end, that she did not say good-bye to us and that there were

199

only strange faces to meet her dying eyes. I was haunted for weeks and months by the anguish of her solitude. I imagined —I heard—that loving soul of hers utter its last despairing cry and sink back again, forsaken by all but God; and it is that cry that re-echoes in the last pages of my *Porte Étroite*.

As soon as I had finished my year of *Rhétorique*, Albert Démarest proposed to paint my portrait. I have already said that I had a kind of tender and passionate admiration for my cousin; he stood in my eyes for art, courage and liberty; but though he showed me the greatest affection, I was never wholly satisfied and kept measuring the little space I occupied in his heart and thoughts in an impatient desire to find some way of increasing his interest in me. No doubt Albert's desire to moderate my feelings was as great as mine to exaggerate them. I vaguely suffered from his reserve, and I cannot help thinking to-day that he would have done me a greater service by breaking through it.

His proposal surprised me. At first it was merely a matter of posing for a picture he wanted to send to the Salon, in which there was the figure of a violinist. Albert armed me with a violin and bow, and for several long sittings I crooked my fingers over the strings and struggled to shadow forth the soul of the violin and my own.

"Try to look agonised!" he said. And indeed it was not difficult, for the strained position very soon became a torture to maintain. My bent arm grew numb and the bow threatened to drop from my fingers.

"A rest now! I see you're exhausted."

But I was afraid I should never get the right pose again, if once I gave it up.

"No, no. I can hold out a little longer. Go on."

But an instant later, the bow dropped. Albert put down his

palette and brushes and we began to talk. He told me the history of his life. My uncle and aunt had for a long time crossed his wish to take up painting as a profession, so that he had not begun to work seriously till very late. Now, at forty, he was still feeling his way, stumbling, hesitating, continually retracing his footsteps, never advancing except over ground he had already covered. Quick to feel, but with a heavy and awkward brush, he painted nothing that was not lamentably inferior to his real self; he was conscious of his own deficiencies, but the wild hope that the very excess of his emotion would enable him to overcome them filled him with excitement every time he began a fresh picture. In a trembling voice and with tears in his eyes, he would describe his "subject" and make me promise not to mention it to anyone. Albert's subjects had not as a rule much to do with painting; lines and colours were called in to his assistance and his despair at finding them so unmanageable was great. His tremors and misgivings, in spite of all his efforts, were manifest and gave his pictures, independently of what he wanted to say in them, a sort of touching grace which was really their most valuable quality. With a little more confidence and a little more ingenuity, his very awkwardnesses might have stood him in good stead; but, out of conscientiousness and modesty, he took the utmost pains to correct them and merely succeeded in making his first charming impulses look commonplace. In spite of my inexperience at that time, I was obliged to acknowledge that Albert, notwithstanding all the treasures of his heart, did not figure as a hero in the world of art; but in those days, I too believed in the sovereign efficacy of emotion and shared his hope of suddenly seeing one of his "subjects" blossom out into a triumphant success.

"You see," he said, "I should like to put into painting the feeling that Schumann expresses in his *Mondnacht*. This

my idea: there will be a kind of hill with the recumbent figure of a woman, veiled in the mists of the setting sun, and
with arms outstretched towards a winged creature flying
down to her. I should like to put into the quivering of the
angel's wings"—here his hands imitated the beating of wings
—"something tender and passionate like the melody." And
he sang:

> *"Es war als hätt der Himmel*
> *Die Erde still geküsst . . ."*

Then he showed me some sketches for the picture, in which
a plentiful allowance of clouds concealed as best they could
the figures of the angel and woman—or in other words—the
inadequacy of the drawing.

"Of course," he said, by way of excuse and comment, "I
shall have to work from models." Then he added with a worried look: "You can't think what a nuisance the question of
models is in our profession. To begin with, they are horribly
expensive . . ."

Here I must open a parenthesis: after the death of his father, Albert would have been very comfortably off if he had
not secretly undertaken certain private responsibilities of
which I must now speak, and the fear of not being equal to
them constantly harassed and obsessed him. This fear of expense, indeed, was part of his nature; he had never been without it.

"It's no good," he used to say; "I can't help it. I have
always been sparing. It's a fault I'm ashamed of, but I have
never been able to cure myself of it. When I went to Algeria
twenty years ago, I took with me a little sum of money I had
set aside for the journey; my fear of spending too much was
so great that I brought almost the whole of it back; like a

fool, I denied myself every pleasure while I was out there."

In a person so fundamentally generous, this was certainly not avarice, but rather a form of modesty. And every penny he spent on his painting (for he was never sure of selling) was a matter of self-reproach to him. In his anxiety not to waste his canvas or use too many paints, he stinted himself miserably. He stinted himself above all over his models.

"And then," he went on, "I can never find models to suit me; not exactly; they are people who never understand what you want of them. You can't imagine how stupid they are. They never manage to look as you wish them to. There are painters, I know, who interpret; and others who don't care a straw for the sentiment of the thing. As for me, I'm always hampered by what I see. And on the other hand I haven't imagination enough to do without a model altogether . . . And then—it's ridiculous, I know—but all the time they're sitting, I'm worried by the fear of tiring them; I keep wanting to ask them to rest the whole time, and it's all I can do not to."

But the chief difficulty was one that Albert did not dare tell anyone and which I only came to understand two years later. For fifteen years, unknown to all his own people and even to his brother, Albert had been living with a young woman whom he regarded as his wife, and whose love was jealous enough to dislike his shutting himself up for hours with a model presumably young and pretty, and as scantily clothed as was necessary for the angel form of *Mondnacht*.

Poor dear Albert! I don't know which of us was the more moved the day he confided to me the history of his double life. His love was perfectly pure, noble and faithful—perfectly unassuming too and unselfish. He had set up the woman whom he already called his wife and whom he afterwards married, in a little flat in the Rue Denfert, where he did his utmost to surround her with every comfort; she, on her side, did her utmost to add to their scanty income by doing fine needlework and embroidery. When he introduced me into their home, what chiefly struck me in my cousin Marie, was her extreme distinction; her beautiful, patient, grave face bent pensively over her stitching in the dim light of her room; she never spoke but in a whisper; noise seemed to startle her as much as daylight; and I think it was out of humility that she did not ask Albert to legalise their union, which had long ago been blessed by the birth of a little girl. Albert, in spite of his Herculean appearance, was the most timid of creatures. He shrank from grieving his mother by what she would have certainly considered an unsuitable marriage. He was afraid of any and every hostile criticism, and more especially of his sister-in-law's; or rather, he dreaded the cloud it might cast over his family life. Frank and honest though he was, he preferred the underhand and crooked dealings into which he was forced by this false situation. And his scrupulous nature made him all the more particular not to let anything interfere with what he considered his duty to his mother, so that his heart and time were continually divided and he spent his whole life standing first on one leg and then on the other. My aunt, whose sole companion he had been ever since his father's death and my other cousins' marriages, treated him like a big, feckless baby, and was convinced he could not get on without her; he dined with her one evening out of two and never spent the night outside his mother's house. In order to preserve his secret, Albert used the pretext of a friendship, which, truth to tell, absorbed him almost as much as his love; but the former was a recognised and admitted thing, upon which his mother actually looked with some favour. Whenever Albert did not take a meal at home, he was supposed to be taking it with his friend Simon; it was always with him that he was supposed to be spending his time. Monsieur Simon was unmarried and the friendship of these two old bachelors seemed above suspicion. The same excuse served to cloak Albert's long absences and his conjugal outings during the summer months, which my aunt spent at La Roque or Cuverville.

Edouard Simon was a Jew; but, except perhaps for his features, his racial characteristics could not, I think, have been less marked; or perhaps I was too young to recognise them. He lived in a very modest style, though he was far from ill off; but the only thing he cared for, the only thing he wanted, was to be of help to others. He had formerly been an engineer, but had retired long before this time, and for many years past his only profession had been philanthropy. Equally in touch with workmen in want of a job and employers in want of workmen, he had organised a kind of free employment agency in his own house. His day was spent in visits to the poor, interviews and engagements of various sorts. It was less, I think, the love of individual men that actuated him than the love of humanity at large and the still more abstract love of justice. His charity had the appearance of a social duty; and this is really a very Jewish trait.

Confronted by a life of such active, practical virtue, and its evident results, poor Albert felt ashamed of his day-dreams, which his friend, it had to be admitted, was incapable of understanding.

"I need encouragement—support," Albert would say sadly. "Edouard pretends to take an interest in what I am doing, but it is only because he is fond of me; in reality, he only sympathises with what is useful. Oh, I should have to paint a chef-d'œuvre to make me feel I'm not utterly worthless!"

Then he would pass his huge, veined, hairy hand over his forehead, which was beginning to grow bald, and a moment

205

later I saw his shaggy eyebrows all ruffled and tears standing in his big kind eyes.

I was perhaps not very sensitive at first to the beauties of painting—certainly sculpture appealed to me more—but I had such a wish, such a longing to understand, that my senses soon became sharpened. One day that Albert had left a photograph lying on the table in order to test me, he was delighted because at the first glance I recognised it to be a drawing of Fragonard's; and then in my turn I was astonished at his astonishment, for it seemed to me impossible that anyone should mistake it. He nodded his head and smiled as he looked at me.

"I must take you to the chief's," he said at last. "It will amuse you to see his studio."

Albert had been one of Jean-Paul Laurens' pupils, and always called him the "chief," regarding him with the feelings of a dog, a son and an apostle. Jean-Paul Laurens lived at that time in a somewhat incommodious apartment with two large studios attached to it, one arranged as a drawing-room where Madame Laurens received her guests, and the other in which the "chief" worked. Every Tuesday evening, the curtains between the two studios were drawn. Only a few intimates came to these weekly evenings—old pupils for the most part; there was a little music; there was talk; everything was as cordial and simple as could be; it was nevertheless with a beating heart that I first entered a world so different from any I had ever known . . . All around was harmony, severe, purple, dusky, filling me at first with an almost religious awe; here, everything I saw seemed soothing to the eyes and mind, and conducive to some delicious kind of studious contemplation. That day, my eyes were suddenly opened, and I then and there realised the ugliness of my mother's rooms; I felt as if some of it must be clinging about me, and the sensation of my unworthiness was so strong that I believe I should have fainted from shame and shyness, if it had not been for my old schoolfellow, Jean-Paul Laurens' eldest son, who with the greatest cordiality tried to put me at my ease.

Paul-Albert and I were exactly the same age; but my school career had been so constantly interrupted that I had long since lost sight of him—ever since the time, indeed, when we had been in the lowest class together. I remembered him as a charming, unruly dunce. He used to sit on one of the back benches and spend his whole time in class covering his copybooks with fantastic drawings, which I thought perfect marvels. Sometimes I got myself punished on purpose, so that I might have the pleasure of being sent to sit beside him. He used the chewed end of his penholder, dipped in ink, as a paint-brush; he was so absorbed in this work as to have every appearance of diligence, but if the master ever took it into his head to ask him a question, Paul looked so startled, so dazed and so wild-eyed, that the whole class would burst out laughing. I was certainly glad to meet him again and be remembered by him, but I was still more tormented by the fear that he would take me for a bourgeois. Since sitting for Albert (he had just finished my portrait) I had become very much taken up with my personal appearance; my desire to look exactly what I felt myself to be, what I wanted myself to be— namely, an artist—was so great that it prevented me from having any existence of my own and turned me into a *poseur*. Looking into the mirror of a little bureau at which I worked (it had come to us from Anna and my mother had had it put into my room), I used to gaze unwearyingly at my own features, study them, train them like an actor, try to catch on my lips and in my eyes the expression of all the passions I longed to feel. Above all things, I wished to make myself loved; I gave my soul in exchange. In those days, I could not write— I had almost said *think*—or so I fancied, apart from this little

207

mirror; in order to become aware of my emotions, of my thoughts even, I must first, I fancied, read them in my eyes . . . Like Narcissus, I hung over my own image, and all the sentences I wrote at that time have become a little deflected by that unnatural attitude.

My acquaintance with Paul Laurens soon ripened into friendship. I will put off speaking of that, however, till I come to the journey we made together a year or two later. I must now return to Albert.

It was not only affection that made Albert confide in me. He had another motive which he soon confessed. His daughter was now twelve years old and very musical. Albert, whose fingers were as clumsy on the piano as his paint-brushes on the canvas, imagined he might make up for his own failure in her person; his hopes and ambitions were shifted on to Antoinette.

"I want to make a pianist of her," he said. "It will console me. I suffered too much from not having worked when I was young. It is time for her to begin."

Now my mother's eyes had at last been opened to the fact that the piano-lessons I had so far been given were most inadequate and that I might very well profit by something better. Some eighteen months earlier, therefore, she had entrusted my musical education to Marc de la Nux, a master of the utmost talent, with whom I immediately made astonishing progress. Albert asked me if I would in my turn give my little cousin lessons and so pass on to her some reflection of M. de la Nux's brilliant teaching; he was afraid of applying to the master himself on account of the expense. I began my task at once, much puffed up by the importance of my rôle, and by Albert's confidence, which I did my best to deserve. These lessons, which I gave twice a week for two years and which I made it a point of honour not to miss, were of as much profit to me as to my pupil, who finally passed into the hands of de la Nux himself. If I ever had to earn my living, I should become a teacher, a piano teacher for choice; I have a passion for teaching and, if only the pupil is worth taking trouble with, inexhaustible patience. I have more than once made the experiment and am vain enough to believe that my lessons were as good as those of the best masters. If I have said nothing as yet of what M. de la Nux's lessons did for me, it is because I was afraid of being too diffuse, but the moment has now come.

Mademoiselle de Goecklin's, Monsieur Schifmacker's, and especially Monsieur Merriman's lessons had been more repellent than I can well say. From time to time, I saw Monsieur Dorval, who took care that the "sacred fire," as he called it, should keep burning; but even if they had been regular, his lessons would never have taken me very far. Monsieur Dorval was too egotistical to teach well. But what a pianist Monsieur de la Nux might have made of me, if only I had gone to him earlier! Unfortunately, my mother shared the prevalent opinion that in the first stages all masters are equally good. From the very first lesson, Marc de la Nux started on a radical reform. I was under the impression that I had no musical memory, or very little; I could never learn anything by heart except by repeating it over and over again, constantly referring to the text, and feeling lost as soon as I took my eyes off it. De la Nux set to work in such a way that in a few weeks I was able to play several of Bach's fugues without once opening the book; and I remember my astonishment when I discovered that the one I was playing in C sharp, was really in D flat. His teaching gave everything life and clearness, made everything fall in with the harmonic necessities, subtly decomposed and recomposed whatever was obscure; at last I understood. I imagine it must have been with something of the same transport that the Apostles felt the Holy Ghost descend upon them. Up till then, it seemed to me, I had done nothing but repeat without comprehension the sounds of some divine language, which now I had suddenly become capable of speaking. Every note now had its own significance, became a word. With what enthusiasm I practised! I was filled with such zeal that the most unattractive exercises were my favourites. One day, after my lesson, when I had made way for the next pupil, I waited on the landing outside to listen to him; the door was shut, but it did not prevent me from hearing. He was probably no older than I and was studying the same piece—Schumann's great Fantasia; he played it with a vigour, a brilliancy, a certainty which were still far beyond me, and I sat on the stairs a long while, sobbing with jealousy.

Monsieur de la Nux seemed to take the greatest pleasure in teaching me, and his lessons often lasted long after the allotted hour. It was not till later that I heard he had tried to persuade my mother that it would be worth while my sacrificing the rest of my education, of which, according to him, I had had quite enough, and devoting myself to music; he begged her to let him undertake me entirely. My mother had hesitated, had had recourse to Albert's advice, and finally had taken upon herself to refuse, thinking there was something better for me to do in life than interpret other people's works; and she begged Monsieur de la Nux not to mention his proposal to me (I should say it was entirely disinterested) so that I might not be upset by vain hopes and ambitions. It was not till years after that I learnt all this from Albert, when it was too late to go back on the decision.

In the course of the four years I spent under Monsieur de la Nux, a great intimacy sprang up between us. Even after he had stopped giving me lessons (to my immense regret he told me one day that he had taught me to do without him, and all my protests could not persuade him to go on with lessons he thought useless), I still continued to visit him frequently. I had a kind of worship for him, the same respectful, humble affection which I had a little later for Mallarmé and which I never felt for any but these two. Both the one and the other were in my eyes the personification of saintliness in one of its rarest forms. I looked up to them with all the ingenuous reverence of youth.

Marc de la Nux was not only a teacher; his personality was one of the most striking I ever met with and his whole life admirable. He took me into his confidence and I made notes of many of the conversations I had with him, especially towards the end of his life; I still think them of extreme interest, but there is no room for them here and I can only give a very rapid sketch of him.

Marc de la Nux was born in Reunion Island, like his cousin, Leconte de Lisle. It was to his West Indian origin, no doubt, that he owed his thick, almost frizzy hair (which he wore rather long and tossed back from his forehead), his olive complexion and dreamy eyes. His whole personality was a queer compound of fire and listlessness. His hand, unlike the hand of any other pianist I have ever known, melted in yours as you pressed it, and his long disjointed body seemed made of the same boneless stuff. While giving his lessons, he used either to pace up and down or lean against a grand piano he kept in the room but did not use for practising. He would stand with his elbows on this, stooping forward, his prominent forehead resting on one hand. He wore a long, tight-fitting frock-coat of a romantic cut, a high collar and a muslin cravat wound twice round his neck and tied high up in a tiny bow; in certain lights, which showed up his high cheekbones and the hollow of his cheeks, he was extraordinarily like Delacroix' portrait of himself. At times a kind of inspiration, of enthusiasm, possessed him, and then his face was really beautiful. He rarely consented—from a feeling of modesty I think—to sit down to the piano, or if he did, only for a passing illustration; on the other hand (with me, at any rate), he liked taking out a violin which he usually kept hidden away, declaring he was very bad at it, though in the sonatas we read together he played his part much better than I did mine. I shall say nothing here of his crankiness, for it would lead me too far, but I cannot resist giving one little example, which paints the whole man.

He thought his grandchildren were very badly brought up.

"For instance," he said, as he opened his heart to me, "I'll just give you an example: little Mimi spends the night here every Wednesday" (she was the younger of his two granddaughters). "There was a clock in the room she slept in and she complained of it; she said the ticking prevented her from sleeping. Do you know what Madame de la Nux did? She took the clock away. What do you think of that? It's absurd! How will the child ever get accustomed to it?"

And this reminds me of a delightful saying of Mademoiselle de Marcillac's, one day when I dropped in upon her at Geneva in the middle of a party of old maids. One of them was talking of her little niece and saying she had a particular horror of cockchafer grubs—those big white maggots. Her mother was determined she should conquer this repugnance.

"Do you know what she did? She actually made the poor child eat them!"

"But," cried Mademoiselle de Marcillac, "it was enough to give her a loathing of them for the rest of her life!"

Perhaps the connection is not very clear. Well, never mind!

The Ecole Alsacienne, though excellent in the lower classes, was supposed at that time to be less good in the higher. *Rhétorique* did at a pinch, but my mother was advised that it would be better for me to attend my *philosophie* at one of the regular *lycées* and she decided on the Lycée Henri IV. I myself, however, had resolved to prepare my next examinations alone or with the help of a few private lessons. (Had I not once before made good five years' want of schooling by two years' work of this kind at home?) The study of philosophy seemed to me then to require an atmosphere of quiet meditation impossible to find in a public school and among a mixed company of schoolfellows. So, at the end of my third month at the *lycée*, I left it. Monsieur L . . ., whose lectures I had attended at Henri IV, undertook to guide me through the labyrinth of metaphysics and to overlook my work. He was a small man—in his mind, that is, for though his legs were long and thin, his ideas were short and set; his flat, dead voice was enough to nip the greenest and most promising of thoughts in the bud; but even before he began to express the thought he was dealing with, one felt he had stripped it of all its bloom and all its shoots and that only in the form of a bare concept could it find any place in a mind as barren as his . . . His teaching was the quintessence of dulness. It gave me the same feeling of disillusionment I had experienced before over Monsieur Couve's confirmation classes. What! was this the exalted science I had hoped would be the illumination of my life—the intellectual summit from which it would be possible to survey the universe? . . . I consoled myself with Schopenhauer. I plunged into the *World as Will and Idea* with unspeakable rapture, read it from end to end and re-read it with such intense application of mind that for many months no outside appeal was able to distract me. Later on, I put myself to school with other masters whom I greatly

213

preferred—Spinoza, Descartes, Leibnitz, and last but not least, Nietzsche; I think, in fact, that I freed myself from Schopenhauer's influence pretty soon; but it is to him I owe my initiation into philosophy, and to him alone.

I failed in June in the second part of my *baccalauréat*, but managed to scrape through in the following May. This, I considered, brought the first part of my education to an end. I had no desire to push it any further, or to go in for any more examinations, either in law or letters, and resolved to launch out on my own career at once. My mother, nevertheless, extracted a promise from me to go on working with Monsieur Dietz for another year. No matter! from that moment I felt strangely free, without encumbrances or pecuniary anxieties of any kind—at that age, indeed, I had very little conception of what it would be like to be obliged to earn one's living. But no; not free, for I was bound both by my love and by the book which, as I have already said, I was planning, and which I looked upon as the most imperious of duties.

Another resolution I had taken was to marry my cousin as soon as possible. My book seemed to me at times to be nothing but a long declaration, a profession of love; I meant it to be so noble, so pathetic, so peremptory, that when it was published our parents would withdraw their objections to our marriage and Emmanuèle would no longer refuse me her hand. Meantime, my uncle, her father, had just died from a stroke; she and I, as we watched at his bedside and bent over him in his last moments, had been brought very near together. This loss, I thought, was a final consecration of our engagement.

But though my spiritual needs were so urgent, I knew well enough that my book was not yet mature, that I was not yet capable of writing it; and so it was without too much impatience that I looked forward to some further months of study, training and preparation—and especially to more reading (I used to devour a book a day). A short journey between whiles, my mother thought, would be a profitable way of spending the holidays; I thought so too; but we agreed less well when it came to deciding where I should go. Mamma voted for Switzerland; she consented to letting me travel without her, but not entirely by myself. When she suggested my joining a party of tourists belonging to the Alpine Club, I flatly declared that such companionship would drive me crazy, and moreover that I had taken a violent dislike to Switzerland; it was to Brittany I wanted to go, with a bag on my back and no companions at all. My mother began by saying such a thing was out of the question. I called Albert in to the rescue, feeling sure that since he had made me read Flaubert's *Par les Champs et par les Grèves*, he would understand my wishes and plead in my favour . . . My mother yielded at last; but she was determined, if not to go with me, at least to follow me. It was agreed we should meet at different halting-places every two or three days.

I kept a journal of my trip and a few pages of it were published in a review called *La Wallonie;* but they had to be considerably re-handled, for even at that time I had the greatest difficulty in combing out my thoughts. Moreover, I thought anything I could express easily must be commonplace and uninteresting. Other recollections of this trip may be found in the *Cahiers d'André Walter*. I have no desire, therefore, to say anything more about it here. There is one incident, however, I will recall:

I was walking along the coast, going by short stages from Quiberon to Quimper, when I came one evening to a little village called, I think, Le Pouldu. It consisted of no more than four houses, two of which were inns; I thought the humbler of the two the more charming, and I went into it, for I was very thirsty. A servant-girl showed me into a whitewashed room, and left me sitting with a glass of cider before me. A number of unframed canvases standing with their faces to the wall were all the more conspicuous because of the scarcity of furniture and the absence of wall-papers . . . No sooner was I alone, than I ran up to the pictures, turned them round one after the other, and gazed at them with increasing amazement; I was under the impression they were mere childish daubs, but their colours were so bright, so individual and so gay that all desire to continue my walk left me. I wanted to see what kind of artists were capable of producing such amusing freaks; I gave up my first plan of reaching Hennebon that evening, engaged a room and enquired what time dinner was.

"Do you wish to dine by yourself or in the same room as the other gentlemen?" asked the maidservant.

"The other gentlemen" were the painters of the canvases; there were three of them and they soon made their appearance with their easels and paintboxes. Needless to say I had asked to dine when they did—that is, if they had no objection. They soon made it very obvious they were not in the least put out by my presence, by showing not the least concern for it. They were all three bare-footed, in brazen dishabille and with clarion voices. During the whole of dinner, I sat gasping with excitement, drinking in their words, longing to speak to them, to tell them who I was, to find out who they were and to tell the tall one with light eyes that the tune he was singing at the top of his voice and in which the others joined in chorus, was not Massenet, as he thought, but Bizet.

I met one of them later on at Mallarmé's—it was Gauguin. The other was Sérusier. I failed to identify the third—Filiger, I think.

I spent that autumn and winter doing some trifling work for Dietz, paying visits, talking to Pierre Louis, and making plans for a review over which we spent our impatient ardour. In the spring, I felt the moment had come; but in order to write my book, I had to have solitude. I found some temporary lodgings in a little hotel on the tiny lake of Pierrefonds. But before two days had gone by, Pierre Louis unearthed me and I was obliged to go further afield. I started for Grenoble and searched the neighbourhood from Uriage to Saint Pierre de Chartreuse, and from Allevard to—I have forgotten where; most of the hotels were still shut, the châlets were let, and I was beginning to despair when I discovered, near Annecy and almost on the banks of the lake at Menthon, a charming cottage, surrounded with orchards, the owner of which agreed to let me two rooms by the month. I arranged the larger one as a study and sent to Annecy for a piano, feeling it impossible to live without music. I took my meals in a kind of summer restaurant on the borders of the lake, where, thanks to the earliness of the season, I was the only guest for a whole month. Monsieur Taine lived near by. I had just discovered his *Philosophie de l'Art* and his *Littérature Anglaise;* but I refrained from going to see him, partly from shyness, and partly for fear of being distracted from my work. In the complete solitude in which I lived, I succeeded in raising my fervour to white heat and in maintaining myself in the state of ecstatic inspiration which I considered the only fitting one in which to write.

When I open my *Cahiers d'André Walter* to-day, their inspired tone exasperates me. I was fond at that time of using words that leave the imagination full license, such as *indefinite, infinite, inexpressible;* I called them in to my assistance just as Albert had recourse to mists to hide those parts of his model he found a difficulty in drawing. The fact that words of this kind abound in German made me consider it a particularly poetical language. I did not realise till much later that the distinctive characteristic of the French language is its striving after precision. Except for the light the *Cahiers* cast on the uneasy mysticism of my youth, there are very few passages of this book I should wish to preserve. And yet at the time I wrote it, I thought this book one of the most important in the world, and that I was depicting a psychological crisis of the most general and momentous interest; how could I have realised in those days why it was a personal one of my own? My Puritan upbringing had taught me to make a monster of the flesh; how could I have realised in those days that my own nature shrank from the most generally admitted solution quite as much as my puritanism censured it? And yet, as I was obliged to acknowledge, the state of chastity was an insidious and precarious one; as every other relief was denied me, I fell again into the vice of my early childhood and every time I fell, I despaired afresh. With a great deal of love, music, metaphysics and poetry, this was the subject of my book.

I have already said that I saw nothing beyond it; it was not only my first book, it was my *Summa;* with it, I thought, my life must be completed and concluded. But yet at moments, my soul freed itself with an exultant bound from the moribund weight it had too long dragged behind it, and leaving my hero to founder in his madness, caught glimpses of dazzling possibilities. I imagined a series of *Lay Sermons*, in the style of Father Grétry's *Sources*, in which, after an immense détour right round the world, I should lead the most recalcitrant souls back to the God of the Gospels (who was not quite what people usually imagined, as I should demonstrate in a sequel, which would be more purely religious). I also planned a tale, inspired by Anna's death, which was to be called *The Essay of Holy Dying*, and which afterwards became the *Porte Étroite*. Finally, I began to have a suspicion that the world was vast and that I knew nothing of it.

I remember a long walk I took one day beyond the further end of the lake; I was both exalted and exasperated by my solitude; the longing of my heart, as I strode quickly along (so quickly that I seemed to myself to be flying—I was really almost running) was so vehement that I called aloud for a comrade whose passionate enthusiasm should be twin brother to mine, and I told him what I felt, and spoke to him aloud, and broke into sobs because he was not with me. I decided that Paul Laurens should be this comrade (though at the time I scarcely knew him, for what I have said about him and my introduction to his father's studio must be referred to a later date), and foresaw in an extraordinary flash that we should one day set off alone together to follow the call of the road.

When, towards the end of summer, I returned to Paris, my book was finished. Albert, to whom I immediately read it, was dismayed by its immoderate piety and the abundance of scriptural quotations. How abundant they were may be judged from what still remains of them after I had followed his advice and deleted two thirds . . . Then I read it to Pierre Louis. It had been agreed that each of us was to leave a blank page in his first book for his friend to fill in; it was a similar courtesy that made Aladdin leave his father-in-law the task of decorating one of the balconies of his palace. The story tells us that the father-in-law never succeeded in making the balcony match the rest of the building; and in the same way, we two were equally incapable, I of writing one of his sonnets, or he of writing a page of my *Cahiers*. But in order not to give up the idea altogether, Louis proposed to write a sort of introduction which would give the book a really posthumous appearance.[1]

At that time, the papers were full of pressing appeals to the youth of the day. My book, I thought, was an answer to Paul Desjardins' *Devoir Présent*. An article by Melchoir de Vogüé, addressed "to young men of twenty," convinced me the world was awaiting me. Yes, my book, I thought, was the answer to such a great and present need, to such a definite demand of the public's, that I was surprised someone else did not think of writing and bringing it out before me. I was afraid of appearing too late and fumed against Dumoulin, the printer, to whom I had long since returned the final proofs, and who would not deliver the volume. The truth was, as I learnt later, that my book had put him in a very embarrassing situation. Dumoulin, who had been recommended to me as one of the best printers in Paris, was extremely Catholic and orthodox in his opinions, and anxious to appear so; he had accepted this piece of work without having looked at the text; and now rumours reached him that the book smacked of heresy. He hesitated for some time and then, for fear of compromising himself, borrowed the signature of a brother printer.

This limited edition was to be very carefully got up and was intended to be the first; but I was at the same time preparing a cheaper one in order to satisfy the demand of the general public, which I imagined would be considerable. But Dumoulin's scruples and his negotiations with the obliging brother printer had lasted so long that, in spite of all my precautions, I could not prevent the cheap edition from coming out first.

I was dismayed by the number of misprints it contained,

[1] The short preface, signed P. C. (the initials of Louis' first pseudonym, Pierre Chrysis) only appeared in Perrin's edition.

and was obliged to admit besides, that the sale amounted to next to nothing, so that as soon as the smaller edition was ready I made up my mind to have the other pulped. I took it to the sacrifice myself, after having collected it from the binder's almost entire—minus, that is, about seventy press copies—and was delighted to receive a little money in exchange. It was paid for by weight. But all this is of no interest except for bibliophiles . . .

Yes, its success was nil. But I am so constituted that I took pleasure in my very disappointment. There lies at the bottom of every failure a lesson for him that hath ears, and I heard it. I instantly gave up wishing for a triumph that had slipped from my grasp; or at any rate, I began to wish for it in a different form. I became convinced that the importance of applause lies in its quality and not in its quantity.

Some talk I had at this time with Albert hastened me in a resolve very congenial to my nature, and made me adopt an attitude which has since been severely criticised—that of holding aloof from success. Perhaps the moment has now come for me to explain it.

I have no wish to make myself out more virtuous than I am: I have passionately desired fame; but I soon came to the conclusion that success in its usual manifestations is only an adulterated imitation of it. I like to be liked on good grounds, and if I feel the praise vouchsafed me is the result of a misunderstanding, it gives me pain. I can find no satisfaction in trumped up favours. What pleasure can there be in compliments made to order, or dictated by reasons of interest, social connections, or even friendship? The mere idea that I am being praised out of gratitude or in order to gain my suffrage or disarm my criticism, immediately deprives the praise of all value; I want none of it. What I care for most of all is to know what my work is really worth, and I have no use for laurels that have every prospect of soon fading.

My change of front was sudden and complete; there was certainly some pique in it; but the pique did not last long, and, if it was the original motive of my attitude, had no share in its maintenance. This attitude, as I soon realised, though it may have been taken for a pose, tallied so exactly with my character, I felt myself so much at home in it, that I never attempted to change it.

I had had a mortifying number of copies of my first book printed; for the future, I would print only just enough—and even less than enough. I intended henceforth to sift my readers: I intended, encouraged by Albert, to do without blazoning; I intended . . . But I think there was a good deal of amusement and curiosity in my case: I intended to run a chance no one had ever run before. I had enough to live on, thank Heaven, and could snap my fingers at the idea of gain; if my work is worth anything, I said to myself, it will last; I can wait.

I was strengthened in my determination to baffle my critics, and even my readers, by a kind of natural moroseness, and by that diversity in my moods which makes me, the moment I am delivered of one book, fly to the opposite extremity of myself (for the sake of equilibrium too) and write another which will be the least likely to please any readers that have been attracted by the former.

"You will never get me to believe," cried my old cousin, the Baronne de Feuchères, (what! haven't I mentioned her yet?) "you will never get me to believe that if once you succeed in a style, you won't stick to it."

But that was just it; I had rather not succeed than stick to one style. Even if it leads to honour and glory, I detest following a road already laid out. I like chance, adventure, the unknown; I like not to be where I am expected to be—for it allows me to be where I please and to be left in peace there. What I prize above all other things is to be able to think in freedom.

One evening, after the publication of the *Cahiers*, as Adolphe Retté was besmearing me with his gross compliments, I felt irresistibly impelled to cut them short (for in all I do there is a great deal more instinct than deliberation—I cannot act in any other way) and I suddenly got up and left. This happened in the Café Vachette, or the Café de la Source, where I had gone with Louis.

"If that's the way you take compliments," said Louis when we next met, "you won't get any."

And yet I like compliments; but clumsy ones exasperate me; if I am not flattered in the right place, I become as prickly as a hedgehog; and rather than be stupidly praised, I prefer not be praised at all. I am easily inclined too to believe that people exaggerate; an incurable modesty shows me at once in what I have failed; I know where I fall short and where the weak point lies; and as I fear nothing so much as self-deception and consider conceit fatal to intellectual development, I take unremitting care to *under* rather than *over* estimate my value, and put all my pride in humbling myself. But it would be a mistake to think all this is studied; the movement I am analysing is spontaneous. If the springs are complicated, how can I help it? I do not court complication—it is within me. No act in which I fail to recognise all the contradictions that inhabit me seems to me a real act of mine.

Now that I re-read all this, I am dissatisfied with it. I ought to put forward an extreme fear of fatigue as one of the explanations of my shyness of society and my abrupt withdrawals. The minute I cannot be perfectly natural in it, I find all company exhausting.

The cousin I have just spoken of was née Gide and was the widow of the General Feuchères who has given his name to a street in Nîmes. In the days of my youth, she lived in the Rue de Bellechasse on the second floor of a fine private house. There was a verandah at the front door, and as you were crossing the courtyard to get to it, the concierge rang twice on an invisible bell to give warning of your arrival, so that when you got upstairs, you found the door open and a tall footman standing behind it ready to show you in. This bell gave exactly the same crystalline sound as a glass cheese-cover which was only used at home on occasions when there were "people" to dinner; and so everything connected with my cousin Feuchères was associated with ideas of luxury and ceremony.

When I was quite a child, she used to receive my mother and me in a small room furnished with mahogany furniture. I remember in particular a large bureau, on which I kept my eyes fixed for I knew that at a given moment my cousin would take out of it a box of preserved fruit and hand it round, just as oranges and chocolates are handed round in the entr'actes at the theatre. It was an agreeable interruption to the visit, which seemed to me interminably long; for my cousin used to take advantage of my mother's unwearying patience to pour out the tiresome story of her grievances against her daughter, or her banker, or her lawyer, or her clergyman; she was on bad terms with all and sundry. She took great care, therefore, not to hand round the preserved fruit too soon, but chose the moment when her visitors' patience showed signs of failing. Then she lifted her skirt, took out a bunch of keys from the pocket of her silk petticoat, selected one that opened the drawer of a what-not that stood near her, found another key in this drawer, which opened the drawer of the bureau, and finally pulled out the box of preserved fruit together with a bundle of papers to read to my mother. The box was nearly empty, so that you only dared help yourself very discreetly; my mother abstained altogether; and as one day I asked her why:

"Well, my dear," she said, "your cousin didn't exactly press me."

After I had taken my fruit, cousin Feuchères put the box back in the bureau again, and the second act of the visit began. The papers she produced in this way I myself had to listen to a few years later, when I was considered sufficiently ripe of understanding. These papers were not only letters addressed to herself and duplicates of her answers, but also accounts of conversations she had noted down, recording not so much the other person's words as her own replies, which were of extreme nobility, and remarkable at once for lapidary terseness and infinite eloquence: I have a suspicion that, like Livy, she wrote what she would have liked to say rather than what she actually said, and that that was why she wrote it.

"So this is what I answered," she began in a theatrical voice—and then you knew you were in for it.

"Come, to-day he has been a good child; he is getting a big boy now," she said one afternoon as we were taking leave. "He didn't once ask when it would be time to go. *He* is beginning to take an interest in it all too."

And the time came when I was considered old enough to visit her without my mother. There was no more question of preserved fruit. I was of an age to be confided in; and I felt considerably flattered when my cousin took out her papers for me.

It was in the Avenue d'Antin (she had changed houses), in a magnificent apartment of which she occupied barely more than one room, for she had her meals in her bedroom. On

225

the way to it one caught a glimpse, by peering through some glass doors, of two grand drawing-rooms where the shutters were kept closed. One day she took me into one of them to show me a great portrait by Mignard, which she intended "to leave to the Louvre." She was constantly thinking how she could best disinherit her daughter, the Comtesse de Blanzey, and I think there were one or two people by no means unwilling to help her. Her stories were not uninteresting, but spoilt by being too extravagant. I remember in particular an account of an interview she had had with Pastor Bersier; she was telling him some story or other of an attempt to poison her, made, so she alleged, by her daughter:

"But it's fit for the stage!" he had exclaimed.

"No sir," had been her answer, "for the Assizes!"

She repeated these words in a tragic voice, drawing herself up as she sat in her armchair. It was a big armchair, with ear-pieces. She hardly ever left it; I can see her now. Her chalk-white face was surrounded by the coils of a jet-black wig, on the top of which sat a lace cap. She was dressed in a puce-coloured silk dress which rustled every time she moved; her long hands, covered with black mittens, were almost hidden in wide pleated ruffles. She liked crossing her legs in such a way as to show a small foot; it was shod in stuff the same colour as her dress and peeped out from the lace edging of her drawers, which reached almost to the bottom of her skirt. Her other foot was snugly tucked away into a kind of footmuff placed in front of her.

She was nearly a hundred when she died and more than ninety when she told me these stories.

X

Directly after the publication of my *Cahiers*, I entered
upon the most confused period of my life—a *selva oscura*,
like Dante's—from which I only succeeded in disengaging
myself when I left for Africa with Paul Laurens. A period of
dissipated energies and distracted thoughts . . . I should be
only too glad to skip it altogether, if I did not hope that the
contrast of its darkness would shed some light upon what follows; just as I find some explanation and some excuse for my
dissipation in the state of moral tension in which I had been
kept by the long effort of elaborating my *Cahiers*. If even
the simplest statement I make immediately arouses in me a
desire to assert and maintain the contrary, it may be easily
imagined what a reaction the exaggeration of such a book
was bound to provoke. I seemed to have got rid of the dis-
quietude I had painted by the very act of painting it; my
mind for a time now could find no room for anything but
trivialities, or be guided by anything but the least spiritual,
the absurdest vanity.

I had not been able to find out what Emmanuèle thought
of my book; all that she let me know was that she rejected the
offer that followed it. I declared that I would not consider
her refusal as final, that I was prepared to wait, that nothing
would make me give her up. Nevertheless I ceased for a while
writing her letters which she had ceased to answer. This silence, this vacancy of my heart made me feel I had been cut
adrift, but friendship came in time to fill the hours and take
the place left empty by love.

I continued seeing Pierre Louis almost every day. He lived
at that time with his brother at the end of the Rue Vineuse,
on the second floor of a low corner house which looks on to
the little Square Franklin. The view from his study window

stretched as far as the Trocadéro, and even farther. But we had no eyes for the outside world, occupied as we were with ourselves, our plans and dreams. Pierre Louis, during the year he had been at the Lycée Janson, had struck up a friendship with three of his schoolfellows, of whom two, Drouin and Quillot, soon became my intimate friends. My relations with Franc Nohain, the third, though always pleasant, were only intermittent.

I find it hard to explain how it is I have no wish to speak in these memoirs of friendships which nevertheless took up so great a place in my life. Perhaps it is simply the fear of being led on to say too much. It was they who made me feel the truth of that saying of Nietzsche's that every artist has at his disposal not only his own intelligence but his friends' too. My friends penetrated further than I into many regions of the mind where I was unable to follow them and where they served me as prospectors. If I went part of the way with them out of sympathy, I myself instinctively took care not to specialise; so that there was not one of my friends whom I did not recognise as my superior in his own domain; but their intelligence was no doubt more circumscribed than mine; and while I understood less than each of them separately what he understood best, I felt as though I understood all of them together, and from my central standpoint, where all their roads converged, could take a circling glance down each of them in turn towards the various prospects they opened out to me.

And this would be nothing but a commonplace—for every mind makes itself a centre, and one always thinks the world is grouped about oneself—if I had not prided myself on becoming the best friend of each of my friends. I could not bear to think that any of them had a more intimate confidant than myself, and to all of them I offered my whole self, just as from each one I exacted a like gift. I should have considered the least reserve shocking and impious; and when some years later, after I had come into my mother's money, I was asked to help Quillot, whose business was on the verge of bankruptcy, I did it without reservation and without enquiry; I thought it only natural to give him everything he asked for and would have given him still more without even troubling to find out whether by so doing I was really rendering him a service; so that to-day I wonder whether it was not perhaps the action itself that attracted me and whether what I cared for was not rather friendship than my friend. My call was an almost mystic one, and Pierre Louis, who was clear-sighted enough, used to laugh at me. One afternoon, when I had come punctually to a rendezvous he had given me, he hid in a shop in the Rue Saint-Sulpice and watched me for an hour on end—the wretch!—while I paced up and down in the rain near the fountain, waiting for him, though all the time I had a presentiment he did not mean to come. Finally, I admired my friends more than I did myself; I could not imagine better ones. The kind of faith I had in my predestination as a poet made me welcome whatever happened to me and look at everything I met upon my path as if it had been sent providentially and had been singled out by some divine choice on purpose to win me over, assist and perfect me. I still retain something of this disposition, and in the worst adversities instinctively look round for what may amuse or instruct me. I even push the *amor fati* so far that I cannot bring myself to believe that any other event, any other issue would have suited me better. Not only do I consider whatever is is good, I consider it best.

And yet, as I meditate over those bygone days, I think how much I should have profited by the friendship of a naturalist. Had I come across one at that time, my taste for natural science was so keen that I should have thrown over literature tened to follow his lead. Or if I had met the circle of which Mallarmé was the centre and into which I had been introduced by Pierre Louis, they all piqued themselves on being musical; but I used to think that what Mallarmé himself, and his circle too, really looked for in music was still literature. Wagner was their god. They wreathed him with explanations and commentaries. Louis had a way of enjoining me to admire such and such an exclamation or interjection which made me take a loathing to all "expressive" music. I fell back all the more passionately upon what I called "pure" music—that is to say, music that does not claim to mean anything; and in my reaction against Wagnerian polyphony, I preferred—I still prefer—a quartet to an orchestra, a sonata to a symphony. But I was already occupied to excess with music; my style was unctuous with it . . . No, the friend I needed was perhaps someone who would have taught me to be interested in other people, and taken me out of myself—a novelist. But in those days, I had no eyes but for the soul, no taste but for poetry. It is true that I was indignant when I heard Pierre call Guez de Balzac "Balzac the Great," out of scorn for the author of the *Comédie Humaine*; but nevertheless he was in the right when he told me to put questions of form in the forefront of my preoccupations, and I am grateful to him for this advice.

I really think that if it had not been for Pierre Louis, I should have continued living in solitude like a savage; not that I had no desire to go into literary society, and find friends there, but an invincible shyness held me back, and the fear which still paralyses me of boring or being in the way of the people I feel most drawn to. Pierre, more spontaneous than I, more enterprising, certainly cleverer too and with a more mature talent, had made an offering of his first poems to those among

230

our elders whom we condescended to admire. At his instance, I resolved to take my book to Hérédia.

"I have spoken to him about you," repeated Louis; "he is expecting you."

Hérédia had not yet brought out his sonnets in book form; the *Revue des Deux Mondes* had printed a few of them; Jules Lemaître had quoted others; the greater number were still unpublished, preserved jealously in our memories as a precious deposit and thought all the more splendid because they were unknown to the vulgar. My heart beat, as for the first time I rang the bell at the door of his apartment in the Rue Balzac.

I was dismayed at first to find how little Hérédia resembled my idea of a poet. There was no silence in him, no mystery; his stammering, trumpeting voice had no modulations. He was a little man, with a fairly good figure, though he was rather short and roundabout; but he walked with an air and a strut, his chest out, his waist in, and made his heels ring on the ground at every step. His beard was cut square and his hair *en brosse*, and he wore eyeglasses when reading, over which, or rather round which, he cast a curiously dim, misty glance, without a gleam of malice in it. Being unhampered by excessive thought, he was able to reel out the first thing that came into his head, which made his conversation delightfully racy. He was interested almost exclusively in the outside world and in art; what I mean is that in the domain of abstract speculation he was completely at sea, and the only thing he grasped about other people was their behaviour. But he was widely read, and as he was unaware of his deficiencies, he never felt at a loss. He was more of an artist than a poet, or rather, more of an artisan than either. I was terribly disappointed at first; then I began to ask myself whether my disappointment did not come from a false conception of art and poetry, and whether simple perfection of workmanship was not a more valuable thing than I had hitherto supposed. His welcome was so warm that it took one some time to see that his mind was a little less open than his arms; but his devotion to literature was so great that even if there were things he could not understand by means of the spirit, I think he still managed to grasp them by means of the letter, and I do not remember ever to have heard him say anything silly.

Hérédia was at home every Saturday afternoon. At four o'clock his smoking-room began to fill up with a stream of diplomats, journalists, poets, and I should have died of shyness if Pierre Louis had not been there. The ladies of the family also received on the same day; the habitués occasionally passed from the smoking-room into the drawing-room or vice versa; as the door opened for a moment one heard a chirping and piping of voices and laughter; but the fear of being caught sight of by Madame Hérédia or one of her daughters, to whom I had been introduced, and to whom I knew I ought to have paid my respects oftener, kept me rooted at the other end of the smoking-room, hidden in the smoke of cigars and cigarettes as in an Olympian cloud.

Henri de Régnier, Ferdinand Hérold, Pierre Quillard, Bernard Lazare, André Fontainas, Pierre Louis, Robert de Bonnières, André de Guerne never missed a Saturday. I met the six first again at Mallarmé's on Tuesday evenings. Louis and I were the youngest of them all.

At Mallarmé's the habitués were more especially poets; or sometimes painters (I am thinking of Gauguin and Whistler). I have described the little room in the Rue de Rome—partly drawing-room and partly dining-room—in another book; our age has grown too noisy for it to be easy nowadays to imagine the calm and almost religious atmosphere of the place. Mallarmé certainly prepared his talk beforehand; and it was often not very different from the most carefully written of his *Divagations;* but he spoke with such art, there was so little of the professorial in his tone, that every fresh proposition he brought out seemed like an entirely new idea which he had only just that moment hit on, and which he was not so much asserting as submitting to your judgment, interrogatively almost, with his forefinger raised—as much as to say: "Mightn't we also say . . . ?" or, "Perhaps . . ." and ending up almost every sentence with a "Don't you think so?" And no doubt it was on this account he had so much hold on some people's minds.

He often interrupted his "divagation" with an anecdote or a bon-mot; it was always told to perfection, with all the anxious feeling for elegance and preciosity, which made him so deliberately divorce his art from life.

Occasionally, when there were not too many people gathered round the little table, Madame Mallarmé would linger on at her needlework, with her daughter beside her. But the tobacco-smoke soon put them to flight; for in the middle of the round table at which we sat, was placed an enormous jar of tobacco, into which we all dipped, rolling ourselves endless cigarettes; Mallarmé himself smoked without stopping, but preferred a little clay pipe. At about eleven o'clock, Geneviève Mallarmé would come back with glasses of grog; for there was no servant in this very simple household, and the Master himself went to answer the door whenever the bell rang.

I will now sketch a few of the young men who flocked about these two leaders, and with whom I came to be on terms of good fellowship. In those days, instead of trusting to the guidance of our own minds, we seemed to be more or less consciously obeying a vague kind of *mot d'ordre.* The movement in progress was a reaction against realism, with an ac-

233

companying backwash against the Parnassian school as well. Supported by Schopenhauer, to whom I could not understand that some people should prefer Hegel, I considered everything that was not *absolute*—that is to say, the whole prismatic diversity of life—*contingent* (this was the fashionable word). It was very much the same with every one of my companions. But our error did not lie in trying to extract some beauty and some truth of a general order out of the inextricable medley presented at that time by *realism*, but rather in deliberately turning our backs upon reality. I personally was saved by a greedy appetite . . . But I must return to my companions.

Henri de Régnier was certainly the most conspicuous of them all. His appearance was already remarkable. He concealed under a charming, though slightly supercilious, cordiality of manner, an unfailing, if discreet sense of his own superiority. Tall, thin and loose-limbed, he managed to make his very awkwardness graceful. At first sight of him, one was struck by the height of his forehead and the length of his chin, his face and his fine hands, which he was always putting up to twist his long, light-brown, drooping moustache. A single eye-glass completed the picture. Leconte de Lisle's monocle had set the fashion and several young gentlemen in our set wore one. At Hérédia's and Mallarmé's, Régnier, out of deference, scarcely opened his mouth; that is to say, he would cleverly and lightly drop into the conversation (I am speaking of Mallarmé's) no more than the airy word or two that was just enough to keep the ball rolling. But in tête-à-têtes his talk was exquisite. Not a fortnight passed without my receiving some such note as this from him: "If you have nothing better to do, come and see me to-morrow evening." I am not sure that nowadays I should take so much pleasure in those evenings, but at the time I liked nothing better. I cannot remember that we either of us talked much; and in those days I had not begun to smoke; but there was something indolent in his manner, an odd charm in his voice (it was less musical than Mallarmé's, more sonorous, with a tendency to become incisive as soon as it was raised) a way of presenting his opinions—I dare not call them thoughts, for thoughts were greatly looked down upon—in the most fantastic and disconcerting guise, a kind of mischievous amusement in people and things . . . well! whatever it may have been, the time passed quickly and when midnight struck, I was sorry to leave.

My readers will understand that in making these portraits, I have collected and put together observations scattered over a period of ten years and more. And it was not till a good deal later . . . I remember an evening—Régnier seemed preoccupied; he dropped his monocle; his eyes had a far-away look.

"What's the matter, my dear fellow?" I said at last.

"Oh," he answered with a shrug of his shoulders and in a voice at once solemn and farcical, "I'm preparing to double the cape of my thirtieth birthday."

I there and then thought him very old. What a long time ago it is!

Francis Vielé-Griffin was at that time his most intimate friend. People used often to mention their names together and even to confuse their poetry; for a long time the only poetry which in the public's eyes allowed of any difference was regular verse; all *vers libres* were alike. It is the same thing whenever a new technique is introduced—either in music or painting or poetry. And yet no more divergent beings than these two can be imagined; their friendship, like Louis' and mine, was based on a misconception. Nothing could be franker, more honest, more spontaneous than Griffin; far be it from me to imply that Régnier was the reverse, cunning, false or deceitful; no indeed! But careful and elaborate cultivation had so taken control of his tenderest, best, most natural feelings, and had given them such polish and gloss and pliability, that in the end he seemed never to feel anything by surprise, or to experience any emotion he was not already master of and had not determined beforehand to experience. There are people, some of whom I have known, who strive to attain this state, which they consider the highest of all; I have often thought they reached it a little too easily, too quickly, and always to their detriment; in other words, I think this ideal is only good for those who strive to attain it unsuccessfully. Certainly Griffin made no such attempt. He expressed himself humorously, in whimsical sallies, and though he had the sincerest love for our country and the sweet speech of France, there was something raw and unruly in his bearing, which had in it an unmistakable tang of the New World. A slight burr in his voice, almost like a Burgundian accent (his charming compatriot Stuart Merrill had the same), gave singular spiciness to his simplest words; if only he had not been too fond of paradox, his way of talking would have been delightfully genial. He was extraordinarily pugnacious by nature; out of generosity, a great setter to right of wrongs; at heart something of a Puritan; he could not away with the extreme, often affected, license of the literary circles he frequented. He would run atilt against French alexandrines, Catulle Mendès, latter-day morals, the present age and so on, and used often to wind up a story with these words, accompanied by a hearty laugh—for he was amused even by his own indignation:

"No, but, really, Gide, what are we coming to?"

He had a very round, very open face, and a forehead that seemed to run back into the nape of his neck; he tried, however, to conceal his premature baldness by training a flat lock of hair across his head from one temple to the other; for, in spite of his free and easy manners, he had a great notion of decorum. His complexion was high-coloured, his eyes a forget-me-not blue (some people who knew him very well assure me his eyes were hazel, but I cannot think of them as anything but forget-me-not blue). He was obviously very strong, though he had a sausage-like appearance in his little black coats; his trousers always looked too tight and his arms ended off too soon in hands that were rather wide than long. It was said of him that one evening after a dinner-party, he had made a bet that he would jump over the dining-room table with his feet together, and this he had done without the smallest breakage. Such was the legend; but it is true that if anyone expressed any desire for it, he would jump over the chairs in a drawing-room without taking a run—not so bad for a poet.

He was the first person to write to me about the *Cahiers d'André Walter*. I kept it in mind and tried to show I was grateful. I should have liked to talk to him better, but his flow of paradox disconcerted me terribly; I found it impossible to compete with him, and consequently felt like a fool, while he was soon left to do all the talking himself; for he was one of those people who can only talk well if they don't listen to you. It has sometimes happened to me to go and see him with some definite thing I wanted to say, and to come away without having been able to get in three words.

He had another little failing which made my relations with him slightly awkward, and that was a touchiness which was always on the lookout for offence but not always very reasonable. As he was in constant fear that people were going to slight him, I was in constant anxiety not to appear slighting. As often as not this preoccupation landed him in some outrageous blunder, which covered him with confusion, until his intrinsic good nature got the better of it; a hearty laugh then swept away all unpleasantness and one found oneself looking once more into the crystal clearness of his eyes. One example will show what I mean better than any explanations. (I repeat that I am telescoping here the recollections of over ten years.)

I had succeeded Léon Blum as literary critic on the staff of the *Revue Blanche;* my function was to review the prose books, while Gustave Kahn did the verse. I must here recall that in some circles Gustave Kahn passed as "the inventor of the *vers libre*"; this was a much debated point at the time and caused great heart-burning to more than one, Griffin amongst others, who maintained that the *vers libre* would have done just as well without Kahn, that it had come into the world by itself, or at any rate, that it had some other father . . . When the *Légende Ailée de Wieland* came out, Griffin sent it to me, as he did his other books. I was sorry that it was not in my province to review it and, thinking no harm, I slipped an unfortunate alexandrine into my letter of thanks:

"Would I might poach on Gustave Kahn's domains."

No doubt Griffin thought I was alluding to the domain of *vers libres* as belonging to Kahn, and his blood boiled; at any rate, a day or two later, I received the following note which stupefied me with amazement:

February 20th, 1900

"Dear André Gide
I have been thinking over your letter for the last forty-eight hours.
I must ask you to explain by return of post what was your meaning and purpose in using the strange words:

238

> *'Would I might poach on Gustave Kahn's domains!'*
> *Awaiting your answer,*
> *I have the honour to be*
> *Your obedient servant etc. . ."*

We were both of us too genuinely well-intentioned and our liking for each other was too sincere for this misunderstanding to last long.

This impulsiveness of Griffin's, which was one sign of the generosity of his character, led me into an error, serious in itself and in its consequences. I am referring to the disparaging article I wrote on Régnier's book, *La Double Maîtresse*. I rather foolishly followed Griffin in this, and I afterwards heartily regretted it. Griffin thought that Régnier was going on a wrong tack in this book. A little while before, in the *Trèfle Blanc*, he had shown another side of himself, a fresher, more Arcadian side, and one much more akin to Griffin. Griffin was not in the least bookish, and perhaps his best contribution to letters was the breath of open air and freedom he brought with him—a kind of artless spontaneity, a kind of freshness which, it must be confessed, our literature at that time was greatly in need of. *La Double Maîtresse*, for all its grace, was, he thought, a falling-off; exquisite as it was, he saw nothing in it but literature and the affectation of depravity; he worked on me so much that he persuaded me I should be doing French letters and Régnier himself a notable service by bringing him back to the fold (as if such a thing were possible!) and by frankly pointing out his backsliding. Let me make myself clear: I have no wish to deny, or even to lessen my responsibility for the severe article I wrote; but I have seldom had occasion to regret more not having followed my natural taste, or been more sorry that I indulged my desire to react against, to resist my inclinations (though that is natural to me too),

239

instead of simply giving way to them. Needless to say Régnier continued to follow his to the delight of his readers; and the only effect of my article was that the excellent terms we had been on till then were considerably cooled. For the rest, even without the article, we should no doubt have soon found other reasons for disagreeing; our tastes were too different.

Hérold was certainly one of the most assiduous in visiting Mallarmé, Hérédia, Bonnières, Judith Gautier and Leconte de Lisle. I can speak of the two latter only by hearsay, as I did not visit them at all, and Bonnières very rarely; but I know that wherever I did visit, I was sure to meet Ferdinand Hérold. He never left you without making a fresh appointment, and the wonder is he had any time left for reading or writing; but as a matter of fact, he wrote a great deal and had read everything. He had an inexhaustible fund of information on all the subjects our passions played with in those days: the kind of sonnet called *bigorne*,[1] for instance, or the rôle of the saxophone in the orchestra—on such things as these he could discourse for miles on end; for at whatever hour you left Mallarmé's house, or a party, or the theatre, he always walked home with you. My mother had a special liking for him on this account, for she began to be anxious when she knew I was out alone later than twelve o'clock at night, and she counted on Hérold's not abandoning me till I reached my own door. He did his best to give his jolly baby-like face a masculine air by means of an enormous beard; he was the best of good fellows and the most faithful of friends; always at hand when he was wanted, and very often when he was not. It seemed as if he had to wait for other people to be there in order to exist himself. Ferdinand Hérold had held his head a little higher and stuck his beard out a little further ever since the publication of his article on—or rather against—

[1] A freak sonnet, beginning and ending with a tercet.

Respect, in which he proved that, contrary to Solomon's opinion, Wisdom only begins when the fear of God ceases. And as all respect, whether of parents, customs, authorities or what not necessitates some degree of blindness, it is only by ridding himself of respect that a man can hope to progress towards the light. The anti-militarism of Quillard, Lazare and Hérold (and not theirs alone) was pushed to the point of regarding every sort of uniform with horror. Uniform, according to them, was equivalent to domestic livery and was an outrage against personal dignity. I should be sorry to disoblige them by talking of their internationalism, for after all perhaps I am doing them wrong in supposing they held these opinions in the past, but the fact is that as they were my own, I was certainly under the impression that they shared them. And moreover, I could not conceive that anyone who had attained a certain degree of intelligence and education could hold any others. It is easy to understand that in these circumstances I looked upon military service as an unbearable calamity, rightly to be avoided, if possible, by any means short of desertion.

Hérold was sometimes flanked by his brother-in-law, an enormous Belgian called Fontainas, who was, I expect, the best and kindest of men—not stupid either—as far as one could judge from his silence. He seemed to have discovered that the best way never to say anything foolish was never to say anything at all.

What shall I say of Count Robert de Bonnières? His young wife had a reputation for beauty which had a good deal to do with the warmth of the reception he everywhere met with. I think he had been a journalist. At the time I am speaking of he had just published a novel called *Le Petit Margemont*. I never read it, but the habitués of Hérédia's salon were pleased to say that its qualities were those of the best French tradi-

241

tion. He was then working at a volume of short stories in octosyllabic verse, and was addicted to reading them aloud. He was fairly good-natured, I think, but hot-tempered, and one day at Hérédia's, where he had been reading aloud his latest effort, I was very near stirring up a storm . . . It was the story, I remember, of a haughty beauty who accidentally, or deliberately, drops her glove; the gallant knight she has scorned picks it up, in spite of some danger or other—I can't exactly remember what, but isn't there something of the kind in Schiller?—and then, when the lady relents, he, in his turn, passes haughtily on his way;

"Passe aussi son chemin, ma chère."

This was how the story ended. I, who was usually as silent as Fontainas himself, was suddenly seized by a spirit of extreme audacity:

"Aren't you afraid of the '*sse aussi son*'?" I asked.[1]

All the company looked at each other; and what saved me was that at first nobody understood. When what I meant dawned on them, there was a roar of laughter, and what could poor Bonnières do? I think he afterwards altered the line.

Bonnières was supposed to be very clever; this reputation gave him immense self-assurance. He had opinions upon everything under the sun, and they were impossible to shake, because he was never known to listen to anyone but himself. Heavens! how his peremptory tones used to irritate me, when he laid it down as a law that:

"It ought always to be possible to sum up an author's work in a single formula. The more easily this can be done, the

[1] The two words *aussi son* preceded by the last letters of *passe* make the unfortunate consonance *saucisson*, French for *sausage*.

more likely it is to survive. What can't be fitted into the formula is bound to perish."

One day, after a more than usually pressing invitation, I decided to go and see him, when, to my horror, he seized me by the buttonhole, and thrusting his face into mine, as was his way, asked me if I had got my formula yet? I drew back terrified, pretending not to understand; but he refused to let me go.

"Yes," he kept on, "supposing you wanted to sum up your future work in a single phrase, in a single word, what would that word be? Do you know? Can you say?"

"Of course!" I cried impatiently.

"Well then, what is it? Come on! Out with it! Everything depends on that!"

And the absurd thing was that I really had my formula, and it was simply a sensitive reluctance on my part that made me hesitate to expose the pure secret of my life to this ridiculous old ass. At last, goaded to desperation and really shaking with rage, I stuttered out in a voice of white-hot fury:

"We must all play our parts."

He looked at me in stupefaction, and at last let go my buttonhole.

"All right, my dear boy!" he cried (he was much older than I); "All right! Play away!"

I should really appear too foolish, if I did not give some explanation of my "formula." It was my dominating thought at the time and all the more imperious from being my latest love. The moral rule, according to which I had hitherto lived, had of late begun to give place to what I felt, vaguely as yet, was a richer, more varied, more coloured vision of life. It was beginning to dawn on me that duty was perhaps not the same for everyone, and that possibly even God himself might loathe a uniformity to which all nature was in contradiction, but towards which, it seemed to me, the Christian ideal tended when setting out to subdue nature. I now admitted only individual moralities, with imperatives that were sometimes opposed. I was convinced that everyone—or at least every one of the elect—had a part to play in the world which was his very own and unlike any other; so that every effort to submit to a common rule became in my eyes treachery; yes, treachery; and I likened it to the sin against the Holy Ghost "which shall not be forgiven," the sin by which the individual loses his exact, irreplaceable significance, the "savour" which cannot be given back to him. I had attached to the journal I kept at that time the following Latin sentence, to serve as motto— I have forgotten where I found it:

"Proprium opus humani generis totaliter accepti est actuare semper totam potentiam intellectus possibilis."

The truth was I was intoxicated by the diversity of life now first beginning to dawn on me, and by my own proper diversity . . .

But I had meant to keep to other people in this chapter. I return to my subject.

Bernard Lazare, whose real name was Lazare Bernard, was a Jew from Nîmes; he was not really short, but looked small and inexpressibly unpleasant. His face seemed all cheeks, his body all stomach, his legs all thighs. He cast a caustic glance at things and people through a single eye-glass and seemed to have a bitter contempt for everyone he did not admire. The most noble sentiments animated him; that is to say he was in a constant state of indignation against the caddishness and blackguardism of his contemporaries; but he seemed to be in need of this state of things and only to become conscious of his own existence by being in violent opposition, for as soon as his indignation waned, there was nothing left of him but a pale reflection, and he wrote the *Miroir des Légendes*.

Lazare's and Griffin's quarrelsome tempers ran in harness together in the *Entretiens politiques et littéraires*. This little review with its blood-red cover was, I must say, very well run, and I was extremely flattered at having my *Traité du Narcisse* printed in it. I have always been incredibly lacking in a quality that lies at the root of a great many audacious actions—the faculty, that is, of gauging my credit in other people's minds; I always underestimate it, and am not only incapable of making any claims, but feel so honoured by the smallest token of appreciation that I can scarcely hide my amazement—a weakness which, even at fifty years of age, I am only just beginning to get over.

Bernard Lazare frightened me; I vaguely felt there were puzzling possibilities in him which could have nothing to do with art; this feeling was no doubt not peculiar to me, and to some extent estranged, if not Quillard and Hérold, who were eventually swept into the same current of ideas, yet certainly Régnier, Louis and myself.

"Did you notice Régnier's tact the other day?" Louis asked me; "he was on the verge of forgetting himself and treating Lazare like a real pal. He was going to tap him on the knee, and only just remembered in time. Did you see how his hand stopped in mid-air?"

And when Lazare, at the time of the Dreyfus case, drew his sword with a flourish and played the important part the whole world heard of, we realised he had found his real line at last, and that up to that time he had been merely waiting in the outer courts of literature—as so many people do all their lives.

Albert Mockel, whom I have not yet mentioned, was the editor of a small but important Franco-Belgian review called *La Wallonie*. As each individual member of a school (and we were certainly that) gets his taste sharpened and refined by

245

rubbing up against the others, it was rare for any of us to commit an error of judgment; or at any rate, the error then was that of the whole group. But besides this collective taste, Mockel had the most refined artistic feeling of his own. He pushed refinement to the verge of tenuity; the rarefaction of his thought made you feel your own was coarse and vulgar.[1] His speech was so exquisitely subtle and full of such delicate allusions that in order to follow, one had as it were to run after him on the tips of one's toes. With his excessive honesty and scrupulosity, the conversation, more often than not, became a mere dizzy pursuit of definitions. A quarter of an hour of it left one as flattened out is if one had been under a steam-roller. And in the intervals he wrote his *Chantefable un peu naïve*.

Besides all these friends whom I often met at Hérédia's, Mallarmé's or elsewhere, there was another, a poor young fellow I used to see regularly. I can scarcely call him a friend, but I had a curious kind of affection for him. He was called André Walkenaer, and was the grandson of the learned author of an excellent life of La Fontaine; he was a sickly, weakly creature too intelligent not to realise the value of all that had been denied him; but nature had given him only the shrillest of voices and only just enough of it to bewail his lot. He had been through the Ecole des Chartes and was under-librarian in the Mazarine library. He was connected by marriage with my aunt Démarest, and it was in her house I first met him at dinner. I had not yet finished my *Cahiers d'André Walter*, that is to say, I was a little under twenty; André Walkenaer was a few months older. I was immediately flattered by the consideration and attention he showed me, and in order not to be outdone encouraged myself in the fancy that in many

[1] Mallarmé used to tell of a lady who was so extraordinarily distinguished that, 'When I say good morning to her, I always feel as if were saying *m—e*'.

246

particulars he had an extraordinary likeness to the imaginary hero of a book I had vaguely planned, which was to be called *L'Education Sentimentale*. It is true that Flaubert had written one with the same title; but mine fitted it much better. Walkenaer was naturally very much excited about the book in which his portrait was to figure. I asked him if he would agree to come and sit to me, as he would to a painter. We fixed a day. And so for three years on end, during the whole time I was in Paris, André Walkenaer came to my house every Wednesday from two o'clock to five—unless I went to his, and sometimes our sitting lasted till dinner-time. We talked unwearyingly, inexhaustibly; Proust's way of writing reminds me of the texture of our conversation more than anything else I can think of. We discussed everything under the sun, and no hair was too fine for us to split. Waste of time? I cannot think so: a certain subtlety of thought and style can hardly be attained without some practice in dialectics. As I have said, the poor fellow had very bad health; his constitution was so frail that he only avoided asthma by periodically breaking out into eczema; it was wretched to see his drawn features, and to hear him panting and groaning; he was aching too from a desire to write, and being utterly incapable, he went through the most frightful searchings of spirit. I listened as he spoke of his vain dreams and frustrated hopes, and though no doubt unable to console him, the interest I took in hearing him talk of his sufferings gave them perhaps a *raison d'être*.

He introduced me to another individual who was even more of a shadow than himself, and whose name I will not mention. X. was just substantial enough to flit through a salon, like a tailor's dummy in a suit of impeccable cut. When one went to a party with him, one was astonished not to see him hung bodily up on a hook in the cloak-room together with his coat. Once in the drawing-room, an extraordinary ghost of a piping voice welled up from under his long, silky, honey-coloured beard, and with exquisite suavity gave vent to a flow of incredibly inept platitudes. He began his life every day at teatime, going the rounds of his acquaintance, and playing the part of news-monger, go-between and listener. He would not rest until he had introduced me into some of the circles Walkenaer was also to be found in. Very fortunately, I had none of the qualities which would have enabled me to shine in society; in the drawing-rooms into which I misguidedly wandered, I must have looked like a strayed night-bird; my frock-coat, it is true, was well enough cut; and my long hair, my high collars, my drooping attitude attracted some attention; but my conversation must have been sadly disappointing, for my wits were so dull, or at any rate, so unready, that I was reduced to silence whenever I ought to have sparkled. At Madame Beulé's, at Madame Baignères' (who was by no means stupid), at the Vicomtesse de J.'s. ("Oh, Monsieur X . . .!" she would say, "do recite us Sully Prudhomme's *Vase Cassé*.")[1] She was always mangling names and titles in this way and used to speak of her admiration for the English painter John Burns (meaning, I suppose, Burne-Jones), I only put in an occasional terrified appearance.

At Princess Ouroussof's, it was more lively; at any rate, one was amused. There was no constraint, and the wilder the talk, the more satisfaction it gave. The princess, an opulent beauty dressed in Oriental costume, put everyone at ease by her affable volubility and by appearing to be so much amused at everything herself. The craziness of the talk was really almost fantastic and one wondered whether the hostess was

[1] The real title of this well known poem is *Le Vase brisé*.

quite aware of some of the enormities that were uttered; but a kind of jolly cordiality, which she unfailingly kept, discouraged irony. In the middle of a grand dinner-party, as the footman in livery was handing round some delicious dish, she would call out in her deep contralto voice:

"How's your swelling, Casimir?"

I don't know what possessed me one day that I happened to be calling on her, suddenly to open her piano and embark on Schumann's *Novellette* in E. I was incapable at that time of playing it at the proper pace. To my great surprise, she criticised the *tempo* quite justly and gently pointed out some of my mistakes, showing that she knew and understood the piece to perfection. Then:

"If you like my piano," she said, "come and practise on it. I shall be delighted and you won't be disturbing anyone."

The princess hardly knew me then, and this proposal, which for that matter I declined, instead of putting me at my ease, rather embarrassed me; I only mention it as an example of her charming, impulsive manners. But as there was a rumour that she had once had to be shut up, I was never long in her company without being afraid her flightiness might degenerate into actual madness.

I took Oscar Wilde once to one of her dinners; Henri de Régnier has somewhere described the occasion and how the princess suddenly gave a loud shriek and declared she had seen a halo round the Irishman's head.

It was at another of her dinners too that I met Jacques-Emile Blanche—the only one of all the persons I have mentioned in this chapter whom I still see something of . . . But there would be so much to say about him . . . I must put off till another time too the portraits of Maeterlinck, Marcel Schwob and Barrès. I am afraid I have already overdone the density of that "selva oscura" in which I lost myself on emerging from childhood, with all my vague aspirations and the eager questing of my fervour.

Roger Martin du Gard, to whom I have shown these Memoirs, finds fault with me for never saying enough in them, and for leaving the reader with his appetite unsatisfied. And yet I have meant all along to say everything. But in making confidences, there is a limit which cannot be overstepped without artifice, without strain; and what I aim at above all is to be natural. No doubt there is in me some intellectual need that inclines me to simplify everything to excess for the sake of tracing my lines with greater purity; all drawing necessitates choice; but what hampers me most is having to represent states that are really one confused blend of simultaneous happenings as though they were successive. I am a creature of dialogue; everything in me is conflicting and contradictory. Memoirs are never more than half sincere, however great the desire for truth; everything is always more complicated than one makes out. Possibly even one gets nearer the truth in a novel.

II

AND NOW I HAVE TO RELATE FACTS, MOTIONS of my heart and mind, which I desire to set in the same light in which I first saw them, without letting the judgment I afterwards brought to bear on them be too apparent. Especially as that judgment has varied more than once and that I look on my life with an eye that is alternately indulgent or severe, according as my inward sky is bright or clouded. And lastly, though it has occurred to me of late that an actor of considerable importance—namely the Devil—may perhaps have played a part in the drama, I shall nevertheless recount that drama without alluding to an intervention which I did not identify till much later. The circuitous ways I followed, the blinding dazzlement of happiness towards which they led, is what I now propose to tell. At that moment, when I was in my twentieth year, I was beginning to have the conviction that nothing could happen to me that was not fortunate; I kept this conviction until a few months ago [1] and I consider the event that suddenly made me doubt it as one of the most momentous of my life. Yet even after such doubting, I recovered myself—so imperious is the call of my joy, so strong my belief that the circumstance which at first sight seems the most unfortunate, is, on closer examination, also the one most likely to instruct us, that there is a soul of goodness in things evil, and that if more often than not we

[1] Written in the spring of 1919.

fail to recognise happiness, it is because it comes wearing a different face from the one we were expecting. But I am anticipating, and I shall spoil my story if I represent myself as having already attained a state of happiness which I hardly imagined possible, which, above all, I hardly dared imagine permissible. When later on I knew more of life, everything no doubt seemed simpler; I was able to smile at the immense torments little difficulties caused me, and call by their right name propensities which were still vague and which terrified me because I could not discern their contours. At the time of which I am speaking, I had everything to discover; I had to invent both the torment and its cure, and I cannot say which of the two I thought the more monstrous. My Puritan education had taught me to attach so much importance to certain things, that I could not conceive that the questions which agitated me were not of passionate interest to humanity in general and to each individual in particular. I was like my own *Prometheus Ill-Bound* who could not understand how it was possible to live without an eagle, or without being devoured by it. For that matter, I unconsciously liked my eagle; but I was beginning to come to terms with it. Yes; my problem remained the same, but as I advanced in life, I thought it less terrible, and looked at it from an angle that was less acute. What problem? It would be very difficult to define it in a few words. But to begin with, was it not a great point that a problem existed? Reduced to the simplest possible expression, it was this:

In the name of what God or what ideal, do you forbid me to live according to my nature? And where would my nature lead me if I simply followed it? Up to the present, I had accepted Christ's code of morals, or at any rate, a kind of Puritanism which I had been taught to consider as Christ's code of morals. By forcing myself to submit to it I had merely caused a profound disturbance in my whole being. I would not consent to live lawlessly, and I required my mind's assent to the demands of my body. Even if those demands had been more usual, I doubt whether I should have been less troubled. For as long as I thought it my duty to deny my desire *everything*, what I desired did not matter. But I gradually came to wonder whether God really exacted such constraints, whether it was not impious to be in continual rebellion, whether such rebellion, was not against Him, and whether, in the struggle that divided me, it was reasonable to consider the opponent always in the wrong. It dawned upon me at last that this discordant duality might possibly be resolved into harmony. And then I saw at once that that harmony must be my supreme object, and the endeavour to acquire it the express reason of my life. When in October '93 I embarked for Algiers, it was not so much towards a new land that my impulse sped me, as towards *that*—towards that Golden Fleece. I was resolved in any case to go on a journey, but I had hesitated for some time as to whether I should not accept my cousin George Pouchet's invitation to accompany him on a scientific cruise to Iceland; and I was still hesitating when Paul Laurens was given a travelling scholarship, which obliged him to go abroad for a year; the choice he made of me as a companion decided my fate. And so my friend and I started off on our journey, fired by no less lofty an enthusiasm than that which thrilled the gallant youth of Greece, setting sail on the Argo.

I have already said, I think, that we were exactly the same age; our height, our looks, our figures, our tastes, were the same. From having constantly mixed with art-students, Paul had acquired a slightly bantering air of self-assurance which concealed great natural timidity; and also the habit of expressing himself with the agility of a tight-rope dancer; this verbal dexterity filled me with admiration and delight, but with despair too, when I compared it with the paralysed stiffness of my own wits.

I saw perhaps less of Paul than of Pierre Louis; but I think my affection for the former was more real and more capable of development. There was something aggressive, romantic, and antagonistic about Pierre, so that the terms we were on were always exceedingly unstable. Paul's character, on the contrary, was all give and take; it shifted and veered with mine. In Paris, I hardly ever saw him except in company with his brother, who had a more uncompromising disposition and, though he was younger than we were, used to hustle and bustle us so that conversation when he was there became rudimentary. Twice a week a fencing lesson I took at their house in the evenings gave us an opportunity for readings and long talks. Paul and I felt our friendship steadily increasing and discovered with delight all sorts of fraternal possibilities in each other. We had both reached the same stage in our lives, but there was this difference between us, that his heart was disengaged and mine occupied by my love; but I had determined not to let this stand in my way. After the publication of the *Cahiers*, my cousin's refusal, though it had not exactly discouraged me, had at any rate obliged me to postpone my hopes; but, as I have already said, my love was of a quasi-mystic nature and it was perhaps a deceitful suggestion of the devil's (though it was impossible for me to realise it at the time) that made me consider the admixture of anything whatever carnal in it would be a profanation. However that might be, I had resigned myself to dissociating pleasure and love; and even thought that this divorce was desirable, that pleasure would be purer and love more perfect if the heart and senses were kept apart. Yes, Paul and I were resolved when we started . . . And if anyone were to ask me how it is possible that Paul, who had been brought up, morally it is true, but

in a Catholic and not a Puritan family, should have kept his
virginity till he was past twenty-three, living as he did in a
circle of artists and with the constant provocation about him
of students and models—I should answer that it is my story
I am telling and not his, and that besides such cases are much
more frequent than one supposes; for people generally dislike
having them know. Timidity, shame, distaste, pride, ill-
judged sentimentality, nervous fright caused by an unfortunate experience (this was Paul's case I believe) all these things
may stop a young man on the verge. Then follow doubt, dis-
quiet, romanticism and melancholy; we were tired of all this;
we were determined to shake ourselves free from all this. But
our predominant feeling was one of horror for anything
peculiar, odd, morbid and abnormal. And in the conversations
we had before starting, we urged each other, I remember, to
pursue an ideal of equilibrium, plenitude and health. It was
I believe, indeed, my first aspiration towards what is now
known as "classicism"; how contrary this was to the Christian
ideal I began life with, it is impossible to say; and I realised
this so thoroughly that I determined not to take my Bible
away with me. This, which may perhaps seem a trifle, was
of the highest importance: up till that time not a day had
gone by without my going to the Holy Book for both sustenance and counsel. But it was just because this sustenance
seemed to have become indispensable, that I felt I must do
without it. I did not bid farewell to Christ without a wrench
at my heart, so that I ask myself now whether I ever really
left him.

We stayed a few days at Toulon with the Latils, family
friends of Paul's. I caught cold there and was beginning to
feel unwell even before we left France, though I said nothing
about it. I should not have mentioned this, if the question of
health had not been so important in my life, and particularly

257

so during the period that began with this journey. I had always been delicate; for two years running the army medical board had pronounced me unfit for military service, and the third time I went up had definitely rejected me; the word "tuberculosis" was what the paper said, and I don't know whether I had been more delighted at having been let off my service or frightened by the reason given. I knew besides that my father had already . . . In short, the kind of treacherous cold I caught at Toulon alarmed me so much that I almost hesitated whether I should not let Paul sail by himself and join him a little later. Then I abandoned myself to my fate, which is almost always the wisest thing to do. Besides which I thought the warmth of Algiers would set me to rights and that no climate could be better for me.

In the meantime Toulon was welcoming the Russian squadron; the harbour was decked with flags, the town illuminated, and strange rejoicings overflowed its smallest alleys; thus, from stage to stage of our journey, and even at its very start, countries and peoples, so we fancied, made merry to greet us, and nature herself grew brighter at our coming. I cannot remember how I came to let Paul go by himself to the night-fête given on one of the men-of-war; it was either that I felt too unwell or else that the spectacle of debauchery and drunkenness in the little streets attracted me more.

We spent the next day with the Latils, at La Simiane, their magnificent place on the coast, where Paul remembers my telling him the subject of what afterwards became my *Symphonie Pastorale*. I talked to him too of another more ambitious plan, which I ought to have carried out before letting it be devoured by my scruples. One should only become aware of the difficulties of a subject progressively and in the course of working at it; if one realises them all at the outset, one

258

loses heart. My plan then was to write the imaginary history of a people, of a country, with its wars and revolutions and changes of government and outstanding events. Although the history of every country is different from that of every other, I flattered myself I should be able to trace lines that would be common to them all. I should have invented heroes, sovereigns, statesmen, artists, and an apocrypha-literature; I should have described and criticised its tendencies, traced the evolution of its different styles, quoted fragments of its chefs-d'œuvre . . . And all this to prove what? That mankind might have had a different history, that our manners and customs and morals might have been different, our tastes, codes and standards of beauty different—and nevertheless remained human. If I had really embarked upon this subject, I should perhaps have come to grief, but without a doubt I should have enjoyed myself immensely.

We had a fairly calm crossing from Marseilles to Tunis. Our cabin was stifling and the first night I perspired so profusely that the sheets stuck to me; I spent the second night on deck . . . Great flames of sheet lightning flickered in the distance in the direction of Africa. Africa! I repeated the mysterious word over and over again; in my imagination it was big with terrors, with alluring horrors, with hopes and expectations; and throughout the hot night I turned my longing eyes towards the sultry promise of that lightning-swathed horizon.

Oh, I know a journey to Tunis has nothing very extraordinary about it; no; but the extraordinary thing was *our* going there. In truth, the cocoa-palms of the atolls would fill me with no greater amazement to-day—and to-morrow, alas, with less—than the sight of the first camels I saw from the deck of our boat. There they were on the strip of low land that curved round the narrow channel we had entered, silhouetted against the sky like a demonstration on a black-board. I had of course expected to see camels, but I had never succeeded in imagining them so queer; and then, when our ship drew up alongside the quay, that shoal of golden fish it sent spirting and flying out of the water! And the crowd straight out of the Arabian Nights, which came hustling round to seize our luggage! We were at that stage of life when every novelty is intoxicating delight. With what gusto we enjoyed both our thirst and the quenching of it! Every-thing was astonishing beyond all hope. How innocently we fell into all the traps of the touts! But how lovely the stuffs of our haïks and burnouses were! How delicious we thought the coffee the shopman offered us, and how generous of the shopman to offer it! On the very first day, as soon as we made our appearance in the bazaar, a small guide of about four-teen years old, took possession of us and escorted us into the shops (we should have been indignant if anyone had sug-gested he was given a commission); then, as he talked French fairly well, and moreover was charming, we made an appoint-ment with him for the next day at our hotel. He was called Ceci and came from the island of Djerba, said to be the isle of the Lotus-eaters. I remember our anxiety when he did not turn up at the appointed hour. And a few days later, when he came into my room (we had left the hotel and taken a little apartment of three rooms in the Rue Al Djezira) carrying the things we had just bought, I remember my mixed and troubled feelings when he half undressed in order to show me how to drape myself in a haick.

Captain Julian, whom we met at General Leclerc's, put some army horses at our disposal and offered to go riding with us outside the walls. Up till that time I had never rid-den except in a riding-school, where we pupils, after filing drearily past while the riding-master criticised our seat, had trotted gloomily backwards and forwards for an hour on end in a gloomy covered-in hall. My little chestnut Arab was perhaps a thought too spirited to be quite to my taste, but when I resigned myself to giving him his head and letting him gallop to his heart's content, my delight was immeasurable. I soon found myself alone, having lost my companions and my way, and feeling very little inclined to find either the former or the latter again before evening. The gold and purple of the setting sun was flooding the immense plain that lies between Tunis and Mt. Zaghouan and is marked out at long intervals by the huge ruined arches of the Roman aqueduct; I imagined it was the very same that in ancient days had brought the limpid waters of the Nymphaeum to Carthage. A pool of brackish water looked like a lake of blood; I followed its desolate shores and startled a few birds I took for flamingos.

We had intended to stay in Tunis till the beginning of winter and then travel to Biskra via the South, for we were inexperienced enough to think nothing of bad weather and to be afraid only of the heat. But Captain Julian, who spoke from knowledge, persuaded us, in view of the approaching cold weather, not to delay our departure. He revised our itinerary, prepared our relays and gave us quantities of introductions for every stage. If I remember rightly a military escort was to accompany us across the Chott El Djerid. We embarked on our journey through the desert with a childish want of foresight, trusting to our stars, and convinced that everything we undertook must turn out successfully. For twenty-five francs a day we procured the services of a guide and of a coachman who was to drive us in an enormous landau —a kind of gorgeous coach with four horses—and take us to Sousse in four days. There we were to consider whether it would not be better to dismiss the landau and take the Sfax and Gabè's diligence. The guide and coachman were both Maltese, young, superb and stalwart, with brigand-like airs that delighted us. I am still amazed we were able to get such an equipage for so small a sum; but of course we had to pay the four days' return journey as well. And now all was ready —the relays arranged for, and our luggage and provisions roped on to the back of the landau. As we sank back in a heap of rugs and burnouses, Paul and I looked like two Russian boyards:

"And those about them were amazed at the modesty of their tips," said Paul, ably putting the situation in a nutshell.

We were to sleep at Zaghouan, and all day long we watched the mountain in front of us slowly drawing nearer and nearer and gradually growing pinker and pinker. And the vastness of the country, its monotony, its iridescence, its emptiness, its silence slowly sank into our hearts . . . But oh, the wind! . . . If it stopped blowing, the heat was overpowering; if it rose the cold was perishing. It blew like the flowing of water in a big river, swiftly and steadily; it pierced one's wraps, one's clothes, one's very flesh; I was chilled to the bone. I had not properly recovered from the indisposition I had suffered from at Toulon, and fatigue had made it worse; but I would not give in. I felt it too hard not to do whatever Paul did and I went with him everywhere; but I expect that but for me he would have done more, and that he held back out of kindness and delicacy when he saw my strength beginning to fail. I was constantly having to take precautions, constantly afraid of being not warmly enough, or too warmly, clad. In these circumstances, it was folly to launch off across the desert. But I would not give up the idea, and besides, I fell a victim to the lure of the South, to that mirage of mildness with which it blinds us.

Zaghouan, however, with its charming orchards, its running waters, its sheltered situation in a fold of the mountains, would have had a great many advantages, and I should no doubt soon have got well, if I could have brought myself to stop there.

But how was it possible not to imagine that still further south . . .? We arrived at the inn famished and exhausted. As soon as we had finished supper we prepared to go to bed, with the one idea of getting off to sleep as quickly as possible, when a spahi (he may have been a turco—I know nothing about uniforms) came with a message to say that the commanding officer (I know nothing about ranks either, and have never been able to count stripes) had already been informed of our arrival, that he was looking forward to seeing us and could not allow us to lodge anywhere but in the camp. He added that there were several cases of cholera in the village and that it would be imprudent to stay in it. This invitation did not at all suit our book; we had already taken out our things for the night; we had to start early the next morning and we were dropping with sleep; but how was it possible to refuse? I think nevertheless we tried to and only gave in when a second spahi appeared with another summons, so we were obliged to pack up our bags again; they were put on to a mule that was waiting at the door and we set off behind it. The camp was about a mile away; there we found several officers who seemed to have had nothing better to do than to wait for us; they meant to carry us off to a Moorish café, which provided the only entertainment in the place, with its songs and dances. I excused myself on the ground of fatigue, and Paul went with them alone. One of the officers offered to show me to our dormitory; but no sooner had the others gone than he stuck me down at a table in front of him and, pulling out a voluminous packet of MS., forced me to listen for over an hour while he read aloud a work on Arabic dialects.

That night in camp, however, was not unprofitable, for there I made my first acquaintance with bugs. When the officer thought I had been sufficiently plagued, he conducted me, more dead than alive, to a kind of enormous shed, very dimly lighted by a tallow dip, in a corner of which were two camp beds. The creatures rushed to the feast as soon as the candle was put out. I did not realise at first they were bugs and thought some practical joker had sprinkled the sheets with an irritant. There was a struggle for some time between sleepiness and itching, but itching was the stronger and sleep retired discomfited. I wanted to relight my candle but looked in vain for matches. I remembered having noticed an alcarazas on a stool at the head of my bed. By the light of the moon, which was shining in by a window, I took a long draught from the alcarazas; then soaking my handkerchief, I tried to cool my fever, and drenched the neck and wristbands of my nightshirt with water. After that, as it was hopeless to think of sleep any more, I groped for my clothes in the dark and dressed.

On the threshold I met Paul just coming in:

"I can't stand it any longer," I said. "I'm going out."

"Don't forget we're in a camp. You don't know the password. You may be fired on, if you go too far."

The moon was flooding the camp with its silent light, and for some time I paced up and down in front of the shed door; I felt as if I were dead, a floating ghost, light and unsubstantial as a dream or a memory; if the sentinel I saw over there were to challenge me, thought I, I should fade away into the night. I must have gone in unconsciously and lain down on my bed again in my clothes, for it was there reveille woke me.

We were told our carriage was waiting for us at the inn. The morning air had never seemed to me more delicious than after that feverish night. The white walls of the houses of Zaghouan, which the evening before had struck a note of blue against the rose-coloured sky, were now tinted like hydrangeas in the softer azure of the dawn. We left Zaghouan without having seen the Nymphaeum, so I am able to imagine it is one of the most beautiful places in the world.

On the second day, our road was more often than not a half-obliterated track, and immediately after leaving the mountains it plunged into a region more arid still than the one we had passed through the day before. Towards the middle of the day we came to a cavernous rocky cliff, peopled by bees and streaming with honey—at least, so our guide told us. We reached the model farm of Enfida in the evening and spent the night there. On the third day we arrived at Kairouan. The holy city rises suddenly and unexpectedly straight out of the desert; its immediate surroundings are ferocious; not a trace of vegetation except nopals—those extraordinary plants like green rackets, covered with poisonous prickles—whose thickets are said to be the haunt of cobras. Near the town gate, at the foot of the ramparts, a magician was making one of those terrible serpents dance to the sound of his flute. All the houses of the town had been freshly white-washed, as though in honour of our arrival. I prefer these white walls, with their shadows and strange reflections, to any but the mud walls of the southern oases. I was glad to think that Gautier disliked them.

We had letters of introduction to the principal personages of the town, and rather imprudently made use of them, for it greatly curtailed our liberty. We went to dinner at the caliph's to meet some officers; it was all very splendid and gay; after dinner, I was set down to a wretched piano and had to rack my brains for music for the guests to dance to . . . Why do I tell all this? I know well enough it isn't interesting. Merely, I think to put off for a little what is coming.

We spent the whole of next day at Kairouan. There was a gathering of Aïssaouas in a little mosque, which surpassed in frenzy, in strangeness, in beauty, in nobility, in horror, anything I have ever seen since; in my six other journeys to Algeria, I have never met with anything approaching it.

We started off again. I was feeling more and more unwell every day. Every day, the wind grew colder and colder and blew incessantly. When we arrived at Sousse after another day in the desert, I was breathing with such difficulty, and beginning to feel so uncomfortable, that Paul went to fetch the regimental doctor. (For once our letters of introduction were of some use.) It was plain enough he thought my condition serious. He prescribed a revulsive to relieve the congestion of my lungs and promised to come again next day.

Needless to say there was no further question of our continuing our trip. But I thought Biskra would not be a bad place in which to spend the winter, so long as we gave up the idea of reaching it by the longest and most adventurous route. If we returned to Tunis, the train would take us there prosaically, but practically, in two days. In the meantime, I must first of all rest, for I was not fit as yet to travel.

I ought now, I suppose, to describe my state of mind when I heard the doctor's opinion, and say to what extent I felt alarmed. I cannot remember that I was much concerned; either because at that time I was not really afraid of death, or because my idea of death was vague and remote, or because my state of apathy was such that I was incapable of feeling any strong reaction whatever. Moreover, the elegiac strain does not particularly suit me. I gave myself up to fate therefore, without feeling much regret except that I was in-

266

volving Paul in my break-down; for he would not hear of leaving me alone and continuing his journey without me; so that the first result of my illness, and I might almost say its reward, was to bring home to me the inestimable value of his friendship.

We stayed at Sousse only six days. But on the dreary background of those monotonous days of waiting, there stands out a little episode which was of great importance in my life. And if it is indecent to relate it, it would be still more dishonest to pass it over.

At certain hours of the day, Paul left me to go and paint; but I was not so poorly as to be unable sometimes to go and join him. For that matter, during the whole time of my illness, I did not keep my bed, nor even my room, for a single day. I never went out without taking a coat and a rug with me : as soon as I got outside, some boy would appear and offer to carry them. The one who accompanied me on that particular day was a young brown-skinned Arab whom I had already noticed on the previous day among the troop of little rascals who loitered in the neighbourhood of the hotel. He wore a chechia on his head like the others and nothing else but a coat of coarse linen and baggy Tunisian trousers that stopped short at the knee and made his bare legs look even slenderer than they were. He seemed more reserved or more timid than his companions, so that as a rule they were beforehand with him; but that day, I don't know how it was, I went out without any of them seeing me, and all of a sudden it was he who joined me at the corner of the hotel.

The hotel was situated in a sandy district on the outskirts of the town. It was sad to see the olive-trees, so fine in the surrounding country, half submerged here by the drifting sandhills, a little further on one was astonished to come upon a stream—a meagre water-course, springing out of the sand just in time to reflect a little bit of sky before reaching the sea. A gathering of negresses squatting over their washing beside this trickle of fresh water was the subject Paul had chosen before which to plant his easel. I had promised to meet him there, but when Ali—this was my little guide's name— led me up among the sandhills, in spite of the fatigue of walking in the sand, I followed him; we soon reached a kind of funnel or crater, the rim of which was just high enough to command the surrounding country and give a view of any- one coming. As soon as we got there, Ali flung the coat and rug down on the sloping sand; he flung himself down too, and stretched on his back, with his arms spread out on each side of him, he looked at me and laughed. I was not such a simpleton as to misunderstand his invitation; but I did not answer it at once. I sat down myself, not very far from him, but yet not very near either, and in my turn looked at him steadily and waited, feeling extremely curious as to what he would do next.

I waited! I wonder to-day at my fortitude . . . But was it really curiosity that held me back? I am not sure. The secret motive of our acts—I mean of the most decisive ones—es- capes us; and not only in memory but at the very moment of their occurrence. Was I still hesitating on the threshold of what is called sin? No; my disappointment would have been too great if the adventure had ended with the triumph of my virtue—which I already loathed and despised. No; it was really curiosity that made me wait . . . And I watched his laughter slowly fade away, his lips close down again over his white teeth and an expression of sadness and discomfiture cloud his charming face.

"Good-bye, then," he said.

But I seized the hand he held out to me and tumbled him on to the ground. In a moment he was laughing again. The complicated knots of the strings that served him for girdle did not long trouble his impatience; he drew a little dagger from his pocket and severed the tangle with one cut. The garment fell, and flinging away his coat, he emerged naked as a god. Then he raised his slight arms for a moment to the sky and dropped laughing against me. Though his body was perhaps burning, it felt as cool and refreshing to my hands as shade. How beautiful the sand was! In the lovely splendour of that evening light, what radiance clothed my joy! . . .

In the meantime it was getting late. I had to join Paul. No doubt my countenance bore traces of my rapture and I think he guessed something; but as—out of discretion, perhaps— he did not question me, I said nothing.

I have so often spoken of Biskra that I will not repeat myself here. The set of rooms surrounded with terraces (I have described them in the *Immoraliste*) which were put at our disposal by the Hotel de l'Oasis, were actually those that had been arranged for Cardinal Lavigerie, who was on the point of occupying them when he expired at the Pères Blancs' mission house. I slept in the Cardinal's own bed, in the biggest room, which we also used as a sitting-room; a small room next it served as a dining-room, for we had no intention of taking our meals with the other inmates of the hotel. The dishes were brought us on a hot-plate by a young Arab called Athman whom we had taken into our service. He was not more than fourteen, but very tall, though not very strong; his height, however, gave him an appearance of importance among the other boys who used to come to our terraces after school hours to play at marbles or spin their tops; Athman indeed was a head taller than any of them, so that his patronising airs seemed almost natural; for that matter, his swagger was charmingly good-tempered, and even droll, as though to imply that if perhaps he was a little ridiculous, it was not altogether unintentionally. He was besides the best and most honest boy in the world, incapable of taking advantage of anyone and with as little ability to make money as a poet—always ready on the contrary to spend and give away all he had. When he told one his dreams, one understood Joseph's. He was very fond of stories, knew a great many and told them in a slow, clumsy way Paul and I fondly thought was oriental. He was indolent, greatly given to wool-gathering, and possessed to a high degree the charming faculty of exaggerating his happiness and wafting away the cares of the moment in dreams, hopes and smoke. He helped me to understand that if the Arab people, artistic as they are, have produced so few works of art, it is because they do not attempt to hoard their joys. There is much to be said about this, but I have resolved not to digress.

Athman lodged in a third room next door to the dining-room—a tiny little room opening on to a minute terrace which brought the apartment to an end; this was where he used to clean our shoes, and this was where Paul and I found him one morning, sitting cross-legged on the ground like a Turk, and dressed up in his finest clothes, as if he were going to a feast; he had made a circle round him of twelve candle-ends, all lighted, though it was broad daylight, and alternating with little nosegays arranged in small tin cups. In the heart of this modest magnificence sat Athman, brushing and polishing our shoes with rhythmic energy, and singing at the top of his voice something or other that sounded like a hymn.

He was not so happy when he accompanied Paul across the oasis, carrying his easel, paint-box, camp-stool and umbrella. He would suddenly stop short, sweating and panting, and exclaim with the utmost conviction: "Oh, here's a beautiful subject!" in an attempt to bring his master's vagabond humour to a standstill. So Paul would tell me with great amusement when he came home.

I felt totally unfit to go with them, and watched them set off not without a touch of melancholy. I could not manage more at first than the public gardens, which began at our door. In truth, I was a poor thing; my lungs, or "heart's fan," as Athman called them, did their work grudgingly and it was an effort to breathe. As soon as we arrived at Biskra, Paul had sent for Dr. D., who brought his thermocautery and began at once to use it; after which he came back every other day. After about a fortnight's application of "pointes de feu" to the chest and back alternately, followed by a liberal sprinkling of turpentine, the congestion kindly consented to become localised; it then passed abruptly from the right lung to the left, to Dr. D.'s stupefaction. There was no question of taking my temperature, but from some of the symptoms I can remember, I feel convinced I was feverish morning and evening. I had had a good piano sent me from Algiers, but the running up of the smallest scale put me out of breath. Incapable of work, and even of prolonged attention, I dragged miserably through the day, my only distraction, my only joy being to watch the boys at play on our terraces, or in the public gardens, if the weather allowed of my going out; for the rainy season had now set in. And it was not with any one of them in particular that I fell in love, but with their youth indiscriminately. The sight of their health sustained me and I had no wish for any society but theirs. Perhaps I found in their simple ways and childish talk a mute counsel to trust more confidently to life. Under the combined influence of climate and illness, I felt my austerity beginning to melt and my frowning brows unbend. At last I realised how much pride lay concealed in this resistance of mine to what I had once called temptation, but which I called so no longer, now

271

that I had ceased to fight against it. "More obstinate than faithful," Signoret had once said of me; I prided myself indeed on being faithful; but henceforth I placed all my obstinacy in clinging to the resolution Paul and I had made to "renormalise" ourselves. Illness did not weaken my determination. And I should like it to be understood how largely resolution entered into what I am about to relate; if I am to be accused of giving way to my inclinations, let it be understood, I repeat, that they were the inclinations of my mind and not of my body. My natural propensity, which I was at last forced to recognise, but which I would not as yet assent to, was increased by resistance; I merely strengthened it by struggling, and in despair of vanquishing it, I thought I might succeed in cheating it. Out of sympathy for Paul, I even went so far as to invent imaginary desires; that is to say, I adopted his, and each of us encouraged the other. A winter resort like Biskra offers particular facilities in this respect; a troop of women live there who make a trade of their persons; the French government treats them, it is true, like the usual prostitutes of vulgar brothels; registration is enforced on them for purposes of supervision (thanks to which Dr. D. was able to give us the necessary information about each of them), but their manners and habits are different from those of ordinary licensed prostitutes. By an ancient tradition, the tribe of the Oulad Naïl exports its daughters every year when they are barely nubile, and a few years later they return with a dowry that enables them to purchase a husband, who accepts, without considering it dishonourable, what in our countries would cover him with ridicule or shame. The real Oulad Naïl have a great reputation for beauty; so that all the women who practise the profession in those parts call themselves by that name; not all of them however return to their own country, so that there are women of all ages among

272

them, some being extremely young; these, before they are nubile, share the lodging of some elder sister or friend, who protects and initiates the younger; the sacrifice of their virginity is the occasion for rejoicings in which half the town takes part.

The troop of the Oulad Naïl at Biskra is confined to one or two streets, known as the Holy Streets. A euphemism? I think not. The Oulad often figure in semi-profane, semi-religious ceremonies; very venerable marabouts show themselves in their company; I do not want to be too positive, but I am under the impression the Mahommedan religion does not view them unfavourably. The Holy Streets are also the streets of the cafés; at night they become animated and the whole population of the oasis throngs them. The Oulad exhibit themselves to the desires of the passers-by in groups of two or three, sitting at the foot of little flights of steps that lead straight from the street to their rooms. Motionless, sumptuously dressed and adorned, with their necklaces of gold coins and high head-dresses, they look like idols in their niches.

I remember walking down these streets a few years later with Dr. Bourget of Lausanne.

"Young men ought to be brought here to give them a horror of debauchery," exclaimed the worthy man, bursting with disgust. (Every Swiss carries his glaciers inside him.) Oh! how little he knew of the human heart!—of mine at any rate . . . Exotic beauty can best be compared to the Queen of Sheba, who came to Solomon "to prove him with hard questions." There is nothing for it. Some people fall in love with what is like them; others with what is different. I am among the latter. Strangeness solicits me as much as familiarity repels. Let me add besides, and with more particularity, that I am attracted by "Phoebus' amorous pinches" on a brown skin; it was especially for me that Virgil wrote:

"Quid tunc si fuscus Amyntas?"

Paul came back one day very much excited: as he was walking home he had met the troop of Oulad going to bathe at Fontaine-Chaude. One of them, whom he described as being particularly charming, had managed to escape from the group at a sign from him; an appointment had been made. And as I was not yet in sufficiently good health to go to her, it was settled she was to come to us. Although these women are not confined to their lodgings, which have nothing in common with a brothel, they are obliged to conform to certain rules: there is a fixed hour after which they are not allowed out: they must escape, if they wish to, before it; Paul accordingly went to lurk behind a tree in the public gardens, and lie in wait for Meriem, on her return from the bath; he was to bring her back to me. We had decorated the room, prepared the meal we meant to take with her, and given Athman a holiday. But the hour had long since gone by; I waited in a state of inexpressible agitation; Paul came back alone.

The reaction was all the more cruel because there was no real desire at the back of my resolution. I was as disappointed as Cain when he saw the smoke of his offering beaten back to earth: the holocaust was not accepted. We felt we should never again find such another occasion; I felt I should never again be so well prepared. The door which hope had pushed ajar for a moment was too heavy; it had slammed back again; it always would: I was shut out for ever. I must put a good face on it, I said to myself, and the best thing to do, no doubt, is to laugh; and besides we took no little pride in showing our buoyancy under the blows of fate; our humour was apt enough and the meal which had begun lugubriously ended in merriment.

Suddenly there was a noise like the fluttering of a wing against the window. The outside door opened gently . . .

Of all that evening this is the moment of which I have kept the most thrilling recollection: I can still see Meriem outlined on the dark background of the night; I see her standing there hesitating; then she recognises Paul and smiles, but before coming in, she steps back, and leaning over the balustrade of the terrace behind her, waves her haïk in the dark—a signal to dismiss the maid-servant who had brought her to the foot of our staircase.

Meriem knew a little French; enough to tell us the reason she had not been able to join Paul, and how Athman soon after had shown her where we lived. She was wrapped in a double haïk which she let fall at the door. I cannot remember her dress, for she soon shed it; but she kept her bracelets on her wrists and ankles. I do not remember either if it was not Paul who began by taking her to his room, a separate little pavilion at the other end of the terrace; yes, I think she did not come to me till dawn; but I can remember Athman's lowered eyes next morning as he passed in front of the Cardinal's bed and his amused, prudish, comic "Good morning, Meriem!"

Meriem was amber-skinned, firm-fleshed. Her figure was round but still almost childish, for she was barely sixteen. I can only compare her to a bacchante—the one on the Gaeta vase, for instance—because of her tinkling bracelets too, which she was continually shaking. I remember having seen her dance in one of the cafés of the Holy Street, where Paul had taken me one evening. Her cousin En Barka was dancing there too. They danced in the antique fashion of the Oulad, their heads straight and erect, their busts motionless, their hands agile, their whole bodies shaken by the rhythmic beating of their feet. How much I liked this "Mahommedan

275

music," [1] with its steady, obstinate, incessant flow; it went to my head, stupefied me like an opiate, drowsily and voluptuously benumbed my thoughts. On a platform beside the clarinet player sat an old Negro, clacking his metal castanets, and little Mohammed, in a lyrical ecstasy, thumping on his tambourine. How beautiful he was! Half naked under his rags, black and slender as a demon, open-mouthed and wild-eyed ... Paul had bent towards me that evening (does he remember it, I wonder?) and whispered in my ear:

"Do you suppose he doesn't excite me more than Meriem?"

He had said it in jest, without meaning it, for he was only attracted by women; but what need had he to say it to me of all people? I did not answer; but this avowal had haunted me ever since; I had taken it as mine; or rather it was already mine, even before Paul had spoken; and if that night I was valiant with Meriem, it was because I shut my eyes and imagined I was holding Mohammed in my arms.

After that night I experienced an extraordinary sensation of calm and comfort. And I do not only mean the feeling of rest that sometimes follows upon pleasure; it is certain that Meriem had then and there done me more good than all the doctor's revulsives. I should hardly dare recommend this treatment; but my case was so much a matter of nerves that it is not surprising my lungs were relieved by so radical a diversion, and a kind of equilibrium established.

Meriem returned; she returned for Paul; she was to return for me, and the appointment was already made, when we suddenly received a telegram from my mother, announcing her arrival. A few days before Meriem's first visit, I had had a hæmorrhage; I had not attached much importance to it myself, but it had greatly alarmed Paul. He had told his parents about it and they had thought it their duty to tell my mother;

[1] Allusion to a poem by Verlaine.

no doubt too they were anxious for my mother to come and relieve him in his attendance upon me, for they must have thought the time of a young man with a travelling scholarship might be more profitably employed than in the capacity of sick-nurse. Be that as it may, my mother arrived.

I was of course glad to see her and show her the country; we were nevertheless dismayed; our life together was beginning to be so well organised; should we have to interrupt this re-education of our instincts when we had only just started upon it? I swore we should not, that my mother's presence should change nothing in our habits, and that to begin with Meriem should not be put off.

When I afterwards related the story of our adventure to Albert, I was foolishly surprised to find that a man I had thought broad-minded was moved to indignation by the joint possession that had seemed so natural to Paul and me. Our friendship had even taken pleasure in it, had been strengthened by it as by a fresh bond. And we were not jealous either of the strangers to whom Meriem granted or sold her favours. The fact was we both looked upon the carnal act at that time with cynicism, and on this occasion at any rate, no sentiment of any kind was mixed with it. Albert, on the contrary, less as a moralist than as a romantic of the generation that had been brought up on the poetry of Musset, would only admit sensual enjoyment as a recompense of love, and considered simple pleasure contemptible. As for me, I have already said how much both actual events and my own natural inclinations encouraged me to dissociate love from desire—to such a degree indeed, that I was almost shocked by the idea of mixing them. But I am not trying to make my ethics prevail; it is not my apology I am writing, but my story.

My mother then arrived one evening in company with our old Marie, who had never made so long a journey. The rooms

277

they were to occupy—the only ones in the hotel—were on the other side of the courtyard and opened straight on to our terraces. If I remember rightly, it was that very evening that we were expecting Meriem; she arrived almost directly after my mother and Marie had retired to their rooms; and at first everything went off without a hitch. But in the early morning . . .

A remainder of shame—or rather of respect for my mother's feelings—had made me close my door. Meriem went straight to Paul's room. The little pavilion he occupied was so situated that one had to cross the terrace from end to end in order to reach it. In the early morning, when Meriem knocked at my window as she passed, I rose hastily and waved her good-bye. She stepped furtively away and melted into the reddening sky like a ghost that fades on the first crowing of the cock; but just at that moment, that is to say, before she had vanished, I saw the shutters of my mother's room open and my mother lean out of her window. Her glance followed Meriem's flight for a moment; and then the window closed. The catastrophe was upon us.

It was obvious a woman had come from Paul's room. It was certain my mother had seen her, had understood . . . What could I do but wait? I waited.

My mother took her early breakfast in her room. Paul went out and then she came and sat down beside me. I cannot remember her words exactly. I remember I had the cruelty to say, with a great effort, both because I did not want the blame to fall on Paul alone, and also because I intended to safeguard the future:

"But you know, she doesn't come only for Paul. She's coming back."

I remember her tears. I think indeed she said nothing. I think she found nothing to say and could only cry; but her

278

tears touched and saddened my heart more than any reproaches could have done. She wept and wept; I felt she was inconsolably, infinitely sad. So that if I had the face to tell her Meriem was coming back, I had not the courage afterwards to keep my word, and the only other experiment I made at Biskra was outside our hotel with En Barka in her own room. Paul was with me, and for him as well as for me this fresh attempt was a miserable failure. En Barka was much too beautiful (and I must add a good deal older than Meriem); her very beauty froze me; I felt a kind of admiration for her but not the smallest trace of desire. I came to her as a worshipper without an offering. The case of Pygmalion was reversed, for it was the woman who became a statue in my arms; or rather, it was I who turned to marble. Caresses, provocations, nothing availed; I was mute, and left her without having been able to give her anything but money.

In the meantime spring was laying its touch upon the oasis. Faint whispers of delight began to stir under the palm-trees. I was feeling better. One morning I ventured to take a much longer walk than usual; the country, for all its monotony, had an inexhaustible attraction for me; I too felt I had begun to live again; that I was indeed alive for the first time, that I had left the Valley of the Shadow of Death and was awakening to real life. Yes, I was entering upon a new existence where every joy was to be welcomed and none resisted. An azure haze lent distance to the foreground and made every object imponderable, immaterial. I myself, a creature without weight, walked slowly on, like Rinaldo in the garden of Armida, soul and body quivering, dazzled and amazed with a wonder beyond words. I heard, I saw, I breathed as I had never done before; and as the blended stream of sounds, perfumes and colours flooded my empty heart, I felt it dissolve in passionate gratitude.

"Take me, take me body and soul," I cried, sobbing out my worship to some unknown Apollo; "I am thine—obedient, submissive. Let all within me be light! Light and air! My struggle against thee has been vain. But now I know thee. Thy will be done! I resist no longer. I am in thy hands. Take me!"

And so, my face wet with tears, I entered an enchanting universe full of laughter and strangeness.

Our stay at Biskra was drawing to an end. My mother had come to relieve Paul so that he might be free to continue his journey without anxiety about me; but when she proposed to take his place, for my health still necessitated a great deal of care, he declared he had no intention of leaving me. This was a fresh proof of his friendship, given without my having shown him I should be heartbroken by his departure. So it was my mother and Marie who returned to France, while Paul and I embarked at Tunis for Sicily and Italy.[1]

We did no more than pass through Syracuse; I saw neither, the Cyane nor the avenue of tombs, nor the quarries; I was too unwell to look at anything, to see anything; and it was not till some years later that I dipped my hands in the fountain of Arethusa. We were in a hurry too to get to Rome and Florence; and if we stayed a few days at Messina, it was only to take breath, for this first stage of our journey had utterly exhausted me. Heavens! how tiresome this business of health was! It put a stop to all our finest schemes; we had perpetually to be considering it; it was far more hampering, certainly, than the question of money; fortunately, in that respect we

[1] To be more accurate, we left Tunis with the intention of going to Tripoli, as some sort of compensation for all the things my ill-health had obliged us to give up. But this last plan went the way of the others. The crossing was so bad that our courage failed us, and when we got to Malta, we went straight on to Syracuse.

had nothing to complain of; my mother had increased the amount put to my credit, so that I might want for nothing. Continually suffering as I did from cold, from heat, from discomfort, I dragged Paul with me to the best hotels. It was not till later that I made acquaintance with the queerness of small inns, the adventures, the encounters, which are so delightful in Italy, and which I now think the best part of travelling. But at any rate, what opportunities for interminable talks our tête-à-tête dinners gave us! We put all our ideas to the test, weighed them, assayed them, sifted them; we gazed at them reflected in each other's minds, watched them develop and mature, tested the flexibility of their remotest tendrils. I firmly believe that if I heard those conversations again to-day, I should not think them less admirable than I thought them then; at any rate, it is certain I have never found so much enjoyment in talking.

I was not able to see anything of the neighbourhood round Naples; my tiresome health interfered with everything, even with carriage drives. I again dragged about as miserably as in the worst days at Biskra, perspiring in the sun, shivering in the shade, and only able to walk on perfectly flat ground. In such circumstances it may be guessed what I thought of the Seven Hills of Rome. During that first visit of mine to the Eternal City, I saw hardly anything but the Pincio; I passed the best hours of the day there, sitting on a bench in the garden; and even so, by the time I reached it, I was panting and exhausted, though it was only a short distance from the Via Gregoriana, where I had taken a room, on the left hand side of the street as you come back from the Pincio. Although the room was large, Paul, in order to feel more at liberty, had settled at the end of the same street in another room with a little terrace, where he hoped to work. But it was in my room that he received the "Lady," the name we gave a high-class prostitute, who was introduced to us by one of the Villa Medici students. I believe, indeed, I had a try at her myself, but the only thing I can remember is my disgust for her distinguished manners, elegance and affectation. I had only been able to put up with Meriem because she was a cynical little savage; with her, at any rate, one knew what to expect; in her talk, in her behaviour, there was nothing that aped love; with the other woman I profaned the most sacred feelings of my heart.

In Florence I was too unwell to visit the galleries or churches; for that matter, I was as little ready to profit by the lessons of the old masters, as I had been able to appreciate Raphael in Rome. Their work, I thought, belonged to the past; but as nothing really touches me to the quick that is not of present importance, it was not till some years later, when I was more attentive and better educated, that I understood their teaching and was able to recognise it as a living force. I think Paul also failed to study them with enough attention and sympathy; when he went to the Uffizi, he spent all his time in front of Giorgione's portrait of the Knight of Malta; he made an excellent copy of it, no doubt, but it taught him nothing but a few tricks of the trade.

It was in Florence we parted company, not to meet again till near the end of summer at Cuverville. From Florence, I went straight to Geneva to consult Dr. Andreæ, a great friend of the Charles Gides', and not only one of the cleverest of men, but one of the best and wisest as well; it is to him I owe my salvation. He very soon persuaded me there was nothing wrong with me but my nerves, and that a cure of hydrotherapy at Champel to begin with, and a winter in the mountains afterwards, would do me more good than all the precautions and medicaments in the world.

Pierre Louis came to see me at Champel. He had taken

tickets for the summer performance at Bayreuth and was on his way there; but he could not bear to be so long without seeing me, and besides he wanted to hear the account of my travels fresh and hot. He had another reason for making this détour—the hope of dropping Ferdinand Hérold by the way. Hérold had attached himself to Louis as a travelling companion and stuck to him like a leech; he had taken places at Bayreuth too as soon as he heard his friend Pierre was going there. They turned up together at the Hotel des Bains where I was finishing my cure. I enjoyed recounting our adventures to Louis; and I had no sooner begun to tell him about Meriem than he took it into his head to start off at once and join her, leaving Hérold to go on alone to Bayreuth. But Hérold did not see this at all and when Louis told him of his new idea:

"I will go with you," cried Hérold at once.

Pierre Louis, no doubt, had many faults; he was capricious, touchy, flighty and domineering; he incessantly tried to make people fall in with his way of thinking and considered he had the right to force his friends to submit to his wishes; but he had impulses of exquisite generosity, and such spirit and fire and dash that the rest was forgotten in a moment. He persuaded himself he owed it to me as a friend to make Meriem his mistress. Accordingly he started off in the middle of July, with Hérold in tow; Meriem had given me a silk handkerchief which I handed over to him to take her as a token from me and serve as an introduction. He also took a barrel organ as a present for Athman; but Athman sold it for a few francs, preferring his flute.

I soon heard that Louis and Hérold had had a good journey, that they had stayed at Biskra just long enough to get fever (for the heat was infernal) and carry off Meriem, with whom they settled just outside Constantine. It was there that Pierre Louis finished writing his exquisite *Chansons de Bilitis*, which he dedicated to me in memory of Meriem ben Atala; this is the meaning of the three mysterious initials that follow my name on the first page of the volume.[1] If Meriem is not exactly Bilitis, since, if I remember rightly, many of these poems were written before Louis left for Algeria, she nevertheless flits through the pages and every now and then her image flashes out at me.

Shall I tell the absurd joke that Louis and I played with Meriem's help? Louis wrote to me one day:

"Meriem asks what you would like her to send you?"

And I answered without a moment's hesitation:

"Hérold's beard."

I must say here, or rather recall, for I have said it already, that Hérold's beard was the most imposing, if not the most important part of his person. One could no more dare imagine Hérold without his beard than a martyr without his halo; and I had asked for Hérold's beard for fun, as one might ask for the moon. But the amazing thing is that one fine morning it arrived; yes, by post; Louis had taken me at my word; Meriem had cut it off while Hérold was obligingly asleep and Pierre Louis sent it me in an envelope, with a parody of two lines out of Bouilhet's *Colombe*, by way of motto:

> *"The great Parnassian was so little feared,*
> *The Oulad Naïl cut off his golden beard."* [2]

It was at Champel that I read my two Parnassian poets the *Ronde de la Grenade*, which I had written about this time— I can't exactly remember where. I wrote it without having

---

[1] This dedication figures only in the first edition.

[2] The following is a translation of Bouilhet's lines:
> *"The great Olympians were so little feared*
> *That tiny children plucked them by the beard."*

any particular theory beforehand and simply with the wish to reproduce as obediently and responsively as possible a rhythm that was ringing in my head. I had already conceived the idea of my *Nourritures Terrestres;* but it was a book which had to write itself, and all I could tell them about it did not gain me much encouragement from my friends. The Parnassus ideal was not mine and neither Louis nor Hérold had any feeling except for the Parnassus ideal.[1] When my *Nourritures* came out two years later, the book met with almost total incomprehension, and did not begin to arouse attention till another twenty years had passed.

Ever since my resuscitation an ardent desire had taken hold of me—a violent desire to live. Not only did the Champel douches help me but also Andreæ's admirable advice;

"Every time," said he, "you see a piece of water into which you can dip, do so without hesitation."

And so I did. O you foaming torrents! You waterfalls, and icy lakes! Shady streams, limpid springs, translucent halls of the sea, how your coolness tempts me! And then how sweet to rest on the yellow sand beside the backward curl of the waves! For it was not the bath alone that I loved, but afterwards the expectant, the mythological waiting for the god's naked and enfolding flame. My body, shot through with rays, seemed to enjoy some chemical benefaction; with my garments I laid aside anxieties, constraints, solicitudes, and as my will evaporated, I felt myself becoming porous as a beehive, and let my sensations secretly distil the honey that flowed into the pages of my *Nourritures.*

I brought back with me on my return to France, the secret of a man newly risen from the grave, and suffered the kind

---

[1] The school of Parnassus, which followed that of the Romantic poets, had for its chief representatives Théophile Gautier, Hérédia, and Leconte de Lisle; their immediate successors were the Symbolists, chief of whom was Mallarmé.

of abominable sickness of heart that Lazarus must have felt after Christ's miracle. Nothing that had occupied me before seemed now to have any importance. How had I been able to breathe the stifling atmosphere of the salons and coteries, where a dusty scent of death was stirred up by all their vain agitation? No doubt I suffered too in my self-conceit at seeing that the ordinary course of things had been so little disturbed by my absence, and that everybody went about his business as if I had never come back. My secret took up so much room in my heart that I was astonished to find I myself took up so little in the eyes of the world. The most I could do was to forgive other people for not realising I was changed; I, at any rate, felt I was no longer the same; I had new things to say, yet it was impossible to speak to these aliens. I wished I could give them my message; I wished I could persuade them to hear it, but not one of them would lend an ear. They continued living; they went on their way regardless, and all the things that satisfied them seemed to me so paltry that I could have cried aloud in despair at my failure to convince them of it.

This state of *estrangement* [1] (which I suffered from particularly when I was with my own people) might very possibly have led me to suicide, if it had not been for the relief I found in describing it ironically in *Paludes*. This book, nevertheless (curious though it now seems to me), did not originally spring from the impulse to project these agonising feelings outside myself; though the impulse, no doubt, subsequently nourished it, the book itself was actually conceived before my return. Some kind of sense of the ludicrous, which had already shown itself in my *Voyage d'Urien*, inspired the opening sentences, and the whole book crystallised round these, almost without my being aware of it. They came to

[1] In English in the text.

me in the course of a walk in a public garden in Milan, where I stayed a few days on my way to Champel:

Path bordered with aristolochia . . .
"Why, when the weather's so uncertain, take only a parasol?"
"It's an en-tout-cas," said she.

It is easy to understand that with such feelings as I have described I was longing to go away again. But it was still too early to take up my winter quarters in the little village in the Jura, that Dr. Andreæ had recommended. (I followed his instructions to the letter and with the greatest success.) In the meantime, therefore, I settled at Neuchâtel.

I found a room to let on the second floor of a temperance hotel near the lake. The dining-room on the first floor filled up about noon with numbers of frugal or needy maiden ladies who took their abstemious meals opposite an enormous placard, inscribed with the following scripture text, well calculated (if I may say so) to elevate and sublimate the pangs of unsatisfied hunger:

THE LORD IS MY SHEPHERD; I SHALL NOT WANT.

And below it was a smaller notice:

RASPBERRY LEMONADE.

This meant it would be useless to expect anything but meagre fare. But I would have put up with far worse privations for the sake of the view I had from my windows! Since those days a great hotel has reared its huge obtrusive mass on the shores of the lake at the very spot on which my eyes loved to linger—where the grey-green surface of the water showed unexpectedly here and there through the thick foliage of ancient limes or elms, which autumn had tinted with gold and which gave the distance a faint haze of indescribable delicacy.

For months I had let my mind run wild, unchecked and undisciplined; I now at last regained control of it, rejoicing to feel it still so active, and full of gratitude to this peaceful land for helping me to collect and concentrate my thoughts. It is impossible to imagine anything less sublime, less Swiss, more temperate, more human than the quiet surroundings of this lake, still haunted by the shade of Rousseau. There are no haughty peaks in the neighbourhood to humble or dwarf the efforts of man, nor to distract the eyes from the homely charm of the foreground. Venerable trees droop their low branches down to the water and sometimes the line of shore wavers among reeds and rushes.

I spent one of the happiest times I can remember at Neuchâtel; I had recovered hope in life; it seemed to me now strangely richer and fuller than my pusillanimous childhood had fancied. I felt it waiting for me; I counted on it without haste. I was not yet tormented by the uneasy demon, bred of curiosity and desire, which since . . . In the quiet garden paths, along the banks of the lake, on the roads and in the precincts of the autumn-laden woods outside the town, I wandered, as no doubt I should do to-day—but at peace. I pursued nothing my mind did not grasp. I was making a study of Leibnitz's *Theodice*, and used to read it as I walked; I should doubtless not take the same extreme pleasure in it to-day: but the very difficulty of following and espousing a mind so different from my own, the very effort it demanded of me, gave me a delightful foretaste of the mental progress I should be capable of as soon as my thoughts were left free to follow their own course. When I got in, it was to find on my table Claus's enormous manual of zoology which I had just bought and which, to my wonder and amazement, raised the mysterious curtain of a world that was even richer—that was less shadowy too—than the world of thought.

According to Andreæ's advice, I spent the winter at La Brévine—a little village near the Swiss frontier on the iciest height of the Jura. The thermometer remained for weeks below freezing point, and on certain nights there were 30 degrees of frost. And yet I, who as a rule feel the cold so terribly, never for a moment suffered from it. I had found some rooms near an inn where I used to take my meals; they were in a kind of farm at the extreme end of the village, near a drinking trough, where I heard the cows come in the morning to be watered. A private staircase led to three rooms, the largest of which I used as my study; a kind of reading-desk (I was fond of standing up to write) stood opposite a piano that had come from Neuchâtel; a single stove, built into the wall heated this room and my bedroom as well; I slept with my feet against the stove, wrapped in wool from head to foot, and with my head well muffled, for I kept my windows wide open. A young Swiss woman of opulent charms did my room for me. Her name was Augusta. She used to talk to me a great deal about her fiancé; but one morning, while she was showing me his photograph, I rashly began to amuse myself by tickling her neck with my quill pen, when to my extreme embarrassment she suddenly collapsed into my arms. With a great effort, I lugged her on to a sofa; then, as she hung on to me, I found myself tumbled on to her bosom between her open legs; seized with disgust, I suddenly called out in pretended terror: "I hear voices!" and escaping from her arms like another Joseph, rushed away to wash my hands.

I stayed at La Brévine about three months without speaking to a soul; not that I was in an unsociable mood, but I found the inhabitants the most churlish I have ever met. Armed with Dr. Andreæ's letters of introduction, I called upon the doctor and the pastor of the village, but I met with not the smallest encouragement to go and see them again, and still less to accompany them, as I had hoped, on their rounds among the sick and the poor. One must have lived in this part of the world to understand the passages of Rousseau's *Confessions* and *Rêveries*, in which he speaks of his stay at Val Travers. Ill-will, spiteful talk, scowling looks, mocks and jeers—no, he invented none of them; I met with them all myself, even to the stones thrown at the stranger by the pack of village children. And one can imagine how their hatred of foreigners must have been excited by his Armenian costume. The mistake, the madness lay in taking this hostility for a conspiracy.

Every day, notwithstanding the hideousness of the country, I forced myself to take long walks. Is it unfair to say its *hideousness?* Perhaps; but I had taken a loathing to Switzerland; not perhaps to the Switzerland of the high plateaus, but to that belt of forest-land, where the fir-trees seem to have infested the whole of nature with a kind of morose and Calvinistic stiffness. In reality, I regretted Biskra; a nostalgic longing for that great featureless land and its people in their white burnouses had pursued Paul and me all through Italy; we had been haunted by the memory of its songs and dances and perfumes, of its children too, and of the idyllic intercourse into which such a voluptuous charm had already insidiously crept. Here there was nothing to distract me from my work, and in spite of my exasperation with Switzerland, I managed to stick to it as long as was necessary in order to finish *Paludes;* with the fixed idea of leaving for Algeria immediately after.

II

It was not till January that I took the boat, after a short stay at Montpellier with the Charles Gides. I intended to settle in Algiers, which I had not yet seen. I had looked forward excitedly to finding spring already there; but when I arrived the sky was gloomy; it was raining; an icy wind, blowing from the heights of the Atlas Mountains or from the depths of the desert, brought with it fury and despair. Jupiter had betrayed me. My disappointment was cruel. Amusing as the town was, Algiers did not come up to my expectations; the impossibility of finding a lodging anywhere but in the European quarter annoyed me. To-day I should be cleverer— hardier too; in those days, the habit of too great comfort and the recollection of my recent illness made me unenterprising and fastidious. At Mustapha, which might otherwise have suited me, the hotels were too luxurious. I thought I might fare better at Blidah. I was reading at that time, I remember, Fichte's *Science of Knowledge*, without any pleasure but that of my own application, and without finding a trace of the qualities that had attracted me in the *Way to a Blessed Life* and the *Vocation of the Scholar*. But I disliked indulging myself and was grateful to anything that demanded of me a certain amount of effort. For relaxation, I had *Barnaby Rudge*, after having devoured one after the other *Little Dorrit*, *Hard Times*, *The Old Curiosity Shop* and *Dombey and Son*.

Before leaving France, I had been mad enough to write to Emmanuèle and to my mother to persuade them both to come out and join me. Needless to say, this proposal met with no success; but I was a little astonished that my mother did not reject it with a mere shrug of the shoulders, as I had feared. My uncle had died a little while before, after a few days' painful illness, during which time Emmanuèle and I had nursed him together, and this bereavement, while leaving my cousins without any other protection but their aunts' (and in particular, my mother's) further strengthened the ties that bound us. I learnt later that my family were very uneasy at that time about the turn my life seemed to be taking. The idea of my marriage with Emmanuèle began to be looked on more favourably, as perhaps the best means of leading me into more disciplined paths; and finally they could not fail to be touched by my constancy.

"One cannot feel sure this marriage would turn out happily," wrote my uncle Charles Gide to my mother, in a letter which was afterwards shown me, "and it would be taking a great responsibility to encourage it. Nevertheless, if it does not take place, they will very likely both be sure to be unhappy," (I transcribe his words exactly) "so that the only choice lies between a certain and a probable evil." As for me, I was convinced the marriage would take place, and the patience with which I waited came from absolute confidence. There was one thing my love for Emmanuèle made me feel sure of, and that was that if *I* had not need of *her*, *she*, at any rate, had need of *me*, and no one but me, to be happy. From whom but me could her happiness come? Had she not given me to understand she had only refused me because she thought she ought not to leave her sisters, or marry before they did? I would wait then; my obstinacy, my confidence would triumph over every obstacle that lay in my way—our way. But although I would not consider my cousin's refusal as final, it had given me great pain; I needed all my fortitude to bear it; and it was at this very moment that my fine buoyancy, too dependent on the smiles of Heaven, and with a sky above from which all blue had been expunged, began to fail me.

Blidah, which later on in the spring I returned to find all loveliness and perfumes, I now thought dreary and unattractive. I roamed up and down the town looking for a lodging, without finding anything to suit me. I regretted Biskra. I had no taste for anything. My despondency was all the greater because I carried it about with me in a place my imagination had peopled with wonders and delights; but it still lay under the gloomy spell of winter, and I with it. The lowering sky weighed on my spirits; the wind and the rain quenched every spark of fire in my heart; I tried to work, but I felt uninspired; I dragged about in unspeakable boredom. To my disgust with the sky was added disgust with myself; I hated and despised myself; I should have liked to do myself an injury; I should have liked to drive my torpor to desperate lengths.

Three days passed in this way.

I was on the point of leaving and the omnibus had already gone to the station with my bag and trunk. I can still see myself standing in the hall of the hotel waiting for my bill, when my eye fell by chance on a slate on which the names of the visitors were written, and I began to read them mechanically. My own first, then the names of various strangers; and suddenly my heart gave a leap; the two last names on the list were those of Oscar Wilde and Lord Alfred Douglas.

I have already related elsewhere that, acting on my first impulse, I took the sponge and wiped out my name. Then I paid my bill and started on foot to the station.

I am not quite sure what it was that made me wipe out my name in this way. In my first account, I put it down to a feeling of *mauvaise honte*. Perhaps, after all, I was merely giving in to an unsociable desire for solitude. During the fits of depression like the one I was then passing through (I am only too liable to them), I feel ashamed of myself, disown, repudiate myself, and like a hurt dog try to creep out of sight.

293

But on my way to the station, I began to reflect, as I walked along, that perhaps Wilde had seen my name, that what I was doing was cowardly, that—in short, I ordered my bag and trunk to be put back into the omnibus, and returned to the hotel.

I had seen a great deal of Wilde in Paris; I had met him in Florence; I have related the whole of this at length in another book and also what follows, but not with all the details I wish to add here.[1] Lord Alfred Douglas's infamous book, *Oscar Wilde and I*, is too barefaced a travesty of the truth for me to have any scruples about telling it now, and since fate willed that my path should cross his at this juncture, I feel it my duty as a witness to give my testimony.

Wilde, up till that day, had observed the most absolute discretion as regards me. I knew nothing of his reputation except from hearsay; but in the literary circles we both frequented in Paris people were beginning to talk. To tell the truth,

[1] Robert Ross, Oscar Wilde's executor and faithful friend, wrote to me as follows, March 21st, 1910:

"I am delighted that you have reprinted your brilliant *Souvenirs of Oscar Wilde*. I have told many friends, since your study first appeared in *l'Ermitage* that it was not only the best account of Oscar Wilde at the different stages of his career, but the only true and accurate impression of him that I have ever read; so I can only repeat to you what I have said so often to others.

"Some day, perhaps, I shall publish letters of Oscar Wilde to myself which will confirm everything you have said—if there can be any doubt as to the truth of what you so vividly describe.

"This may one day become necessary in order to refute the lies of Alfred Douglas. You no doubt heard reported in a recent libel action that he swore in the witness-box that he was unaware of Oscar Wilde's guilt, and that he was the 'only decent friend who remained with Oscar Wilde.' You know perfectly well that Alfred Douglas was the cause of Oscar Wilde's ruin both before and after the imprisonment. I would like to have pretended this was not the case, out of old friendship and regard for Douglas: and the fact that I had quarrelled with him personally would not have affected my determination to let the world think he was really the noble friend he always posed as being. But since he has taken on himself, in his new character of social and moral reformer, to talk about Oscar Wilde's 'sins' (in most of which he participated) and has betrayed all his old friends, there is no longer any reason for me to be silent . . ."

Robert Ross.

Wilde was not taken very seriously and what was beginning to transpire about his real character seemed an affectation the more. People thought him slightly shocking, but rather a joke, something to be sniggered at. I always wonder at the difficulty French people have (most of them, that is) in believing in the sincerity of feelings they do not share. Pierre Louis, however, had spent a few days in London the summer before. I had seen him on his return; though he had not the same tastes, he had been not a little shaken.

"It's not at all what people over here think," he said. "They are most charming young men." (He was speaking of Wilde's friends and of those companions of his who were soon to arouse such suspicion.) "You can't imagine what beautiful manners they have. Just to give you an idea: the first day I was among a party of them, X., to whom I had just been introduced, offered me a cigarette; but instead of just offering it simply, as we should have done here, he began by lighting it and drew one first puff himself before handing it to me. Wasn't it charming? And everything they do is like that. They manage to make everything poetical. They told me that a few days before, they had celebrated a marriage—a real marriage—between two of them, with an exchange of rings and so on. I tell you we can't imagine it; we have no idea what it's like."

But notwithstanding this, a little while later, as Wilde's reputation was becoming more and more blown upon, Louis announced his intention of having it out with him, and started off for Baden (I think) where Wilde was doing a cure, under pretext of asking him for an explanation, but in reality intending to break with him, and he came back having done so.

He described the interview to me:

"You thought I had friends," Wilde had said, according to Louis; "I have nothing but lovers. Good-bye."

Yes, I really think there was a good deal of embarrassment in the feeling that made me wipe my name off the slate. Wilde's company had become compromising and I felt far from comfortable when I came face to face with him again.

Wilde was extremely changed; not in his appearance but in his behaviour. He seemed determined to break through his reserve, and I think Lord Alfred Douglas's presence encouraged him to do so.

I did not know Douglas, but Wilde began at once to sing his praises with extraordinary enthusiasm. He called him *Bosy* so that I did not realise at first to whom these praises referred, especially as he seemed rather affectedly to make a point of praising nothing but Bosy's beauty.

"You'll see him," he kept repeating, "and you'll tell me if it's possible to imagine a more charming divinity. I adore him; yes, I positively adore him."

Wilde covered over his sincerest feelings with a cloak of affectation which many people found intolerable. He would never cease from acting—could not, no doubt; but the character he acted was his own; the rôle itself, which his everlasting demon kept prompting him, was a sincere one.

"What are you reading?" he asked, pointing to my book.

I knew Wilde did not like Dickens; or at any rate pretended not to like him; and as I was feeling in a cantankerous mood, it was with some pleasure I handed him my translation of *Barnaby Rudge* (at that time I did not know a word of English). Wilde pulled an odd face and began by declaring "it was no good reading Dickens"; then, as it amused me to profess the liveliest admiration for him—which, for that matter, was perfectly sincere and which I have kept to this day—he seemed to resign himself, and began to speak of the "divine Boz" with an eloquence which showed that in spite of his professed disapproval, he had considerable esteem for him. But Wilde never forgot to be an artist, and he could not forgive Dickens for being human.

It was not sufficient for Wilde to tell the vile procurer who came to pilot us through the town that evening that he wanted to see some young Arabs, he added "as beautiful as bronze statues," and only saved the phrase from being ridiculous by a kind of poetical playfulness, and by the slight English or Irish accent which he took good care never to lose when speaking French. As for Lord Alfred Douglas, he did not appear, as far as I can remember, till after dinner. Wilde and he dined in their rooms, and I expect Wilde invited me to dine with them, and I expect I refused, for in those days, all invitations made me retire into my shell . . . I cannot remember and I have vowed not to be tempted into furnishing the vacant rooms of my memory. But I agreed to go out with them after dinner, and one thing I remember very well is that we were no sooner in the street than Lord Alfred took me affectionately by the arm and exclaimed:

"All these guides are idiotic: it's no good explaining—they will always take you to cafés which are full of women. I hope you are like me. I have a horror of women. I only like boys. As you're coming with us this evening, I think it's better to say so at once . . ."

I hid my stupefaction at the brutality of this outspoken statement as best I could and fell into step without a word. I could not think Bosy as beautiful as Wilde did; but though he had the despotic manners of a spoilt child, he combined them with so much grace, that I soon began to understand why it was that Wilde always followed so submissively in his wake.

The guide introduced us into a café which, *louche* as it was, had nothing to offer of the kind my companions wanted. We had only been there a few minutes when a brawl broke out at the further end of the room between Spaniards and

Arabs; the former incontinently pulled out their knives, and as the disturbance threatened to spread, everyone either taking sides with the combatants or trying to separate them, we thought it prudent at the first bloodshed to take ourselves off. I can think of nothing more to say about that evening, which was on the whole a rather dismal affair. The next morning I returned to Algiers where Wilde joined me a few days later.

There is a certain way of drawing a great man's portrait in which the painter seems trying to show himself off at his model's expense. I should like to avoid with as much care the opposite mistake of being too flattering; but at the back of all Wilde's obvious faults, it is his greatness I am chiefly conscious of. No doubt nothing was more exasperating than the paradoxes he was continually firing off out of an unceasing desire to appear witty. But some people, when they heard him exclaim at sight of a furniture brocade: "I should like to have a waistcoat of it," or at sight of a waistcoat material: "I should like to hang my drawing-room with it," too easily forgot how much truth, wisdom, and, in a more subtle fashion, how much personal revelation, lay behind his mask of conceits. But with me, as I have said, Wilde had now thrown aside his mask. It was the man himself I saw at last; for no doubt he had realised there was no further need for pretence and that the very thing that would have made others recoil was precisely what attracted me. Douglas had returned to Algiers with him; but Wilde seemed trying to avoid him.

I remember particularly one late afternoon coming across him in a bar. When I went in, he was sitting in front of a sherry-cobbler, with his elbows on a table strewed with papers.

"Excuse me," he said, "these letters have just come."

He opened a few more envelopes, threw a rapid glance

over their contents, smiled, puffed himself out, and then with a sort of cooing chuckle:

"Charming!" he said; "oh, quite charming!" Then, raising his eyes to mine, "I must tell you I have a friend in London who looks after my correspondence for me. He keeps back all the boring letters—business letters, tradesmen's bills and so on—and only forwards the serious letters—the love-letters . . . Oh! this one is from a young . . . what do you call it? . . . acrobat? yes; acrobat; absolutely delicious." (He put an exaggerated emphasis on the second syllable of the word; I can hear him still.) Then he laughed, bridled, and seemed highly amused with himself. "It's the first time he has written to me, so he doesn't like to spell properly. What a pity you don't know English! You would see . . ."

He was continuing to laugh and joke, when suddenly Douglas came into the bar, wrapped in a fur coat, with the collar turned up, so that nothing was to be seen of him but his nose and the glance of his eyes. He brushed past me as though he didn't recognise me, planted himself in front of Wilde and in a hissing, withering, savage voice, rapped out a few sentences, of which I understood not a single word, then turning on his heels, went out. Wilde had let the storm pass over him without a word; but he had turned very pale and after Bosy had gone neither of us spoke for some time.

"He does nothing but make scenes like that," he said at last. "He's terrible. Isn't he terrible? In London a little while ago we stayed some time at the Savoy; we used to take all our meals there and had a marvellous little suite of rooms with a view over the Thames . . . You know the Savoy's a very luxurious hotel, where the best people in London go. We spent a great deal of money, and everyone was furious with us because they thought we were enjoying ourselves, and London hates people who enjoy themselves. But what I meant to say is this: We used to take our meals in the hotel restaurant; it was a big place and a great many people I knew used to go there; but even a greater number who knew me and whom I didn't know—because a play of mine was being acted just at the time; it was very successful and there were articles about me and portraits of me in all the papers. So in order to be quiet with Bosy, I chose a table at the further end of the restaurant a long way from the main entrance, but quite close to a little door which led to the inside of the hotel. And when he saw me come in by this little door, Bosy, who was waiting for me made a scene. Oh! a terrible, frightful scene! 'I won't have you come in by the side door,' he said; 'I won't tolerate it. I insist on your coming in by the main entrance with me; I want everyone in the restaurant to see us; I want everyone to say, "There goes Oscar Wilde and his minion!"' Oh! isn't he terrible?"

But in the whole tale, and even in those last words, his admiration for Douglas and a kind of lover's infatuated pleasure in being mastered, were manifest. And indeed Douglas's personality seemed much stronger and much more marked than Wilde's; yes, Douglas's personality was overweening; a sort of fatality swept him along; at times he seemed almost irresponsible; and as he never attempted to resist himself, he would not put up with anyone or anything resisting him either. To tell the truth Bosy interested me extremely; but "terrible" he certainly was, and in my opinion it is he who ought to be held responsible for all that was disastrous in Wilde's career. Wilde beside him seemed gentle, wavering, and weak-willed. Douglas was possessed by the perverse instinct that drives a child to break his finest toy; nothing ever satisfied him; he always wanted to go one better. The following example will show to what lengths his effrontery would go: I was questioning him one day about Wilde's two sons;

he laid great stress on the beauty of Cyril (I think), who was quite young at the time, and then whispered with a self-satisfied smile, "He will be for me." Add to all this a poetical gift of the rarest quality, which was apparent in the musical tone of his voice, in his gestures, his eyes and the expression of his features; there was apparent too in his whole person what physiologists call "a bad heredity."

The next day or the day after, Douglas returned to Blidah, where he was making arrangements to elope with a young *caouadji* [1] he wanted to take with him to Biskra; for my descriptions of the oasis—where I intended returning myself —had captivated him. But to run away with an Arab is not such an easy thing as he had thought at first; he had to get the parents' consent, sign papers at the Arab office, at the police-station, etc.; there was work enough to keep him at Blidah for several days; during this time Wilde was more at liberty and able to talk to me more intimately than he had hitherto done. I have already set down elsewhere the most important part of our conversations; I have described his excessive assurance, the hoarseness of his laugh, the fierceness of his joy; I have also said that a growing uneasiness sometimes showed through all this extreme vehemence. Some of his friends have maintained that Wilde at this time had no idea what was awaiting him in London, where he returned a few days after our meeting in Algiers; they speak of Wilde's confidence and declare he kept it unshaken until the fatal upshot of the libel case. I beg leave to set against this, not my own personal impression, but Wilde's actual words, which I transcribed with absolute fidelity. They bear witness to a kind of vague apprehension, a presentiment of some kind of tragic event which he dreaded, but at the same time almost longed for.

"I have been as far as possible along my own road," he

[1] The boy who makes and serves the coffee (*caoua*) in Arab cafés.

repeated. "I can't go any farther. *Something* must happen now."

Wilde had always shown a particular liking for Pierre Louis, and seemed to feel his desertion extremely. He asked me if I had seen him since and insisted on knowing what Louis had said about their quarrel. I told him and repeated the sentence I have quoted above.

"Did he really say that?" cried Wilde. "Are you certain those were his very words?"

And as I assured him I had quoted them exactly and that I had been very sorry to hear them:

"You have noticed, haven't you," said he, "that the most treacherous lies are those that are nearest the truth? But certainly Louis didn't mean to lie; he didn't think he was lying. Only he quite misunderstood what I said that day. No, I won't think he lied; but he was mistaken—terribly mistaken as to the meaning of my words. You want to know what I really said? We were in a room in a hotel, and he began by saying dreadful things, making accusations, because I refused to give him any explanation of my conduct; and I told him I didn't recognise he had any right to sit in judgment on me; but that if he pleased he might believe whatever people said about me. Then Louis answered that in that case all he could do was to leave me. And I looked at him sadly, for I was very fond of Pierre Louis, and that was the reason, the only reason, his reproaches grieved me so. But as I felt it was all over between us, I said: 'Good-bye, Pierre Louis; *I wanted a friend; now I shall have nothing but lovers.*' It was upon that he went away, and I don't wish ever to see him again. But you understand, don't you, that it isn't the same thing?"

It was that same evening he explained to me that he had put his genius into his life, and only his talent into his writings; this illuminating sentence, which has since been so often alluded to, is to be found quoted for the first time in my little book *Oscar Wilde*.

Another evening, immediately after Douglas had left for Blidah, Wilde asked me to go with him to a Moorish café where there was music to be heard. I agreed and called for him after dinner at his hotel. The café was not very far off, but as Wilde had some difficulty in walking, we took a carriage which dropped us in Rue Montpensier, at the fourth terrace of the Boulevard Gambetta, where Wilde told the coachman to wait for us. A guide had got up beside the coachman and this man now escorted us through a labyrinth of small streets inaccessible to carriages, until we came to the steep alley in which the café was situated. As we walked, Wilde expounded his theory of guides, and how important it was to choose the vilest, who was invariably the cleverest. If the man at Blidah had not succeeded in showing us anything interesting, it was because he wasn't ugly enough. Ours that evening was a terror.

There was nothing to show it was a café; its door was like all the other doors; it stood ajar, and there was no need to knock. Wilde was an habitué of this place, which I have described in my *Amyntas*, for I often went back to it afterwards. There were a few old Arabs sitting cross-legged on mats and smoking kief; they made no movement when we took our places among them. And at first I did not see what there was in this café to attract Wilde; but after a time I made out a young *caouadji* standing in the shadow near the hearth; he was busy preparing us two cups of ginger tea over the embers —a drink Wilde preferred to coffee. Lulled by the strange torpor of the place, I was just sinking into a state of semi-somnolence, when in the half-open doorway, there suddenly appeared a marvellous youth. He stood there for a time, leaning with his raised elbow against the door-jamb, and outlined on the dark background of the night. He seemed uncertain as to whether he should come in or not, and I was beginning to be afraid he would go, when he smiled at a sign made him by Wilde and came up and sat down opposite us on a stool a little lower than the mat-covered raised floor on which we were sitting, Arab fashion. He took a reed flute out of his Tunisian waistcoat and began to play on it very exquisitely. Wilde told me a little later that he was called Mohammed and that "he was Bosy's"; if he had hesitated at first as to whether he should come in, it was because he had not seen Lord Alfred. His large black eyes had the languorous look peculiar to hashish smokers; he had an olive complexion; I admired his long fingers on the flute, the slimness of his boyish figure, the slenderness of his bare legs coming from under his full white drawers, one of them bent back and resting on the knee of the other. The caouadji came to sit beside him and accompanied him on a kind of *darbouka*. The song of the flute flowed on through an extraordinary stillness, like a limpid steady stream of water, and you forgot the time and the place, and who you were and all the troubles of this world. We sat on, without stirring, for what seemed to me infinite ages; but I would have sat on for longer still, if Wilde had not suddenly taken me by the arm and broken the spell.

"Come," said he.

We went out. We took a few steps in the alley, followed by the hideous guide, and I was beginning to think our evening was to come to an end there, when at the first turning, Wilde came to a standstill, dropped his huge hand on to my shoulder, and bending down—he was much taller than I—said in a whisper:

"*Dear*,[1] would you like the little musician?"

Oh! how dark the alley was! I thought my heart would fail

[1] In English in the text.

304

me; and what a dreadful effort of courage it needed to answer: "Yes," and with what a choking voice!

Wilde immediately turned to the guide, who had come up to us, and whispered a few words in his ear which I did not hear. The man left us and we went on to the place where the carriage was waiting.

We were no sooner seated in it, than Wilde burst out laughing—a resounding laugh, more of triumph than of pleasure, an interminable, uncontrollable, insolent laugh; and the more disconcerted I seemed to be by his laughter, the more he laughed. I should say that if Wilde had begun to discover the secrets of his life to me, he knew nothing as yet of mine; I had taken care to give him no hint of them, either by deed or word. The proposal he had just made me was a bold one; what amused him so much was that it was not rejected; it was the amusement of a child and a devil. The great pleasure of the debauchee is to debauch. No doubt, since my adventure at Sousse, there was not much left for the Adversary to do to complete his victory over me; but Wilde did not know this, nor that I was vanquished beforehand—or, if you will (for is it proper to speak of defeat when one carries one's head so high?), that I had already triumphed in my imagination and my thoughts over all my scruples. To tell the truth, I did not know it myself; it was only, I think, as I answered "yes," that I suddenly became aware of it.

Wilde interrupted his laughter from time to time to apologise.

"I beg your pardon for laughing so; but I can't help it. It's no good." And he started off again.

He was still laughing when we stopped in front of a café in the Place opposite the theatre, where we dismissed the carriage.

"It's too early yet," said Wilde. And I did not dare ask him what he had settled with the guide, nor where, nor how, nor when, the little musician would come to me; and I began to doubt whether anything would really come of his proposal; but I was afraid to question him lest I should show the violence of my desire.

We only stayed a moment in this vulgar café, and I supposed that if Wilde did not at once get driven to the little bar of the Hôtel de l'Oasis where we went next, it was because he did not want the people of the hotel where he was known to have any inkling of the Moorish café and that he devised this intervening stage in order to put a little more distance between the above-board and the clandestine.

Wilde made me drink a cocktail and drank several himself. We lingered for about half an hour. How long I thought it! Wilde still went on laughing, but not so convulsively, and when from time to time we spoke, it was about any trifle. At last I saw him take out his watch:

"It is time," said he, getting up.

We took our way towards a more populous quarter of the town, further than the big mosque at the bottom of the hill (I have forgotten its name) which one passes on the way to the Post Office—the ugliest part of the town now, though once it must have been one of the most beautiful. Wilde preceded me into a house with a double entrance, and we had no sooner crossed the threshold, than there appeared in front of us two enormous policemen, who had come in by the other door, and who terrified me out of my wits. Wilde was very much amused at my fright.

"Oh, no, dear, on the contrary; it proves the hotel is a very safe place. They come here to protect foreigners. I know them quite well. They're excellent fellows and very fond of my cigarettes. They quite understand."

We let the policemen go up in front of us. They passed the

second floor, where we stopped. Wilde took a key out of his pocket and showed me into a tiny apartment of two rooms, where we were soon joined by the vile guide. The two youths followed him, each of them wrapped in a burnous that hid his face. Then the guide left us and Wilde sent me into the further room with little Mohammed and shut himself up in the other with the *darbouka* player.

Every time since then that I have sought after pleasure, it is the memory of that night I have pursued. After my adventure at Sousse, I had relapsed wretchedly again into vice. If I had now and then snatched a sensual joy in passing, it had been, as it were, furtively; one delicious evening there had been, however, in a boat on the lake of Como, with a young boatman (just before going to La Brévine) when my rapture was encompassed by the shining of the moon, the misty magic of the lake, the moist perfumes breathing from its shores. And after that, nothing; nothing but a frightful desert, full of wild unanswered appeals, aimless efforts, restlessness, struggles, exhausting dreams, false excitement and abominable depression. At La Roque, the summer before last, I had been afraid of going mad; I spent nearly the whole time I was there shut up in my room, where I ought to have been working, and where I tried to work in vain (I was writing *Le Voyage d'Urien*), obsessed, haunted, thinking to find perhaps some escape in excess itself, hoping to come out into the fresh air on the other side, to wear out my demon (I recognise his wile), when it was only myself I wore out, expending myself crazily to the point of utter exhaustion, to the verge of imbecility, of madness.

Ah! what a hell I had been through! And without a friend I could speak to, without a word of advice; because I had believed all compromise impossible, and because I had begun by refusing to surrender, I came near sinking to perdition . . .

But what need is there to recall those lugubrious days? Does their memory explain that night's ecstasy? My attempt with Meriem, my effort after "renormalisation," had not been followed up because it had not been in consonance with my nature; it was now that I found my normal. There was nothing constrained here, nothing precipitate, nothing doubtful; there is no taste of ashes in the memory I keep. My joy was unbounded, and I cannot imagine it greater, even if love had been added. How should there have been any question of love? How should I have allowed desire to dispose of my heart? No scruple clouded my pleasure and no remorse followed it. But what name then am I to give the rapture I felt as I clasped in my naked arms that perfect little body, so wild, so ardent, so sombrely lascivious?

For a long time after Mohammed had left me, I remained in a state of passionate jubilation, and though I had already achieved pleasure five times with him, I renewed my ecstasy again and again, and when I got back to my room in the hotel, I prolonged its echoes until morning.

I know well enough that one of these details may provoke a smile; it would be easy for me to omit or to modify it so as to make it seem more likely; but it is not likelihood I am in quest of, but truth; and ought not the truth to be told more especially then, when it appears least likely? Why else should I mention it?

As I was simply giving my measure, and as I had been reading Boccaccio's *Nightingale* into the bargain, I had no idea there was anything surprising about it, and it was Mohammed's astonishment that first made me suspect there was. Where I went beyond my measure was in what followed and that is what seems to me really strange: glutted and exhausted as I was, I had no rest nor respite till I had pushed exhaustion further still. I often experienced later how vain it is for me to try to be moderate, in spite of what reason and prudence advise; for whenever I attempted it, I was obliged afterwards, and in solitude, to labour after that total exhaustion which alone afforded me respite, and which I obtained at no less cost. For the rest, I am not undertaking to explain anything; I know I shall have to depart this life without having understood anything—or very little—about the functioning of my body.

At the first glimmer of dawn, I got up; with sandals on my feet I ran, yes, actually ran, as far as Mustapha and further, feeling no fatigue after my night, but on the contrary, a joyfulness, a kind of lightness of body and soul which did not leave me all day long.

I saw Mohammed again two years later. His face had not changed much. He looked hardly less young; his figure had kept its grace; but the languor of his eyes had gone; I felt something hard, anxious and degraded in them.

"Don't you smoke hashish any longer?" I asked him, certain of his answer.

"No," he said, "I drink absinthe now."

He was still attractive; oh! more attractive than ever; but he was not so much lascivious now as shameless.

Daniel B. was with me. Mohammed led us to the fourth floor of a disreputable hotel; on the ground floor there was a bar at which some sailors were drinking. The bar-keeper asked our names; I wrote *César Bloch* in the book. Daniel ordered beer and lemonade, "for the sake of appearances," he said. It was night. The only light in the room we went into was the candle we had been given to go upstairs with. A waiter brought us the bottles and glasses and put them on the table beside the candle. There were only two chairs. Daniel and I sat down; and Mohammed sat on the table between us.

He pulled up the haïk, which he was wearing now instead of his Tunisian costume, and stretched out his bare legs to us.

Then, while I remained sitting beside the half-empty glasses, Daniel seized Mohammed in his arms and carried him to the bed which was at the other end of the room. He laid him on his back on the edge of the bed, cross-wise, and soon I saw nothing but two slim legs dangling on either side of Daniel, who was labouring and panting. Daniel had not even taken his cloak off. Standing there in the dim light beside the bed, with his back turned, his face hidden by the curls of his long black hair, his cloak falling to his feet, he looked gigantic. As he bent over the little body he was covering, he was like a huge vampire feasting on a corpse. I could have screamed with horror.

It is always very difficult to understand the loves of others and their way of practising love. And even those of animals (that *and even* should be kept for those of men). One can envy birds their song, their flight; say with the poet:

> "*Ach! wüsstest du wie's Fischlein ist*
> *So wohlig auf dem Grund!*"

I can even give the dog devouring a bone some sort of bestial assent. But nothing is more disconcerting than the act, so different from species to species, by which each one takes his pleasure. In spite of M. de Gourmont, who tries to make out disturbing analogies in this respect between man and animals, I hold that this analogy exists only in the regions of desire; and that, on the contrary, it is perhaps in what M. de Gourmont calls "the physics of love" [1] that the differences are most marked, not only between man and animals, but often from one man to another—so much so that, if we were able to

[1] *La Physique de l'Amour* by Remy de Gourmont.

310

see our neighbour's practices, they would often seem as strange to us, as outlandish, and indeed, as monstrous, as the mating of batracians, of insects—and, why go so far afield? —as that of dogs and cats, or as the onanism of fish.

No doubt this is the reason why failures of understanding on this point are so great, and prejudices so ferocious.

For myself, who only take my pleasure face to face, and who am often, like Walt Whitman, satisfied with the most furtive contact, I was horrified both by Daniel's behaviour and by Mohammed's complacent submission to it.

Wilde and I both left Algiers, I think, on the same day, very shortly after this memorable evening; he, recalled to England by the determination to put an end to the accusations of the Marquis of Queensberry, Bosy's father; and I, with the intention of getting to Biskra before Bosy. Bosy had decided to go there with Ali, the young Arab of Blidah he had fallen in love with; he had written me a letter to say he was returning to Algiers and hoped I would wait for him, so that we might travel together, for the long two days' journey would be unbearably dull with only Ali, who, it appeared, knew no more French or English than Bosy knew Arabic. I have such a contradictious temper, however, that this letter merely made me hurry on my departure; either because I disliked lending a hand to this adventure and smoothing the way for someone who thought everything his due, or because the moralist that slumbers in my breast considered it indecorous to strip the roses of their thorns, or simply because my sulkiness carried the day—for one of these reasons, or a mixture of them all—I started. But at Sétif, where I was to spend the night, I received an urgent telegram.

I always welcome with perverse alacrity anything that comes to upset my plans; I will not attempt to explain this

trait in my character, for I cannot understand it myself . . .
In short, I broke my journey and began to wait for Douglas
as whole-heartedly as the day before I had fled from him.
The fact is I had found the journey from Algiers to Sétif horribly long. But I soon found the wait longer still. What an interminable day! And the next, that still lay between me and
Biskra? What will that be like? thought I to myself, as I paced
up and down the tiresome, regular streets of the ugly little
military and colonial town, where it seemed impossible anyone should care to come except on business, or stay except by
order, and where the few Arabs one sees look out of place and
miserable.

I was impatient to see Ali. I expected just a modest little
caouadji, dressed more or less like Mohammed; it was a young
prince who stepped out of the train, in brilliant garments,
with a silken sash and a golden turban. He was not sixteen,
but how stately his bearing, how proud his glance! What con-
descending smiles he bestowed on the hotel servants as they
bowed before him! How soon he had realised that, humble as
he had been the day before, it was now for him to come into
the room first, to sit down first . . . Douglas had found his
master, and in spite of the elegance of his own clothes, he
looked like an attendant, waiting on the orders of his gorgeous servant. Every Arab, however poor, has an Aladdin
within him all ready to blossom forth; at the first touch of
fate—behold him a king!

Ali was certainly very beautiful; fair-complexioned, with
a smooth brow, a well-formed chin, a small mouth, rounded
cheeks and the eyes of a houri; but his beauty had no power
over me; a sort of hardness in his nostrils, of indifference in
the too perfect curve of his eyebrows, of cruelty in the scorn-
ful curl of his lips, checked every trace of desire in me; and
nothing put me more off than the effeminacy of his whole ap-

pearance, which some people perhaps would have found seductive. All this is to show that during the considerable length of time I lived in his society, I felt absolutely untroubled. And even, as often happens, the spectacle of Douglas's felicity, which I did not envy, had the contrary effect of inclining me all the more to chastity—a disposition that lasted after he had gone and during the whole of my stay at Biskra.

The Hôtel de l'Oasis had already disposed of the Cardinal's apartment, which we had occupied the year before; but the Royal had just opened and we found a set of rooms there which, for agreeableness and commodity, were very little inferior to the former: this apartment was on the ground floor and consisted of three rooms, two of which communicated with each other, and were at the end of a passage opening out of doors. We were able to reach our rooms, without having to go through the hotel, by the outside passage door, of which we were given the key, for no one else used it. But I generally got in and out by the window. My room, into which I had a piano put, was separated from Douglas's and Ali's by the passage, and looked on to the new casino, as did Douglas's; there was a fairly large space of ground in front, which when school was over, was used as a playground by the same Arab boys who the year before had come to play on our terraces.

I have said that Ali did not understand French, so I suggested that Athman should serve as interpreter between Douglas and him. Athman, on hearing I had arrived, had thrown up his work, hoping to take up service with me; but I did not know how to employ him. I blamed myself afterwards for venturing to suggest such a post as this for him, but Douglas and Ali's relations were not of a kind particularly to surprise an Arab, and besides, at that time, I was far from having the great friendship for Athman that took up so much room in my life later on, and which he soon began to deserve. He eagerly accepted the offer directly it was made, but I realised before long that it was because he hoped to spend more time with me. The poor fellow pulled a long face when he saw I was resolved not to go out with Douglas, and that, as a matter of fact, he would see very little of me. Douglas drove out every day with him and Ali to one of the neighbouring oases, Chetma, Droh or Sidi Okba, which could be seen from the hotel terraces, glowing like dark emeralds on the russet cloak of the desert. Douglas tried in vain to persuade me to come too. I took no pity on the boredom he must certainly have felt between his two pages, considering it as the fair penalty of pleasure. It's his own fault, thought I, trying to arm myself with factitious severity against what I was only too ready to admit. And as my own penalty, I buried myself in work, with the flattering feeling that I was atoning for something. Now that years have made me more docile, I wonder at all these scruples—the survival of a worn-out ethical creed, which I had ceased to approve, but on which my moral reflexes still depended. On trying to discover the secret springs that made my machine recoil in this way, and as it were involuntarily, I must confess that what I chiefly discover, is a surly, un-accommodating temper. The fact is, I did not like Bosy, or perhaps it would be fairer to say that my interest in him was greater than my liking; in spite of his attentions and his kindnesses, or perhaps because of them, I remained on the defensive. His conversation very quickly bored me; with an Englishman, or a Frenchman who knew a little more about English matters than I did, I dare say it might have been more varied and abundant; but when the ordinary topics were exhausted, Douglas returned incessantly and with disgusting obstinacy to the things I spoke of only with excessive embarrassment—an embarrassment which was increased by his total lack of it. I found it quite enough to meet him at the interminable hotel meals (how charmingly graceful and roguish he looked as he exclaimed, "I really can't do without a little champagne!"—and why did I sulkily refuse the glass he offered me?) or sometimes at tea, in company with Athman and Ali (and I heard him repeat for the hundredth time—it was the repetition that amused him more than the phrase itself—"Athman, tell Ali his eyes are like a gazelle's").

Day by day, he allowed his ennui to creep a little nearer.

This idyll came to an abrupt end. Although it was with some amusement that Bosy saw Ali was beginning to carry on a somewhat suspicious intrigue with a young shepherd of Fontaine-Chaude, he flew into a violent rage when it dawned upon him that he was quite capable of being touched by the charms of the Oulad, and in particular by Meriem's. He could not endure the idea that Ali perhaps went to bed with her; he was not sure that this had actually taken place (for my part, I had not the smallest doubt of it), angrily demanded confessions, regrets, promises, and swore that if these were broken, he would dismiss Ali on the spot. I felt Douglas was not so much moved by real jealousy as by pique. "Boys," he declared; "yes, boys, as much as he likes; but I will not endure his going with women." For that matter, I am not at all sure Ali really desired Meriem; I think it was rather that he felt flattered and thought he would put an end in this way to the accusations of impotence he heard muttered about him; I think he liked giving himself airs, imitating his elders and appearing grown up. He pretended to submit, but Douglas had lost confidence. One day, in a fit of suspicion, he took it into his head to search Ali's trunk, and discovered under the clothes a photograph of Meriem, which he proceeded to tear to pieces . . . It was tragic; Ali was soundly horse-whipped and his howls created a tumult among the people in the hotel.

I heard this uproar, but considered it wiser not to intervene, and remained shut up in my room. Douglas appeared at dinner that night with a livid face and steely eyes; he told me Ali was returning to Blidah by the first train, that is to say, the next morning. He himself left Biskra two days later.

I was then obliged to admit how much the sight of his dissipation had encouraged me to work, by way of protest. Now that there was no need to resist pressing invitations to go driving, I used to go out every day, starting sometimes as soon as it was light, for long exhausting walks through the desert, either following the dry bed of the *oued*, or going up to the big sandhills, where I used often to stay till nightfall, intoxicated with space, strangeness and solitude, my heart lighter than a bird's.

In the evening, at the end of his day's work, Athman came to join me. Since Ali's and Douglas's departure, he had taken up his occupation of guide again—a degrading occupation, for which his pliable disposition only too well fitted him. As thoughtlessly and as unblushingly as he had consented to transmit Douglas's sugared phrases to Ali, he consented in his innocence to introduce the foreign visitors to the Oulad. He used to tell me how he had spent his day, and as my affection for him grew, so did my disgust at these servile offices; his confidence in me grew too, so that every day he told me more and more.

One evening he arrived highly delighted:

"Oh, I've had such a good day!" he cried. Then he explained how he had just earned thirty francs: ten francs commission from an Oulad for bringing her an Englishman, plus an extra ten francs he had added on to the Oulad's pay, plus ten francs from the Englishman for his little services. I was indignant. I did not object to his being a procurer, but I could not endure him to be dishonest. He was astonished at first by what he took for a fit of temper; and all I got from him to start with was regret that he had spoken to me so freely. I had the idea then of appealing to the sense of dignity, which I flattered myself I could find in every Arab. He seemed to understand:

"All right," he grumbled; "I will give the money back."

"I don't ask you to do that," I protested. "Only if you want to be my friend, stop all such shameful trafficking."

"Then," he replied, smiling—and I recognised the docile boy I had grown fond of—"I think I had better give up introducing tourists to women; it pays too well."

"You see," I went on as an encouragement; "if I ask this of you, it's because I want you to be worthy of my friends when you meet them in Paris."

The idea of taking Athman back with me to Paris was slowly shaping in my heart. I began to mention it in my letters to my mother, tentatively at first, and then more decidedly, while her disapproval grew more and more pronounced. It is true I was only too much disposed to rebel against the maternal admonitions; but it must also be admitted that my mother was a little too free with them. Her letters were more often than not a long series of remonstrances; sometimes they relaxed so far as to be clothed in such an amiable formula as: "I don't offer you advice; I merely call your attention to . . ." But these were the phrases that irritated me most; for I knew, as a matter of fact, that if I did not submit when my attention had been called to something in this way, my mother would return unwearyingly to the charge, for we were both equally determined not to yield. Upon this occasion I had tried in vain to persuade her, as I had succeeded in persuading myself, that it was a matter of moral rescue and that Athman's salvation depended on his being transported to Paris, that I had as good as adopted him . . . My mother, alarmed by the emotional tone of my preceding letters, now thought that the desert and solitude had turned my brain. Her fears were brought to a head when I suddenly informed her that I had spent the small sum of money I had inherited from my grandmother in buying a piece of land at Biskra (I have it still). In order to give this whim some appearance of good sense I reasoned in this way: if Biskra becomes a fashionable winter resort, and consequently I cease to care for it, the land will "go up," and I shall make a good thing by selling it; if Biskra continues to be what it is now, namely the place in the world where I most want to live, I shall build a house there and come to live in it every winter. My dream was to arrange the ground floor of my house as a Moorish café and make Athman the manager; in imagination, I had already invited all my friends. I did not mention this last scheme to my mother; the rest was quite enough already to make her think me mad.

My mother, leaving no stone unturned, called Albert in to the rescue and any other of my friends she could apply to. I was exasperated by this coalition which I felt she was raising against me. What letters I got—beseeching, railing, threatening! I should cover myself with ridicule if I brought Athman back to Paris. What should I do with him? What would Emmanuèle think? . . . still I persisted; but at last a distracted letter from our old Marie forced me to give way. She swore she would leave the house on the day my "negro" came into it. What would become of mamma without Marie? I gave in; I had to.

Poor Athman! I had not the heart to bring down at one blow the dream edifice which every day some fresh hope had come to strengthen. It has not often happened to me to renounce a thing on which I have set my heart; a postponement is the utmost that obstacles wring from me; and in spite of everything I finally carried out this fine plan, which in appearance I had resigned; but it was not till four years later.

Athman, in the meantime, realised there was friction somewhere. Not that I spoke of it to him, for I was still confident in the firmness of my determination; but he interpreted my silence, watched my brow grow darker. After Marie's letter, I waited two more days. I had at last to make up my mind to tell him.

We had got into the habit of going every evening to the station at the time the train came in. As he knew all my friends by name now, for I talked to him about them incessantly, we used to play the childish game of pretending we were going to meet one of them. Not a doubt but so-and-so would be among the passengers. We should see him come out of the train, fling himself into my arms and exclaim: "Oh! what a journey! I thought I should never get here. Well! it's over at last!" But the stream of strangers went by; once more Athman and I were left alone, and as we turned homewards we both felt we had been drawn together in a closer intimacy by the absence of this imaginary friend.

I have said that my room was on the ground floor. The Touggourt road, which the Arabs used to take at night on their way back to the village, passed near by. At about nine o'clock, I heard a little scratching at my closed shutters; it was Sadek, Athman's big brother, and one or two others; they came in by stepping over the window-sill. There were syrups and sweetmeats ready for them. We all sat round in a circle listening to Sadek play the flute, in an oblivion of time such as I have never know but there.

Sadek knew only a few words of French, and I only a few words of Arabic. But had we spoken the same language, what more could we have said than we expressed by our looks, our gestures, and above all by that tender way he had of taking

319

my hands, of holding my hands in his, my right hand in his right hand, so that we walked on, silent as shades, with arms intertwined. On that last evening, Sadek and I walked together in this way for a long time; through the street of the cafés, through the street of the Oulad, bestowing a smile here and a smile there, on En Barka, on Meriem, on the little Moorish café that Athman used to call my little casino, because the year before, when Paul went with Dr. D.'s wife to the gambling rooms of the real Casino, which had just been opened, I went to play cards in this little dark sordid place with Bachir, Mohammed and Larbi; then, on leaving the street of the Oulad, and its lights and noise, we went to the watering-pool, on whose edge I had so often used to sit . . .

When the time came to go, in order not to feel I was abandoning everything at once, I offered to take Athman with me, for a day or two at any rate, as far as El Kantara. Spring was awakening under the palms; the apricot-trees were in bloom and humming with bees; the waters were out and irrigating the fields of barley; nothing more lovely can be imagined than the white blossoms of the apricots overshadowed by the tall palm-trees, and themselves, in their turn overshadowing and sheltering the bright tender green of the young crops. We passed two heavenly days in this Paradise, and they have left me no memory that is not pure and smiling. When, on the third morning I looked for Athman to say good-bye to him, he was nowhere to be found and I had to leave without seeing him again. I could not understand his absence; but suddenly, as I sat in the speeding train, a long way already from El Kantara, I caught sight of his white burnous on the banks of the *oued*. He was sitting there with his head in his hands; he did not rise when the train passed; he made no movement; he did not give a glance at the signs I made him; and for a long time, as the train was carrying me away, I watched his little motionless, grief-stricken figure, lost in the desert, an image of my own despair.

I returned to Algiers, where I was to take the boat for France; but I let four or five steamers start without me, on the pretext that the sea was too rough; in reality, my heart was torn by the idea of leaving the country. Pierre Louis had come to join me; he was recovering from an illness, and came from Seville, where he had spent the winter. I even seem to remember that an excess of friendliness and impatience sent him hurrying to meet me and that I saw him appear unexpectedly at my carriage window a few stations before Algiers. Alas! we had not been a quarter of an hour in each other's company (I remember this only too well) before we had already begun to quarrel. I am willing to admit that some of the fault was mine, and from what I have said it may be seen my character at that time was none of the easiest; but still I know that Louis was the only person I quarrelled with in this way, whereas I am pretty sure that I was not the only person with whom Louis quarrelled. He quarrelled about anything and nothing; if his correspondence is published one day, it will show innumerable examples of this. He was incessantly trying to make his opinion or his humour prevail over yours; but I don't think he was particularly desirous you should yield —or at any rate not too soon, and what he liked was not so much having his own way as measuring his strength—not to say fighting. This pugnacity of his went on all day long, and everything served as a pretext for it. If you wanted to walk in the sun, he immediately preferred the shade; he insisted on your giving in; when you spoke to him, he remained stonily silent or hummed an annoying little tune; he hummed still louder if you wanted to be quiet, and the whole thing irritated me unutterably.

He would not let me be till he had dragged me off to a

brothel. From this way of speaking, it might be imagined that I made difficulties; but no; I made a point now of sticking at nothing, so I followed him not too ungraciously to the "Andalusian Stars," a kind of dancing saloon which had nothing Arab, or even Spanish, about it, and which immediately sickened me with its vulgarity. Then as Pierre Louis began by declaring it was just because of its vulgarity that he liked it, I included him too in my loathing. I was not in the mood, however, to let my repugnances get the better of me; an evil wish to see how far I could go and some kind of obscure compost of feelings, made up of all manner of things—except indeed desire—made me renew the attempt which had failed so lamentably the year before with En Barka. This year it succeeded better, so that there was added to my disgust the fear I had caught a dose. Louis amused himself by fanning this fear into a panic; certainly, he insinuated, the Andalusian star I had chosen to shut myself up with, was the prettiest of the constellation (the least hideous, I should say), and therefore, no doubt, the riskiest, which of course was the only explanation of her not being engaged; that it needed a simpleton like me to choose her, for I ought to have been put on my guard by the very fact of her having some remains of youth and grace left to distinguish her from the others, and by the others' laughter when I chose her, but of course I had noticed nothing of all that. And as I exclaimed that he might have warned me in time, he declared that the illness I should soon, no doubt, be suffering from, had nothing very dreadful about it, and that in any case it was the fee one had to pay for pleasure, that to try and avoid it was to try and avoid the common lot. Then, in order to reassure me completely, he named quantities of great men, who without a doubt owed three-quarters of their genius to the pox!

This funereal knell, which strikes me to-day as rather

funny, when I think of what I must have looked like—and especially now that I know it was a false alarm, did not amuse me in the least at the time. A kind of rage against Louis was added to my disgust and fear. Decidedly we could not understand, could not endure each other. This attempt to renew our friendship was, I think, one of the last we made.

The few more days I spent at Algiers after Pierre Louis had left me are among those I should most like to live over again. I have kept no definite memory of them, but only of an extraordinary fervour, joy, frenzy, which woke me every day at dawn, made an eternity of every moment of every hour, and changed whatever came near my heart into something crystalline or ethereal.

The letters I wrote my mother at that time caused her extreme uneasiness, and as she could not believe it possible that the exaltation they breathed was without a definite cause or object, she imagined me with some love-affair or liaison; she did not as yet dare speak of it openly, but I recognised the phantom she was afraid of in the allusions her letters were full of. She implored me to come back, to "break it off."

The truth, if she had known it, would have frightened her still more; for it is easier to break ties than to escape from oneself. To do this indeed, one must first of all wish to; and it was not at the very moment I was beginning to discover myself—and in myself the tables of a new law—that I was likely to have any such desire. For emancipation from rule did not suffice me; I boldly claimed to justify my folly, to base my madness upon reason.

The tone of these last lines will give the impression that I have passed condemnation on all this; but what should rather be read in them is an attitude of precaution, an answer to all the objections I know may be made to me, a manner of letting it be understood that I made them to myself; for I do not think there is any single way of envisaging the question of religion or morals that at some moment of my life has not been mine. In reality, I should have liked to reconcile all and every of the most diverse points of view, for I could not resign myself to excluding anything and was ready to submit to Christ the settlement of the dispute between Dionysus and Apollo. In what manner and with what transports of love, after what wanderings through the desert into which my worship led me, after what insistent pursuit of my own thirst, I returned once more to the Gospels—of all this the time has not yet come for me to speak; nor of the teaching I found in them when I re-read them with a fresh eye and saw them of a sudden illuminated, both in the letter and the spirit. And I was grieved and indignant too to see what the Churches had made of this divine teaching, which in their interpretation of it I could barely recognise. Our Western world is perishing, I said to myself, from the failure or refusal to read it aright; this became my profound conviction, and that my duty was to denounce the evil. I accordingly planned a book which I meant to call *Christianity against Christ;* many of its pages are written and would no doubt have already seen the light, if the times had been calmer, and if I had not been afraid of distressing some of my friends by its publication, and moreover of seriously imperilling my freedom of thought which I prize more than anything else.

These grave questions, which were soon to be my chief concern, did not begin really to preoccupy me until later; but if I had not as yet clearly formulated them, they were nevertheless in my mind and prevented me from lapsing into a state of complacent hedonism and easy acquiescence. But enough of this for the present.

Yielding at last to my mother's expostulations, I went to spend a fortnight with her in Paris before she left for La

Roque, where it was settled I should join her in July, and where I was only to see her again on her death-bed. In those last days of life in common (those we spent in Paris, I mean) the tension between us was relaxed and we enjoyed a truce; it is some consolation to me to remember them as an off-set to the discussions and struggles, which it must be admitted, formed the most obvious part of our relationship. If, in fact, I use the word "truce" here, it is because no lasting peace between us was possible; the mutual concessions which allowed us a little respite could only have been temporary and were based on an agreed misunderstanding. For the rest, I did not think my mother actually in the wrong. She was in her proper rôle, I thought, even when she was most tormenting me; in reality, I could not imagine it possible for any mother, conscious of her duty, not to insist on her son's submission; but as I also thought it perfectly natural the son should refuse to be quelled, and as this seemed to me just as it should be, I was astonished when I sometimes came across an example of perfect agreement between parents and children, as that, for instance, which existed between Paul Laurens and his mother.

It is Pascal, I believe, who says that we never love people for themselves, but only for their qualities. I think it might have been said of my mother that the qualities she loved were not those of the persons she tyrannised over, but those she wished them to acquire. At any rate, that is how I try to explain her unremitting efforts to work on other people, and me in particular; and I was so excessively irritated by this that I am not sure my exasperation had not ended by destroying all my love for her. She had a way of loving me that sometimes almost made me hate her and touched my nerves on the raw. You whom I shock, imagine, if you can, the effect of being constantly watched and spied upon, incessantly and harassingly advised as to your acts, your thoughts, your expenditure, as to what you ought to wear or what you ought to read, as to the title of a book. She disliked, for instance, that of *Les Nourritures Terrestres,* and as there was still time to change it, she never wearied of returning to the charge.

Wretched questions of money too had for the last few months brought an added cause of irritation into our relations: Mamma used to give me a monthly allowance, which she considered ought to be enough for me—three hundred francs, if I remember rightly—two thirds of which I used regularly to spend on books and music. She did not consider it prudent to put the money that came to me from my father —I had no idea what it amounted to—at my free disposal; and she took care not to let me know that at my majority I had a right to it. But it would be a mistake to think that any personal interest was at the bottom of this; she was solely actuated by a desire to protect me from myself, to keep me in leading strings, and, what exasperated me most of all, by a kind of feeling of what was proper and so to speak, *congruous* for me to have, and this she measured by her own estimation of my necessities. The accounts she showed me when I became aware of my rights, were, she tried to make out, all in my favour; people talk of the "eloquence of figures"; with mamma every column was a speech for the defence; she wanted to prove that I should find no advantage in any other arrangement, that my monthly allowance was as much or more than my rightful income; and as my board and lodging were charged to me, it appeared to me that the best way of getting out of the difficulty was to propose, on the contrary, to pay *her* an allowance during any time I should spend with her. It was by this compromise that our differences were settled.

But, as I have said, this fortnight that we spent together after a long separation, was a cloudless one. I certainly brought a great deal of good will to it on my part, as if some presentiment had warned us both that these were the last days we should pass together; for mamma, on her side, was more conciliatory than I had ever known her. The joy of finding me less deteriorated than she had imagined from my letters no doubt disarmed her; I felt in her nothing but a mother's love, and I was happy to be her son.

I now began to wish for the resumption of our life in common, which I had ceased to think possible, and planned to spend all the summer with her at La Roque. It was settled she was to go there first to open the house and it was possible that Emmanuèle might come and join us. For, as if to seal our more perfect understanding, mamma had at last confessed to me that she wished for nothing so much as to see me marry my cousin, whom she had long looked upon as her daughter-in-law. Perhaps too she felt her strength failing and was afraid of leaving me alone.

I was at Saint-Nom-la-Bretêche, staying with my friend E. R. until it should be time for me to join her, when a telegram from our old Marie suddenly summoned me. My mother had had a stroke. I hurried off. I found her lying in bed in the big room I used as my study in the summer; it was the room she preferred when she spent a few days at La Roque without opening the whole house. I am almost sure she recognised me; but she did not have any clear idea of the time or the place or of herself or of the people about her; for she showed neither surprise nor pleasure at seeing me. Her face was not much changed, but her eyes were vague and her features so expressionless that it seemed as though her body no longer belonged to her and she had ceased to control it. It was so strange that I felt more amazement than pity. She was in a half-sitting position, propped up by pillows; her arms were outside the bed-clothes and she was trying to write in a large open account-book. Even now her restless desire to intervene, to advise, to persuade, was still troubling her; she seemed in great mental agitation, and the pencil she held in her hand ran over the blank sheet of paper, but without making any mark; and the uselessness of this supreme effort was inexpressibly distressing. I tried to speak to her, but my voice did not reach her; and when she tried to speak herself, it was impossible for me to make out what she wanted to say. I took away the paper in the hope she might be able to rest, but her hand continued to write on the sheets. At last she drowsed off and her features gradually relaxed; her hands ceased moving . . . And suddenly, as I looked at the poor hands I had just seen labouring so desperately, I imagined them at the piano, and the thought that they too had tried in their unskilful way to express a little poetry, music and beauty, flooded my heart with a great wave of respect and admiration, and falling on my knees at the foot of the bed, I buried my face in the bedclothes to stifle my sobs.

It is not my personal sorrows that draw tears from me; however grief-stricken my heart, my eyes remain dry. There is always one part of me which hangs back, looks mockingly at the other and says: "Come! Come! You're not so unhappy as all that!" On the other hand, I have a great abundance of tears to shed over other people's griefs, which I often feel more keenly than my own; but I have even more for any manifestation of beauty, nobility, abnegation, devotion, gratitude, courage, or sometimes for a very ingenuous, very childlike expression of feeling. And any very vivid artistic emotion too is immediately watered with my tears, to the extreme astonishment of my neighbours, if I happen to be in a picture-gallery or concert-room. I remember the uncontrollable laughter of two English girls in Florence on seeing my streaming eyes in front of Fra Angelico's great fresco at San

Marco; my friend Ghéon, who was with me, wept in unison, and I admit that the sight of our two waterfalls must have been very ludicrous. In the same way, there was once a time when the mere name of Agamemnon opened some secret floodgate in my heart, so great was the feeling of awe and mythological reverence with which the majesty of the King of kings filled me. So that now, it was not my loss that so greatly upset me (and to be quite sincere, I am obliged to confess that my loss afflicted me very little; or perhaps I should say the sight of my mother's suffering afflicted me, but not the idea of her leaving me). No, it was not grief that made me cry, but admiration for that heart that had never allowed anything vile to touch it, and that beat only for others, with an unfailing devotion to duty that was not virtue so much as natural inclination, and with a humility so great that my mother might have said like Malherbe, but how much more sincerely: *I have always held my service such a despicable offering that to whatever altar I bring it, it is with a heart ashamed and a trembling hand.* And above all I admired her for her life which had been one continual effort to draw a little nearer to what she thought lovely or worthy to be loved.

I was alone in the big room, alone with her, watching the solemn approach of death, and feeling the restless beatings of that unflagging heart re-echo in my own. How it still laboured on! I had been present at other death-beds, but I had not thought them so pathetic as this, either because they had seemed to put a more conclusive and natural end to a life, or simply because I had looked at them less fixedly. It was certain she would not recover consciousness, so that I felt no need to summon my aunts; I was jealous of watching by her side alone. Marie and I assisted her in her last moments, and when at last her heart ceased to beat, I felt myself sink into an overwhelming abyss of love, sorrow and liberty.

It was then that I experienced the singular propensity of my mind to let itself be dazzled by the Sublime. I spent the first weeks of my bereavement, I remember, in a sort of moral intoxication which led me to commit the most ill-considered acts; provided I thought them noble, it was enough to ensure them the approval of my mind and heart. I began by distributing as souvenirs to distant relations, some of whom had scarcely known my mother, the trifling jewels and knick-knacks that had belonged to her, and which for that reason I specially prized. Out of exalted love, out of a strange longing for privation, I would have given away my whole fortune at the very moment I became possessed of it; I would have given myself too; the feeling of my inward wealth filled·me to overflowing, inspired me with a sort of heady abnegation. The sole idea of keeping anything back would have seemed to me shameful and I lent an ear to nothing that did not help me to admire myself. The very liberty, which during my mother's life-time I had so craved for, stunned me like a wind from the open, suffocated—perhaps, indeed, frightened me. I felt dazed, like a prisoner unexpectedly set free, like a kite whose string has been suddenly cut, like a boat broken loose from its moorings, like a drifting wreck, at the mercy of wind and tide.

There was nothing now I could attach myself to but my love for my cousin; my determination to marry her was the only light left me by which to guide my life. I loved her certainly; it was the only thing I was sure of; and indeed I felt I loved her more than I loved myself. When I asked for her hand, I was considering her more than myself; and above all I was hypnotised by the vision of an infinitely widening horizon towards which I should lead her, regardless of perils; for

I refused to believe perils existed which my ardour could not vanquish; I should have thought all prudence cowardly— cowardly all idea of danger.

Our sincerest acts are also the least premeditated; the explanation one looks for after the event is idle. A fatality led me; perhaps also the secret desire to set my nature at defiance; for in loving Emmanuèle, was it not virtue itself I loved? It was the marriage of Heaven with my insatiable Hell; but at the actual moment, my Hell was in abeyance; the tears of my mourning had extinguished all its fires; I was dazzled as by a blaze of azure and the things I refused to see had ceased to exist for me. I believed I could give her my whole self and did so without any reservation whatever. Shortly after this, we became engaged.

Printed in the United States
by Baker & Taylor Publisher Services